THE CATHOLIC CHURCH

A Brief Popular History

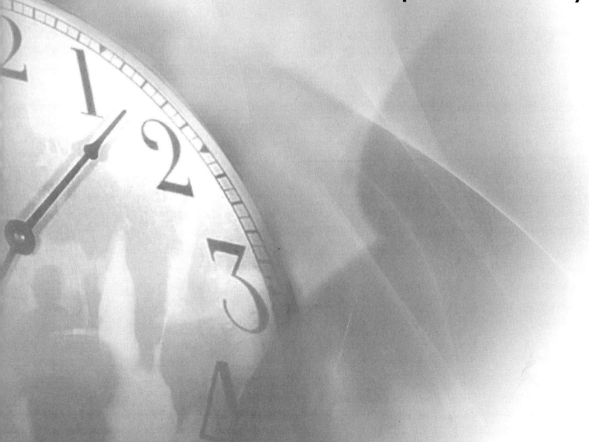

Dedication

This book is dedicated to my son Samuel. May the love of learning light his way forever.

Author Acknowledgments

I wish to acknowledge the Vanderbilt Divinity Library and all who labor there, without whom this work would have been impossible. I send my deepest thanks to the many friends and family members who put up with me during the years that I wrangled this into being.

Publisher Acknowledgments

Thank you to the following individuals who advised the publishing team or reviewed this work in progress:

Jason Bourgeois, PhD, Quincy University, Illinois

Christopher Denny, PhD, Saint John's University, New York

Brennan Hill, PhD, Professor Emeritus, Xavier University, Ohio

John Sheveland, PhD, Gonzaga University, Washington

Special thanks to Jerry Windley-Daoust for his work in the initial development of this text.

THE
CATHOLIC
CHURCH
A Brief Popular History

Cynthia Stewart, PhD

ANSELM ACADEMIC

Created by the publishing team of Anselm Academic.

Cover image royalty-free from Shutterstock.
Interior images royalty free from Shutterstock and iStock.

Printed in the United States of America

7004

ISBN 978-0-88489-967-9

Library of Congress Cataloging-in-Publication Data

Stewart, Cynthia, 1968–
      The Catholic Church : a brief popular history / Cynthia Stewart.
      p. cm.
Includes index.
ISBN 978-0-88489-967-9 (pbk.)
      1. Catholic Church—History. I. Title.

BX945.3.S74 2008
282.09—dc22

                          2007044936

CONTENTS

7 Across a Great Divide: The Eastern Church. 131

8 Shaking Things Up:
The Church Reforms Inside and Out. 149

9 New Ideas, New Problems:
The Middle of the Middle Ages 170

1

History and the Church

Chapter Overview

In this chapter, we will explore:

▶ How learning about the past gives tools for understanding the present

▶ What we mean when we talk about "history" and the sources we use in writing it

▶ Some questions to ask when reading history in general and Church history in particular

History: The Art of Remembering Who We Are

This book is about trying to understand the Roman Catholic Church through its history. That means it has two goals: to better understand the Church's past and to look at how that past has formed the Church as it exists today. Politics, oppression, freedom, debate, wars, prejudice—the history of the Church is also the history of the world. History never just stays in the background, nor is it simply about memorizing names, dates, and events. It is about learning who we are, how we got here, and where we are going. It is about us, the Church, and our world.

Church History: The Art of Learning Who the Church Is

Why is it important to study the history of the Catholic Church? For a Catholic, the answer may seem self-evident. However, if you belong to another faith tradition or to none at all, you may have a harder time seeing the relevance to your own life.

First, Church history is more than just the history of the Church. It goes beyond the record of popes and bishops, councils and cardinals into the story of political intrigue; the rise and fall of empires; and the development of law, science, art, architecture, and literature. It is about saints and sinners, kings and peasants, monks, nuns, poets, and scholars. It is about people who felt they were answering God's call and people who felt they were breaking God's law. It is about people going about the messy business of living and creating a living institution at the same time. Ultimately, Catholic Church history is an essential part of the history of the Western world. Over the last two thousand years, nations and empires have risen and fallen and new ideas have come and gone, but the Church has continued to exist. Its history has been woven into the fabric of the Western world for so long that you cannot separate the two.

In addition, the Catholic Church shares much of its history with that of other Christian churches. Almost all non-Catholic Christian groups trace their history either through a split that occurred between the Eastern and Western Churches in the thirteenth century or through the Protestant Reformation of the sixteenth century. Thus, learning Catholic Church history is also a means of learning the wider history of Christianity.

Ekklesia

The English word *church* comes from the Greek word *ekklesia*, which means an assembly of those who are called forth or summoned. To the ancient Greeks, it meant a gathering of people who held the rights of citizenship. When Jewish scholars translated the Hebrew Scriptures into Greek during the first through third centuries BCE, they used *ekklesia* to talk about the gathering of the people of Israel. If we read the Greek version of Exodus 19:6, we find that when the people meet on Mount Sinai to receive the Law, they are called an *ekklesia*, "a kingdom of priests, a holy nation." With these images in mind, it made sense to early Christians that those who gathered in response to the call of Jesus were an *ekklesia*; in this way, they claimed a heritage that went back to that assembly on Mount Sinai.

So what the term *church* really means is people. However much we may talk about the Catholic Church or any other church as an institution, in reality it cannot be separated from the people who are a part of it. The Church's greatest theologian, Thomas Aquinas, made exactly this point when he wrote that "the church is nothing other than the congregation of the faithful." [1]

All this means that the Catholic Church has played a significant role in creating the world in which we live. Understanding Church history helps us understand our world, which ultimately helps us understand ourselves.

The Church believes its history is of central importance to all of humanity. In the Church's vision, all of human history has value because it is part of the history of salvation, and the Church's history in particular is meaningful because it is a profound part of God's revelation to humanity. The Church claims that the whole arc of its history is simply a way of bringing people into closer unity with God. The following chapters are not an attempt to verify or deny those claims but rather an attempt to look at the claims as they have been lived and see how they have affected and sometimes shaped our world.

Unraveling the Mystery of History

Imagine this scene: You have a fight with a friend. Later, when the two of you have cooled off, you sit down to talk. As you remember it, the fight started because your friend said it was dumb to study art because art could not feed or clothe people; your friend said that art does not help people as directly as science, and you started yelling about art feeding people's souls. So how did the fight really start? The answer may well depend on who is telling the story. History may be about remembering, but people often remember things differently.

If I decided to write about this fight, I would need to know what happened, but after I talked to both you and your friend, I would have two different accounts. Problem? Not really. As a historian, I have the tricky job of sifting through different people's memories of the same event. When you sort through all the sources that talk about a particular incident, they will all usually agree on some facts (like when and where the fight took place and who was involved), but for the "whys" and "hows," mostly what you get is interpretation; even the best interpretations will highlight some things and leave others out. Likewise with writing about events and people—each writer reconstructs a story in a different way. The writer does not create what happened but she does create "history," a particular observation and interpretation of what happened.

There is more. The reader is just as vital to the process of interpreting history as the writer because the reader is constantly sifting through a wealth of information in order to figure out what is most important. When I use a highlighter to help me remember things in a book, I do not highlight everything, just the things I most want to remember. Does that mean the other things are not important? The writer thought they mattered, or he would not have included them. So the writer has one idea about what is important, and the reader has another. The writer may have been creating history by putting things together in a certain way, but the reader is also creating history by pulling things out in a certain way.

Finding the Starting Place

Let's think for a minute about the sources we use to learn history. We have many sources for learning about our nation and our world: books, professors, movies, TV, websites—the list goes on. We also can learn about the history and practices of a religion from books like this one, as well as from people who hold those beliefs.

If I want to know something about Islam, for instance, I could read a book describing that religion's beliefs and practices, talk to a Muslim friend, or read web pages devoted to the topic. My job as a historian would be to figure out which of these sources was most valid and useful. I would be wary of a web page attempting to refute Islam, because as a hostile source, the web page would likely present things in a negative light. Talking with a Muslim might be a good source for understanding how Muslims live their lives, but if I want to know about the origins and development of the religion, the book on Islam might be a better source than my friend. Depending on what it is I want to know, I will decide that some sources are more valuable than others.

It Is All about Asking Questions

Knowing that not all sources are created equal means we have to determine which ones will be most helpful in a given situation. It also means that when we read what is written about historical events and people, we need to ask ourselves some questions:

- What sources did the author use?

- What events and people are included and what is left out?

- Does the author's interpretation fit the facts as you understand them?

- Do you agree with the author's choices and interpretation? Why or why not?

Questions like these help us evaluate a work of history to see if we think it is valid and useful; otherwise we are simply accepting the author's interpretation as fact.

When we look at the Roman Catholic Church, we ought to keep in mind some questions that can help us get a fuller picture of what exactly was going on in the Church at any given moment in its history. I find the following pairs of themes helpful in understanding where the Church was at, what it looked like, what it thought was important, and what it was able to do at various points over the last two thousand years. Think of these themes as windows for looking at the Church. Different windows give different views, but when we are talking about something as rich and varied as the history of the Catholic Church, the more windows we can look through, the better our understanding of that "building" will be.

Knowledge and wisdom. Knowledge is about learning things and wisdom is about understanding them, and both are important in the history of the Church. The Church has always seen itself as the keeper of wisdom, and at times this belief has conflicted with the way secular knowledge was developing. In the early Church, for example, writers debated whether studying philosophy was a true path to wisdom, and the Church had very public conflicts over scientific knowledge and whether it was leading people to devalue the Scriptures. In the modern era, the Church continues to warn against approaches to knowledge geared toward simply determining facts rather than helping people. Looking at where the Church has drawn the line between knowledge and wisdom, and where others have drawn it in relation to the Church, can help us see what the Church has valued at different points in its history.

Political power and social influence. At times, the Church has held extraordinary political power. Kings and emperors gained and lost their thrones based on the actions of the Church's leaders; for centuries, popes ruled the Papal States (part of what is now Italy); there have even been armies controlled by the Pope. Those times eventually ended, but the Church's ability to influence society continues today. From the beginning, the Church has played a role in helping those marginalized by society, and this tradition lives on in the Church's social teachings. Looking at how the Church has used its political power and social influence can point us toward what the Church has most wanted to achieve at different times.

Inside view and outside view. Catholics do not always agree on exactly how they view the Church, but they tend to share a belief in its value as a sign of God's presence in the world. Those outside the Church often view it quite differently. For example, many groups over the centuries have found their beliefs declared heretical because they differed from Church teaching; sometimes people were even put to death over those beliefs. From the Church's "inside" perspective at the time, it had a sacred duty to protect people from teachings that could lead them away from God; from the "outside" perspective of the so-called heretic, the Church was just trying to keep people from speaking a truth it did not like. Understanding the nature and context of differing views about the Church can help us get a fuller view of what role it has played throughout history.

The Catholic Church is a living, breathing, growing and thriving institution. It has been both witness and participant through two thousand years of majesty and beauty, terror and shame, tragedy and even comedy. When we look beyond the names and dates, we see that the history of the Church is a wild ride and a great story.

Questions and Ideas for Understanding

1. Telling the truth does not always involve telling "the whole truth"; you choose what it is important to say. Think about how you might describe a member of your family. How would you decide what things to include and what to leave out? Would you answer differently depending on who was asking the question?

2. It has been said that the news media write the first draft of history. Find two or more media accounts of the same event—a crime, a sports event, a political happening, a war, or whatever else you can find. Briefly describe the stories. Then describe how the accounts agree and how they differ.

3. Imagine you are a historian, and you want to write about a particular period of the Church's history. You have in front of you a number of documents from that time: the personal writings of a priest, a typical Christian, and an atheist; a history text from the court of a Christian king; and a Muslim account of a war against a Christian kingdom. How could each of these sources help you better understand the Church of that time?

Notes

[1]Thomas Aquinas, I Decret. ed Parma 16:305. Quoted in Francis A. Sullivan, SJ, *Salvation outside the Church?* New York: Paulist Press, 1992, p. 47.

2
Laying the Foundation
Jesus and His First Followers

Chapter Overview
In this chapter, we will explore:

▶ The Greco-Roman and Jewish backgrounds of Christianity

▶ The life of Jesus and his first followers

▶ Peter and the founding of the Church

▶ The early Christian community

▶ The Christian Scriptures

Deborah: Who Is This Man, Yeshua?

As you walk to the well in the center of the village, you hear the other women talking—again—about this man Yeshua. It seems like every time you walk out your door, someone is saying his name. Funny, you never even heard of Yeshua while he was alive, but then a man from your village came back from Jerusalem telling stories about Yeshua's life and death. What he says is amazing. People are saying that after he died a criminal's death on a cross, God raised him to life again!

Amid the chatter of the women at the well, you make out your friend Naomi's voice. She is saying this Yeshua must be the long-awaited Messiah, the Lord's Anointed One. Her sister Miriam disagrees: "Blasphemy! The Messiah will come with power. The Romans will not be able to stop him, much less kill him like a common thief."

Naomi catches sight of you. "Deborah, what do you think? Could Yeshua be the One?"

You sigh and reposition the water urn on your head. You have always heard that the Messiah would free his people from Roman rule, that he would make Judea a proud, free nation once more and sit on the throne of his ancestor, the great King David. This Yeshua certainly did not do that. But raised from the dead? If this is so, surely he was special to God. But God's Anointed One?

You silently offer a prayer, asking that the Lord reveal to his people the truth about this man Yeshua. Then you smile at the other women, settle the filled urn once more on your head, and turn toward home.

Yeshua—Jesus—did not free his homeland from Roman rule, yet he did affect the people who gathered around him so profoundly that they continued to believe his message and spread the word about his life even after he died. In this chapter, we will talk about those people, Jesus' first followers, whose belief that Jesus was the Anointed One formed the basis of what would become Christianity. We will meet these people by looking at the world in which they lived. We will see how these first disciples negotiated the transition from followers of a particular man to founders of a worldwide religion. ■

Inside the Empire

To a young Jewish woman like Deborah, the world might have seemed to make little sense. The Jews, who understood themselves to be God's Chosen People, were no longer rulers in their own homeland. Judea was an occupied territory, part of the vast Roman Empire that created a ring around the Mediterranean. While the empire did not cover the entire known world, to the people living within its borders, it must have seemed that way.

The heart of this vast empire was the city of Rome. While each country and each group of people had its own center of culture, politics, business, and religion, Rome had international importance.

It is hard to imagine that a single city could dominate such a large and diverse area, but Rome had the most efficient army the world had ever seen. People usually entered the empire by being conquered, which meant they lost their independence, but lands in the empire could count on protection from their enemies and often gained greater political stability. Individuals could benefit, too, if they managed to become Roman citizens. You were automatically a citizen if your parents were citizens; if not, you could gain the honor if you were a former slave freed by a citizen, if you performed certain kinds of service for the empire, or if you followed the time-honored method of bribery—just pay the person who wrote the list of new citizens. Citizens living outside Rome were exempt from certain taxes the other locals had to pay; the local rulers could not have them beaten or tortured without a legal trial, and if they got in trouble with the law, they could appeal their case to the court in Rome.

The Roman Empire included many different societies, but none had the international impact of Greek culture, known as Hellenism (the Greek word *hellenizein* means "to speak Greek"). Greek influence was so important that we usually talk about the Greco-Roman world: the areas conquered by Rome but influenced by Greece. Rome does not get the laurel for starting the spread of Greek culture, though; that belongs to Alexander the Great, the Macedo-

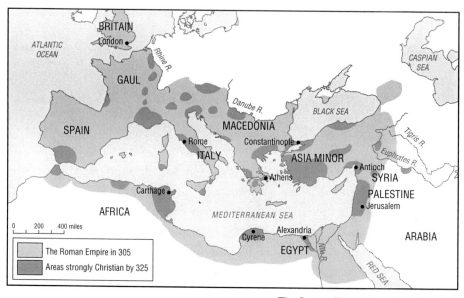

The Roman Empire at the Time of Jesus

nian leader who was a major player before Rome got into the act. Tutored in his youth by the Greek philosopher Aristotle, Alexander was fascinated by the Greek way of life. He began wandering outside of his native Macedonia at the head of an army in about 334 BCE, looking for places to conquer. He quickly gained control of much of the Eastern Mediterranean and Middle East.

Alexander introduced Hellenism wherever he went. He set up city-states on the Greek model, often naming the new cities after himself; the most famous is Alexandria in Egypt. The heart of the city-state was a gymnasium, which was much more than the sports center the name now implies. Men exercised there but also received an education in grammar, rhetoric, and literature. In some ways, the Greek gymnasium resembled a modern college. Alexander also had temples built or converted for worship of the Greek gods, and he set up schools to teach Greek to the native children. This led to the widespread use of Greek as both an official language for government and business and as a common tongue that people from different areas could use in speaking with one another.

Meanwhile, Back in Jerusalem

The people of Judea were familiar with Hellenization—and with the problems it could cause. In the second century BCE, Judea was under the control of the Seleucid Empire, one of the spin-offs of Alexander's empire. For more than a century, the Judeans had been exposed to Greek culture; some people accepted it, some rejected it, but it was not a major source of conflict.

That changed in 170 BCE when the new ruler, Antiochus IV Epiphanes, ordered all the lands under his rule to follow a Hellenistic model. In Judea, he had a gymnasium built, decreed that male children could not be circumcised in accordance with Jewish law, set up a garrison of soldiers in Jerusalem, and even killed people within the Temple walls. The last straw came when he ordered the Temple converted for the worship of Greek gods. It was one thing to be exposed to Hellenistic culture and to accept or reject it by choice but quite another to have it forced on you by a ruler bent on destroying your religious beliefs and a way of life. A Jewish group led by a family known as the Maccabees rose up in revolt in 167 BCE. By 164, they had tossed the Seleucids out of Judea. They cleansed and rededicated the Temple (the event celebrated in the feast of Hanukkah) and returned the land to Jewish rule.

This great victory did not halt the spread of Hellenistic culture throughout Judea, however. Within a few decades after the Maccabean revolt, it was common for members of Judea's upper classes to speak Greek, give their children Greek names, and combine elements of Hellenism with the traditional Jewish way of life. By the time of Jesus, Hellenistic ideas had been a part of Judean society for hundreds of years, and these ideas would have a lasting impact on the Church that developed out of Jesus' ministry.

The Maccabees ruled Judea until 63 BCE, when the Roman general Pompey was asked to settle a dispute over who should rule the area. Not inclined to negotiate, Pompey simply conquered Judea and made sure that whoever was the best friend to Rome was on the throne. The situation deteriorated so that by the time of Jesus, various parts of the homeland were ruled directly through governors like Pilate or indirectly through "client kings" like Herod, who was himself a Jew but maintained his status through support from Rome.

From the Roman viewpoint, Judea was a small and not terribly important part of the vast network of peoples and cultures making up their empire, but the Judeans gave Rome its share of headaches—they never resigned themselves to being part of the empire. This left the Judeans of the first century in a precarious situation: Most people wanted their homeland to be independent, but they knew that if they mounted a revolt and it failed, the Romans would march in and destroy everything Jewish. This fact plays an important part in the Jesus story, as we will see later.

Public Religion and Private Faith

Modern democratic countries see religion as a private matter, but in first-century Rome, who you worshipped was very much a public concern. In the state religion, people worshipped the Roman gods and emperors. No one cared what you really believed, but worshipping the gods and the emperor was your civic duty. All of this would later cause problems for Christians, who would not participate in this form of worship.

Official Roman religion lived side by side with many other religions. Walk around Rome in the first century, and you could find people worshipping Roman gods like Jupiter and Juno, the Greek god Dionysius, the Egyptian Isis and Osiris, the Syrian Cybele, and a host of others. Many of these were mystery religions, which tended to keep their rituals secret, revealing them only to people initiated into the religion. The mystery religions usually focused on a god who had somehow overcome death, either by experiencing a cycle of death and rebirth or by going into the underworld and returning alive. Initiates would receive secret information allowing them to share in the god's overcoming of death and were promised that after their deaths they would be reunited in an idyllic setting with the god. Mystery religions provided the kind of emotional connection to divinity that Roman state religion had no interest in providing. The state religion concentrated on order in society and in the cosmos, but the mystery religions gave life meaning and purpose.

One of the most popular mystery religions was devoted to a Persian god, Mithra. Initiates were baptized into the group, and they shared a common meal of bread and wine as a form of worship. The day of Mithra's miraculous birth was celebrated on the Roman equivalent of December 25, and according to tradition, shepherds brought gifts to the newborn god. If all this sounds familiar, then you may understand why Christianity was regarded by many as simply another mystery religion when it first appeared.

Just One God but a Lot of Ideas

The Greco-Roman world may have seen Christianity as a mystery religion, but it was first understood to be simply another Jewish movement. In Jesus' time, Judaism was full of groups who came together based on their interpretations of the Law, hopes for the coming of the Messiah, or the desire to kick the Romans out of their land. The Jewish historian Josephus tells us about the four main groups in first-century Judaism: the Sadducees, Pharisees, Zealots, and Essenes.

The Sadducees

The Sadducees came mainly from the Jewish upper class, especially the priestly class, and saw Temple worship as the center of Jewish religious life. They believed Jewish observance of the Law had been watered down by overvaluing the oral tradition. People reading and studying the Torah (the first five books of the Hebrew Bible) had developed interpretations that they passed down orally from generation to generation, and as they were passed along, these interpretations came to be thought of as authoritative. But to the Sadducees, everything important was in the Torah's written law, and other writings or oral traditions were not teachings of authority.

The Sadducees were wealthy, powerful, and conservative, and they wanted good relations with their Roman overlords. They took to Hellenism with a vengeance, which sometimes put them at odds with other Jews. Most members of the high council known as the Sanhedrin, which governed Jerusalem under the authority of Rome and oversaw religious disputes, came from the ranks of the Sadducees.

The Pharisees

The Pharisees agreed with the Sadducees about the importance of the Torah, but they thought the oral tradition was also vital. Typically from the middle and lower classes, they were skeptical of Hellenistic ideas. Like most Jews of the time, the Pharisees participated in Temple worship and felt it was a vital part of Jewish life, but they did not feel this fulfilled their religious duties. Righteous living, the Pharisees believed, meant following the Law in every detail.

In the time of Jesus, there were two main groups of Pharisees: one emphasized the letter of the Law; the other, the Law's spirit. While their differences mattered, they still shared the bulk of their basic beliefs. The Pharisees were the most popular group in first-century Judaism. Paul of Tarsus was himself a Pharisee until his experience on the road to Damascus led him to join the young Christian community.

The Zealots

The Zealots worked actively for rebellion, believing the Jews needed to expel the Romans from the land they held sacred. Using the slogan "No king but God!" the Zealots and other like-minded folk set themselves against not only the Romans but also any Jews whom they thought were collaborators. This group gained in popularity during and after the lifetime of Jesus and eventually paved the way for a Jewish rebellion against Rome in 66 CE.

The Essenes

The Essenes were a monastic group that followed a strict interpretation of the Law. Like the Sadducees, they rejected the oral tradition, but they also rejected the Sadducees' worldliness. Like the Zealots, they wanted the Romans out of their homeland, but they were not interested in mounting an armed rebellion; instead, they believed the long-awaited Messiah would come to free them from Roman rule. The Essenes lived apart from the rest of Jewish society, believing it to be corrupt, and they usually remained celibate. While this group is not mentioned in the New Testament (NT), it had a definite presence in the Judaism of Jesus' time.

While these were the main Jewish groups, most Jews did not hold membership in any one of them. Your average person may have felt drawn to one group or another, but he was most likely to consider himself simply an everyday Jew. Still, with the Romans on one hand and all these differences of opinion on the other, tensions ran high in first-century Judean society.

Getting the Word Out: Jesus & Co.

Jesus walked amid these tensions daily, and eventually they led to his execution. The basic facts of the historical account are simple. Some members of the Sanhedrin feared that Jesus' followers would try to proclaim him the Messiah, the King who would throw off the yoke of Roman rule—a move that could provoke a Roman crackdown on Judea. They denounced him to the Roman governor Pilate, who had Jesus executed for treason—for claiming, as the inscription on his cross stated, to be the "King of the Jews."

Over the last two thousand years, countless millions of Christians have believed the Jews killed Jesus and sometimes have committed horrible crimes based on this belief. However, as is often the case, what people have thought and what actually happened are two different things: while a small number of Jews participated in denouncing Jesus as a potential threat, the gospels clearly state that it was the Romans who killed Jesus. And they did so without a second thought, without any terrible excitement or great animosity: they simply put to death a troublemaker who could potentially threaten their rule.

What neither the Jews nor the Romans could have foreseen was that the death of the charismatic leader would not be the end of the movement he started. The people who gathered around Jesus before his death did not just go away after his execution. Jesus' followers continued to believe in him and his message even when he was no longer physically present among them, and it is this belief and these first believers that formed the core of what would become the Church.

Reading the gospel stories two thousand years out of the culture in which they were written, many modern readers think Jesus' healings and teachings were a total break with the Judaism of his day, but that is not the case. The Jews of Jesus' time were familiar with charismatic leaders offering interpretations of the Law. They knew of other miracle workers. Still, those closest to Jesus began to see him as more than just a righteous man. Was he a prophet of God? Could he even be the long-awaited Messiah?

These questions came to a head among Jesus' followers after his death, but they began during the years of his ministry; they had as much to do with what he taught as with the miracles he performed. As a teacher, Jesus had a lot in common with the Pharisees, especially those who followed the "spirit of the Law." Like them, he valued the Temple sacrifices but was more concerned with how people lived their lives. He was much more wary of those who seemed to focus on rules at the expense of spirit. For instance, when Jesus was asked why he allowed his hungry disciples to break the Law and gather food on the Sabbath, he replied, "The sabbath was made for man, not man for the sabbath" (Mk 2:27). Jesus saw the Law as a vehicle to help people draw closer to God, not a ladder that must be climbed in order for that to happen.

Many times the gospels present Jesus as criticizing the Pharisees, calling them "hypocrites" (Mt 23:25) or a "brood of vipers" (Mt 3:7), but we need to understand this from within the culture in which the gospels were written. In the gospels, we see Jesus talking about the Pharisees in much the same way the Pharisees talked about each other: disagreeing and sometimes showing annoyance but still recognizing that what they shared was greater and more important than their differences. Jesus shared the Pharisees' belief that the Torah was sacred and thought that sincerely attempting to follow it was the way to come closer to God, but he went further—Jesus taught that the true meaning of the Torah could be summed up in two phrases: love God, and love your neighbor (Mk 12:29–31). This, to Jesus, was the essence of the Torah, the essence of Judaism, and the essence of what he wanted people to know.

It's Good to Have Friends: The First Followers

As he walked through Judea teaching, healing and telling stories, Jesus gathered about him many who were drawn to his words and actions. Among his first followers were the Twelve who became most closely associated with him.

Other gospels present different lists, but the oldest gospel, that of Mark, lists the Twelve as Simon, later called Peter; Andrew; James and John, the sons of Zebedee; Philip; Thomas; Matthew; James, son of Alphaeus; Thaddeus; Simon the Cananean; Bartholomew; and Judas Iscariot.

When we think of their importance in the history of the Church, it is amazing that these men, Jesus' first disciples (meaning "followers"), were not wealthy or powerful. The disciple John was a member of the priestly class, but most of the Twelve were members of the working class and not leaders. Peter,

"Do This in Remembrance of Me" [1] (1 Cor 11:24): The Eucharist

Just a few days before his death, Jesus and his disciples gathered to celebrate Passover for the last time. Passover commemorates God's freeing of the Israelites from enslavement in Egypt, as told in the book of Exodus. The gospels show Jesus teaching his disciples a new understanding of the food before them as they ate the ritual Passover meal together: "Take it; this is my body . . . This is my blood of the covenant" (Mk 14:22, 24). Paul explains in 1 Corinthians that Jesus asked his followers to continue eating the bread and drinking from the cup as a way of remembering him. This is the foundation of the sacrament that Catholics have come to know as the Eucharist, which comes from a Greek term meaning "to give thanks."

Every Jew grew up knowing the story of the Passover: God sent a series of plagues to force the Egyptians to release their captives. In the final plague, the firstborn of all humans and animals in the land were killed, with the exception of the children of the Israelites. They were saved because they daubed the blood of a lamb on their doorways, indicating to the Angel of Death that theirs was a house to be passed over. After his death, Jesus' early followers soon came to a new interpretation of that story: They saw Jesus as the lamb who was sacrificed so that others could be saved. This idea arising from Passover became central to the early Christian understanding of who Jesus was and what his life meant, and certainly to their celebration of the Eucharist.

For the earliest Christians, celebrating the Eucharist meant sharing a meal, just as the Jews shared a meal as part of their Passover celebration. Jewish Christians almost assuredly did not think the bread and wine were actually the body and blood of Jesus; from a Jewish perspective, this would not have made sense because drinking blood was forbidden under the Law. However, Christians from Gentile backgrounds quickly came to understand Jesus' words literally, and it is this understanding the Church preserves. Catholics consider it one of the mysteries of faith that in the Eucharistic celebration, the bread and wine become the body and blood of Christ: "Christ is thus really and mysteriously made *present*." [2]

By early in the second century, many Christian communities had replaced the actual meal with a ritual meal during the worship service—a ritual meal during the worship service that is strikingly similar to the Catholic Mass today.

Voices from the Past

"One for Whose Sake God Shows Favor to His Entire Generation"

▶ Author: Jewish rabbis

▶ Written: Between the third and sixth centuries, from earlier oral traditions

▶ Audience: Other Jews

Rabbi Chanina ben Dosa lived in Judea in the mid-first century. He was known to his contemporaries as a righteous man whose faith brought about healings and other miraculous occurrences. Here are two stories told about him.[3]

Healing through Prayer

[O]nce upon a time Rabban Gamliel's son got sick. He sent two men of learning to Rabbi Chanina ben Dosa to beg him mercy from God concerning him. [Chanina] saw them coming and went to a room upstairs and asked mercy from God concerning him. When he had come back down he said to them, "Go, the fever has left him." They said to him, "What? Are you a prophet?" He said, "I am not a prophet ... But this I have received from tradition: if my prayer of intercession flows unhesitatingly from my mouth, I know it will

be answered" ... [W]hen they came back to Rabban Gamliel he said to them ... "You are neither too early nor too late but this is what happened: in that moment the fever left him and he asked for water!"

Chanina's Sinlessness

[O]nce upon a time a poisonous snake was injuring people. They went and made it known to Rabbi Chanina ben Dosa. He said to them, "Show me its burrow." They showed him its burrow and he placed his heel upon the mouth of the hole. It came forth and bit him—and it died. He put the snake on his shoulders, went to the House of Study, and said to them, "See, my sons; it is not a snake that kills but sin that kills." Then they said, "Woe to the man a snake attacks and woe to the snake which Rabbi Chanina ben Dosa attacks!" ■

Andrew, and the sons of Zebedee were fishermen, an honest middle-class occupation. Matthew was a despised tax collector working for the Roman government. Some of these men may have had some education; others were probably illiterate. None of them would have foreseen their historical impact as the first people to proclaim the Christian message.

One of the most important people in getting the fledgling Christian community going was the apostle who came to be known as Peter. The gospels show Peter to be a complex person—committed, loyal, hotheaded, dense, and scared. The respect he gained in the early Christian community, and which modern Christians still extend to him, did not come about because he was perfect or because he always understood what was going on but because he stayed with it and kept on trying.

The most frequently mentioned disciple in the gospels, Peter was the first one called, a leader of the other disciples and a special friend of Jesus. He came from the town of Bethsaida in the Galilee, an area with many non-Jewish inhabitants and strongly influenced by Greek culture. Many around Peter spoke Greek rather than the Aramaic common in Judea, and as a prosperous fisherman, he probably knew at least enough Greek to conduct business.

Catholics see Peter as the first Pope in a succession that continues to the present day, but he did not come by that title immediately. Once the hierarchy of the Church began to emerge, people looked to the line of the bishops of Rome to see how the teachings had been passed down. The earliest lists record Linus as the first bishop of Rome and thus the first Pope; Peter was not given that title until the late second or early third century. Nevertheless, there is no doubt that he was honored in a particular way even in the earliest Christian circles.

Later in his life, Peter traveled extensively, telling people the good news about Jesus. Eventually he traveled to Rome, which became the last of Peter's journeys as he was killed during Nero's persecution of Christians in about 65 CE. The executions took place in an area called the Vatican Gardens, and a tradition from the early Church tells us that Peter was buried in a cemetery close by. The Emperor Constantine certainly knew this tradition: in 315, he began building what would eventually become St. Peter's Basilica on that site. If you go to St. Peter's today, you can walk below the basilica floor and see what is thought to be the tomb of this faithful follower of Jesus.

Long before that, though, Peter was simply a tradesman who worked hard to take care of his family, including his wife. Although we know little about Peter's wife—even her name is never given in the gospel accounts—it is clear that she too was among the early followers of Jesus. Paul tells us in 1 Corinthians 9:5 that she went with Peter on mission trips after the resurrection. Her faith would not have come about just by listening to her husband either, since Jesus stayed in her house many times; it seems to have been his base of operations during his ministry. According to the gospel writers, she also saw Jesus heal her mother of a fever and, later that same day, heal a host of people who showed up at her home.

Peter's wife is one of the many faith-filled but usually unnamed women who formed part of the community around Jesus during his life and spread the Christian message to others after his death. The Twelve may all have been men, but women also formed part of the inner core of the group that gathered around Jesus. The Gospel of Luke, for instance, presents Jesus staying at the home of a woman named Mary and her sister Martha when he traveled to Bethany (10:38). We also hear in Luke about Joanna and Susanna, who traveled with Jesus and the Twelve and helped financially support Jesus' ministry (8:1–3). We read about many other unnamed female followers of Jesus, such as the woman who washed his feet with her hair and tears and the women who walked with Jesus on the road to his crucifixion. And no follower of Jesus, male or female, has been more honored among Catholics than Jesus' mother, Mary. Although they are not as often discussed, women were every bit as important in Jesus' life and ministry as were the men who heeded his call.

The best known of Jesus' female followers is Mary Magdalene, a disciple of Jesus and, according to all four canonical gospels, the first witness to the resurrection. The gospels differ on exactly who first saw Jesus after he was resurrected, but all of them list Mary. This led a second-century Christian writer named Hippolytus to proclaim her the "apostle to the apostles" (a title the Church continues to use today), as she was the first one to see and also the first one to tell, which makes her the first spreader of the good news, the first apostle. Mary followed Jesus in his travels and supported his ministry financially. When most of the disciples fled in fear, Mary remained with Jesus until his death. Her role as the first one to hear about the resurrection did not create her status as a disciple; it came about because of it.

During Jesus' lifetime, those who gathered around him were known simply as his followers. A little later, they came to be known as followers of the Way. By about 45 CE, Jesus' followers in Antioch had come to be called Christians (Acts 11:26), which comes from *Christ*, a Greek word meaning "anointed one"; in Hebrew, *Messiah*.

The followers of Jesus did not become known by his name but rather by the title they believed was his, that of the Anointed One whom the Jews had long awaited. With this name, they proclaimed their belief that Jesus played a special role in history and claimed the Jewish heritage as the background of their faith. The term *Christian* was soon proclaimed by the followers of the man from Nazareth, and it is the name by which they came to be known as they traveled outside of Judea to spread their beliefs to others.

Getting the Church Going

The man we know as Peter was born with the name of Simon, but Jesus changed it at a crucial point in the development of the Christian community: the moment the followers first began to see Jesus as more than simply another teacher. When Jesus asked his disciples whom they thought he was, Simon opened his mouth and these words flew out: "You are the Messiah" (Mt 16:16). For a first-century Jew like Simon, this statement carried a lot of meaning: it was a declaration of belief in the God who would free his people yet again and an expression of hope in a very near future that would be better than the present. It was also a political statement because the Messiah was expected to free his people from Roman rule.

Jesus' response to Simon given in the gospels shows a very different understanding of what being the Messiah could mean. Rather than speaking the language of politics, Jesus looked at Simon and declared him to be Peter, a name that means "rock," and told him that "upon this rock I will build my church" (Mt 16:18). Catholics see this as the moment when the Church came into being, as with these words Jesus both gave Peter a promise (that the Church would be built) and entrusted him with a responsibility (to be its leader).

The idea of this promise and responsibility comes easily to Catholics two thousand years after the fact, but to Peter and the others it must have quickly seemed a sheer impossibility. Jesus was crucified, dead, and buried. The followers had not only experienced the devastating loss of their beloved teacher, but many of them also felt the fear of being a known associate of someone executed as a criminal—the same fear that had led Peter so famously to deny Jesus three times just prior to his crucifixion.

Then came stories of the resurrection, and everything began to change.

The idea of resurrection was a hot topic in first-century Judaism. The Pharisees believed in bodily resurrection, seeing some evidence for it in the Scriptural writings outside the Torah; the Sadducees, who looked only to the Torah for guidance, did not accept it. There were probably differences of opinion about the matter among Jesus' followers, but this academic discussion, this question of belief about what might happen in the future, suddenly became a part of their here and now.

Jesus' resurrection is beyond the reaches of historical verification. What people say they experienced is not. In 1 Corinthians, Paul writes that Jesus "appeared to [Peter], then to the Twelve. After that he appeared to more than five hundred brothers at once . . . After that he appeared to James, then to all the apostles. Last of all . . . he appeared to me" (15:5–8). Even if five hundred witnesses did emerge to tell their story, many would have questioned whether the resurrection really happened and what it meant if it did. Nevertheless, we do know that these stories spread and that as more and more people came to accept them as fact, the community of believers grew.

Apparently, it grew rapidly on the day of a Jewish festival known as Pentecost. Acts 2 tells the story of the disciples gathering in Jerusalem to celebrate this feast of thanksgiving for the first fruits of the harvest. Suddenly, "there came from the sky a noise like a strong driving wind . . . Then there appeared to them tongues of fire, which parted, and came to rest on each one of them. And they were all filled with the holy Spirit" (Acts 2:2–4). How did the disciples react? We are told that they went among the people gathered from many lands for the celebration and began telling them about the life, death, and resurrection of Jesus in words the people could understand—they were actually speaking other languages, "as the Spirit enabled them to proclaim" (Acts 2:4).

This day of fire and power has an important place in Catholic theology, because it is the foundation of the doctrine of apostolic succession. While practices varied in the early Church, most Christian communities believed that when the apostles passed on their teachings to the leaders who followed them in the communities they founded, they also passed on their authority to teach. In this way, they ensured the teachings would be remembered and applied in ways that were in keeping with their beliefs. As the communities developed a hierarchy and structure that included bishops, they were the ones who came to be seen as entrusted with this authority.

It is this ability to trace the teachings of the Church and the authority of the bishops back to the apostles that is meant by apostolic succession, but there is an important step behind this, theologically speaking: the reason the apostles had this authority in the first place was that Jesus "entrusted to them his power of sanctifying"[4] when he sent the Holy Spirit to them at Pentecost.

So ultimately, apostolic succession is understood to mean not so much that the modern bishop's authority derives from the apostles as that it derives from Jesus himself. This belief in an unbroken line, from the historical Jesus living and teaching in the small area of Judea to present-day believers all over the world, is a central concept in Catholicism and the Eastern Orthodox Churches, and it is what Catholics mean when they proclaim in church services held every day throughout the world that the Church is apostolic.

Working Out the Kinks: The Council of Jerusalem

Another change also took place at Pentecost. Up until then, Peter and the others had spread their message only among other Jews, but on this day of radical change, Peter began preaching to Gentiles, too. Acts 10 portrays Peter telling the Gentile Cornelius and his family about Jesus and then watching in amazement as the Spirit filled these non-Jews, just as it had filled the apostles at Pentecost. Peter interpreted this as a message from God showing him that people did not have to be Jews in order to be part of the Christian community, and he had Cornelius and the others baptized.

When word got back to the community in Jerusalem that Peter had let Gentiles be baptized without first being circumcised, many were angry. This was a violation of Torah Law, and it was just the first of many. Soon Peter, and later Paul, also started eating with Gentiles—an impossibility for Jews keeping the Law because their food had to be prepared in particular ways. To Peter and others like him, these actions were expressions of a new freedom they felt God had given them to bring others into the fold; to many, though, it was disregard for and contempt of God's law.

As more Gentiles joined the early Christian communities, this issue began to take center stage. In some places, the Jewish and Gentile Christians got along, each continuing in its own traditions but coming together in their belief in Jesus. In other places, the Jewish and Gentile Christians argued about what role the laws of the Torah should play in the community that was coming together because of Christ. Around the year 50 CE, the leaders of the growing Christian community—including Peter, Paul, and James—met at what is called the Council of Jerusalem to debate whether a person had to be a Jew in order to become a Christian. Those gathered at the council decided that Gentiles needed to follow only a few essential rules: they had to "abstain from meat sacrifices to idols, from blood, from meats of strangled animals, and from unlawful marriage" (Acts 15:29). From now on, people were going to be welcomed into the Christian community based solely on their belief in Christ, not on their following of laws. It is hard to overstate the importance of this decision: there is no way the Christian message would have spread so far and so fast if the council had decided that rigor of Torah Law was going to be a necessity for new Christians.

Fishing for Converts

The Christian community grew in Judea and the surrounding areas, and soon missionaries began traveling all around the Mediterranean. The Christians' claim that Jesus had risen became an important part of the message when they began talking to people familiar with Hellenistic religions. It made sense to those familiar with the mystery religions and their stories of dying and resurrecting gods, but it also set the Christian message apart: those other stories were always set in some mythical past, but Christians claimed they were telling the story of a man to whom this had just happened. That a god from some ancient time might do it was one thing, but the idea that a man from Judea could accomplish this was simply shocking.

As the missionaries spread, new communities of believers sprang up, from Asia Minor to Rome itself. There were many of these missionaries, such as Barnabas, Thomas, and James, but none is better known or more highly revered than Paul.

If They Had Only Had Frequent-Flier Miles

Paul did not start out as a Christian, and he was not one of the original members of the community that gathered around Jesus. In fact, until his conversion experience on the road to Damascus (described in Acts 9:1–19), he tells us that he was one of the Jews who thought that the Christian claims were blasphemous and that the people spreading its message needed to be stopped before they led others into danger. His experience led him to a different belief, though, and he moved quickly from persecuting the followers of Jesus to being one of their best missionaries.

For Paul, the central Christian message was not found in Jesus' words but in his death and resurrection. As he saw it, this is what made salvation possible for all people. Before his conversion, Paul believed living a life in communion with God meant following the Law perfectly; but he could not be perfect. When he learned about Jesus, he came to believe being perfect was not the issue: what mattered was faith in Christ's life, death, and resurrection. He no longer saw following the Law as a path to justification, for God, Paul wrote, "justif[ies] the one who has faith in Jesus" (Rom 3:26). Some people of his time, and many more through the centuries, have held that Paul changed the deepest content of the Christian message: rather than proclaiming the coming of the kingdom of God, as Jesus did, he instead proclaimed faith in Jesus as the Christ. The truth of this proclamation is a question for theology, not history, but it is clear that the Church following Paul, and most Christians following the Church, have held belief in Jesus to be the defining point of Christianity.

"Let the Christians . . . Perish as in a Moment"

By 67 CE, missionaries like Paul had helped develop Christian communities throughout the Eastern Mediterranean. Back in Jerusalem, though, troubles were rolling like waves: in that year, the Judeans rose up in rebellion against their Roman overlords—and were crushed. The Roman army marched into Jerusalem, where they desecrated and then tore down the Temple. This was a devastating loss to the Judeans, and it caused a massive upheaval in their religious lives. The Sadducees did not have a role to play without the Temple, the Zealots were either killed in the fighting or completely demoralized, and the Essenes lost some of their monasteries and all of their hope. Each of these groups faded out of Jewish life, which means the only groups within first-century Judaism to survive the destruction were the Pharisees and the Christians.

The Pharisees were able to hold onto their vision of what it means to live a Jewish life because their focus was on righteous living rather than on Temple worship. They became the foundation for Judaism as it has continued to exist to the present day. In the Christian communities, those with Jewish roots mourned for Jerusalem, but their faith survived because it was centered in Christ rather than in the Temple.

Focus On

Putting Pen to Paper (or Stylus to Papyrus): Christian Writings

Jesus' first followers expected him to return almost immediately, so there seemed no need to write down the stories about Jesus and his disciples. But as those followers began to die, Christian communities started to realize the need to preserve those stories—in writing. It is from these stories that the gospels grew.

Just what are gospels? They are not modern biographies, which would not leave a gap of eighteen years in the central figure's life: we hear about Jesus at age 12 and then not again until he is 30! The gospel writers do not record all the happenings in Jesus' life, only those that help the reader see what the story of Jesus means—its significance. Each gospel author was trying to explain Jesus and his message in a way that would make sense to the people of the community for whom he was writing.

The Gospel of Matthew. Written for Jews to explain Jesus as the fulfillment of Jewish prophecies, this gospel shows Jesus' teachings as a new Torah, a new sacred grounding and covenant for those who follow him. This gospel presents Jesus passing his authority on to his followers, which Catholics understand as the origin of the Church's authority.

The Gospel of Mark. This gospel portrays a suffering Jesus who ministers mainly to the people of his homeland. The earliest written, this gospel shows a Jesus who, although the Son of God, brings the same message to God's people as the prophets before him did: "This is the time of fulfillment. The kingdom of God is at hand. Repent, and believe in the gospel" (1:14–15). An early Church tradition tells us this gospel is based on the memories of Peter.

The Gospel of Luke. This gospel was written for a Gentile audience for whom the Jewish prophecies meant nothing. While showing Christianity as the proper fulfillment of Judaism, it emphasizes Jesus' deep compassion and his importance for all people. It also stresses the theme that Jesus' ministry continues through the work of the Church.

The Gospel of John. Here we find the Christian message expressed in terms a Hellenistic audience would understand, where Jesus is presented as the source of wisdom and God's agent in the creation of the world. It was written at a time when tensions between Jews and the Jewish followers of Jesus had led to Jewish Christians being expelled from synagogues, and it reflects the bitterness of this situation.

Mark was written around 70 CE; Matthew and Luke, sometime between 80 and 90 CE; and John, sometime between 95 and 100 CE. Matthew, Mark, and Luke make up the Synoptic gospels—although differing in important details and overall impact, they share a similar chronology of Jesus' life, point to the same major events as important, and share many parallels in reporting what Jesus said and did. John is unique: it has a different chronology and geography, things show up in John not found in the Synoptics and vice versa, and it has an entirely different feel to it. The Jesus of the Synoptics speaks in parables, but in the Gospel of John, symbolism pervades.

These four gospels were not the only stories about Jesus and his teachings written in the early Church, but only these four made it into the canon of the NT. The canon is the authoritative list of writings the Church believes were inspired by the Holy Spirit. ■

Their mutual survival did not unite these two groups, however; in fact, it deepened the divide between them. The Jewish way of life was more than under siege; it was on the verge of being destroyed. The Jews who were able to hold onto their culture and beliefs did not want to see it threatened from within their own community by those who, as they saw it, disregarded the Torah and the Law and everything they held sacred. Within sixty years of Jesus' death, Jews who believed Jesus was the Messiah were being told to leave the synagogue.

Within a generation, the differences separating Jews and Jewish Christians grew even more serious. A group of rabbis came together in a place called Yavneh in about 90 CE to figure out how to continue being Jews without the Temple. One of the things they did was insert a condemnation of Christians into Jewish worship in synagogues; part of it is quoted in the title to this section. Gentiles, meanwhile, had already become the fastest-growing part of the Christian movement. All of these differences simply led the Christian community further from its Jewish roots and closer to its Hellenistic surroundings.

Jesus Said: The Gospel of Thomas

The noncanonical gospel that has had the most profound effect on modern scholarly understandings of Jesus is the Gospel of Thomas. In this gospel, there are no stories about Jesus or other people we associate with Jesus, with the exception of the disciples—who are there only to ask questions. Rather, this gospel is a collection of sayings attributed to Jesus. It includes parables, prophecies, and rules for the Christian community, but its most important theme is the search for wisdom.

Even though the Gospel of Thomas as a whole looks different, many of the sayings resemble those from the NT gospels. Scholars disagree about why this is: some see Thomas as a later reworking and expansion of things found in the NT gospels, while others argue that Thomas is a completely separate source that contains what may be some of the earliest and most authentic sayings of Jesus. In either case, we know Thomas was a favorite of early Christian Gnostics, who believed Christ came to bring humans knowledge about our true selves and how we can return to our divine home (we will talk more about Gnostics in chapter 3). Thomas was traditionally known in Syrian churches as the founder of a number of Christian communities in the East—and the brother of Jesus. While most of Western Christianity has traditionally understood Jesus to be an only child, other strands have seen Jesus as coming from a large family.

Beyond the Gospel Truth

The Christian Scriptures include many writings in addition to the gospels. For example, there is an apocalypse—a vision of the end of a terrible time—known as the Book of Revelation. The most common genre in the NT is the letter. Paul's letters, written in the 50s and 60s CE, are the earliest Christian writings. However, not all the NT letters that carry his name were actually composed by Paul. It was common practice to put the names of teachers and leaders onto the works of their students and followers or to cite some authority as the author of a work. The idea was not to mislead readers but to show an association with some figure whom the reader trusted. There are seven letters carrying Paul's name that everyone agrees were written by him: 1 Thessalonians, 1 and 2 Corinthians, Philippians, Philemon, Galatians, and Romans. Scholars debate whether to include 2 Thessalonians in the list of Paul's correspondence, but almost none would put any of the other letters into that category. Nor are scholars inclined to think that most of the other NT letters attributed to early Christian leaders like Peter and John were actually written by these men themselves. In fact, 2 Peter was probably written around 140 CE, making it the last written of all the books in the NT.

Just as there were gospels other than the four in the NT, many other apocalypses, letters, recorded visions, and other kinds of Christian writing circulated in the first few centuries of the Church's existence but were not included in the canon of the NT. Two such important early Christian works are the Shepherd of Hermas, which records a series of visions and actually is considered canonical in the Ethiopian Orthodox Church, and the Didache, a sort of handbook on how to be a Christian.

So how did the canon actually come to be? We saw that a group of rabbis met at Yavneh in 90 CE to close the canon of the Hebrew Scriptures, but no such event took place for the Christian Scriptures. Instead, we just start seeing consensus over time. The first known list of Christian works that the author considered inspired is called the Muratorian Canon (named after the scholar who discovered it in the early eighteenth century). It lists most of the books now included in the NT. Early Christian writers like Origen and Eusebius detailed their understandings about what should be included in the canon, but it is not until Athanasius in the fourth century that we get a Christian author listing each of the twenty-seven books now accepted as belonging in the NT, though a couple more centuries would pass before everybody would agree with the canon first described by Athanasius.

Questions and Ideas for Understanding

1. Which do you think is more important—for people to preserve their individual culture or for them to come together in a larger unity?

2. Various Jewish groups had to decide the extent to which they were willing to be assimilated into the Greco-Roman culture of their society. Many groups in the United States, especially immigrant populations, face this issue today. Do you think immigrants should assimilate into American culture? If so, to what extent?

3. Some people think a big change occurred with Paul. Jesus, they say, talked about loving God and other people—just look at the Sermon on the Mount in Matthew 5:3–11. But Paul's message was about faith in Jesus and the resurrection—see Romans 8:1–4. Did Paul represent a change, or was this just his way of helping people realize what Jesus really meant?

4. Investigate a modern ethnic group that wishes to break away from a larger political unity, like the Quebeçois in Canada, the Basques in Spain, or the Muslims in the Kashmir region of India. Discuss the origins and development of their claims to separateness and explain what part, if any, religious views play in their politics.

5. Women have been part of the Christian movement from its beginning, but their contributions have often been overlooked. Talk to Catholics from your parents' and grandparents' generations, as well as Catholics your own age, and write a description of women's status in the Church of today based on these interviews.

Notes

[1] Information taken from Joseph Martos, *Doors to the Sacred.* Tarrytown, NY: Triumph Books, 1991.

[2] *Catechism of the Catholic Church*, 1356.

[3] David R. Cartlidge and David L. Dungan, *Documents for the Study of the Gospels.* Philadelphia: Fortress Press, 1980, pp. 158–159.

[4] *Catechism*, 1087.

3

Under Attack

Persecution in the Early Church

Chapter Overview

In this chapter, we will explore:

▶ Changes in the Roman Empire and the Church during the second and third centuries

▶ The problems Christians encountered under Roman law

▶ The persecution of the Church

▶ The writings of Perpetua, a martyr

▶ The way Christian authors dealt with persecution

▶ Martyrdom in the modern era

Origen: When Belief Is More Important than Life

You know you believe, but do you believe enough? No, this is not the time to question. You have seen friends walk to their deaths with heads held high, determined to witness to the truth of the Christian message with their lives. But to lose your father … You know your father did the right thing—it would have gone against everything he believed to sacrifice to the Roman gods to save his life. And it would have gone against everything you believe as well. You even wrote to tell him that he should not change his mind out of love for his family. You miss him already, but you admire him for his courage and conviction, and you love him even more, knowing that he died like he lived—for the gospel.

Today your father was executed for nothing more than believing that the man from Nazareth was the Christ who came to set people free. The Christ showed not only that a life of love might carry a sentence of death but also that death was not the end of the story. Those who stayed true to the end gained so much: freedom from sin and fear, and ultimately reunion with the Eternal Father. No price is too high for that. So you do what you must: You accept the terrible suffering of losing your earthly father—and you accept the work of preparing yourself should you one day be called upon to make the same sacrifice.

The young man in this story is Origen. When Origen was 17, his father was killed during one of the periods of persecution that marked the early centuries of the Church. In this chapter, we will look at the political and social situations in the Roman Empire that led to these persecutions and at the people who faced them. Many of these people became *martyrs*, a word that comes from the Greek for "witness" and refers to those who choose to die rather than renounce their beliefs. We will see how facing imprisonment and death affected the lives and thinking of early Christian communities. We will end this chapter by reflecting on twentieth-century martyrs. ■

Rome on the Verge of a Nervous Breakdown

The second century was not a bad time to be a Roman; in fact, scholars call the period from 96 to 180 CE the Golden Age of the empire. By and large, this was a period of peace and prosperity, with new roads and ports being built, cities growing, and business interests flourishing. People outside Rome, however, had a different experience. For them, it seemed like the empire was always engaged in some war at its borders, and since wars are expensive, the government kept imposing more taxes on and requiring services from the peoples it ruled.

Conditions worsened around the middle of the third century. The empire was under attack by old rivals like the Persians and by new enemies like the Vandals and Goths. For half a century, the empire stood on the verge of collapse.

Leadership in the empire also became hotly contested. During the Golden Age, the transition from one emperor to the next had been relatively peaceful. By 253, however, it seemed like everybody wanted the job and was willing to fight to get it. In the space of about fifty years, at least twenty-five people were recognized in Rome as emperor. In the fifteen years of his rule, the emperor Gallienus had to deal with at least eighteen people who tried to claim his throne.

Things settled down a bit when the reform-minded Diocletian came to power in 284. Faced with all these enemies at the borders, in 293, Diocletian divided the empire into four administrative districts. Along with himself, he appointed a co-emperor and two "lesser" emperors; each of the four ruled over one of the districts. These rulers were able to regain control so that by 301, Diocletian was ready to turn his attention to issues within the empire itself. He reorganized the currency, put wage and price controls in place to deal with inflation, and began a massive persecution of Christians—all part of his attempt to bring peace to society. Happy with his various reforms, Diocletian stepped down from office in 305.

The Word Gets Out

The empire may have been teetering, but the Church was growing. At the end of the second century, there were approximately 220,000 Christians among the 60 million people in the empire; by the end of the third century, the number of Christians had grown to between 4 and 6 million. The word was spreading—and spreading fast.

As the Church grew, diversity became an issue. Some Christian communities favored leadership by bishops in the apostolic line of succession, while others elected their leaders; some placed a high value on prophecy, while others focused on acts of compassion. By the end of the second century, though, most Christian communities had come to accept the doctrine of apostolic succession as the foundation for leadership and were headed by bishops who had priests and deacons to assist them.

The word *bishop* comes from the Greek word *episkopos*, which means "overseer" or "supervisor." The bishop supervised the local community and ensured that the gospel teaching was properly passed down to the next generation. Different Christian communities, however, shared different gospel stories, and how they interpreted those stories differed as well. In an attempt to find unity of belief, bishops within particular regions began coming together to discuss issues and work out their differences. These meetings were called councils (or synods), with the first taking place in 175 CE to deal with a heretical movement called Montanism (more on that later).

Bishops were sometimes helped by presbyters, who at first had mainly an honorary role in the Christian community. Over time, this would change, and presbyters would evolve into priests. Deacons and deaconesses were the bishop's helping hands, members of the community appointed to help care for those in need. The apostles were the first to appoint deacons. Recognizing that they needed to devote more time to preaching, they asked their followers to choose "seven reputable men, filled with the Spirit and wisdom, whom we shall appoint to this task" (Acts 6:3) of managing the community. Women were also called upon to fill this role. Paul talks about "Phoebe our sister, who is [also] a minister of the church at Cenchreae" (Rom 16:1), and 1 Timothy 3 gives specific instructions about the type of women who should be chosen as deaconesses. Most often their duties centered on ministering to other women in the community.

Christians were also looking for the best ways to express their beliefs. One way they settled on was a statement of faith known as a creed. The earliest creed is found in the writings of the bishop Irenaeus in the latter part of the second century. Irenaeus expresses faith in God the Father as Creator of all things; in God's incarnation as Jesus the Christ; and in the Holy Spirit, who had worked through the Hebrew prophets to foretell the story of salvation through Jesus. It may seem like having it all written down would make things easier, but as we will see in the next chapter, words on paper tend to lead to all kinds of interpretations, and creeds became a source of intense infighting among Christians for centuries to come.

As the Church grew, it also began to accumulate wealth. Christians contributed to the upkeep of churches and their ministers, and some individual communities began to own significant amounts of property. This had both positive and negative consequences: it attracted the attention of the emperors, who realized they could make money by persecuting the Church, but it also allowed Christians to minister to the social and economic needs of people in need. (As a rule, Romans felt no responsibility toward the poor, seeing poverty as either the will of the gods or the result of personal folly and not the responsibility of the wealthier members of society.) By early in the second century, Christians had developed an organized system of support, with voluntary offerings collected and given to the bishop, who used them to help those most in need: orphans, widows, those ill or in prison, and travelers.

Deaconesses

Women continued to fill this role as late as the fifth century, but eventually the way deacons were appointed began to change. Being a deacon became a step on the way to becoming a priest, and women were forced to turn their talents to filling other roles in the Church. In the 1960s, the bishops at the Second Vatican Council decided that the ancient understanding of the ministry of deacon in the Church should be revived, and in many modern Catholic communities, we find permanent deacons who are married and hold regular jobs performing these works of service. Women still may not serve as deacons, however; Vatican II did not turn quite that far toward the ancient understanding.

Run-Ins with the Law

People were free to believe what they wanted in the Roman Empire as long as they participated in the sacrifices that were supposed to keep the Roman gods happy. When Christians stood against these sacrifices, they were violating Roman law.

Romans, as well as most other people of the time, thought that when humans were fighting on earth, their gods were fighting in the heavens. If your god was weaker or became angry and abandoned you, you lost. With the empire seemingly always at war, keeping the gods pacified was the top priority. If a group of people refused to do their civic duty and sacrifice, especially if they did this because they were worshiping what the Romans viewed as a competing god, this was seen as a flat rejection of Roman rule. It meant you were probably politically opposed to the empire and would revolt if only you got the chance.

The Jews, however, were a special case. The Romans had come to recognize that the Jews could not perform these rituals and that forcing them to do so caused more problems than it solved. So the Jews were exempted from having to sacrifice, which meant the earliest Christians were exempted as well. As it became clear that Christianity was something separate from Judaism, however, the Romans no longer felt obligated to grant them the exclusion. Writers like the author of the Gospel of Luke tried to show that Christianity was really a continuation and fulfillment of Judaism—and thus covered under the exclusion—but the Romans were not buying it. In addition, religions needed official approval to operate legally, and while Judaism had this status, Christianity did not. It did not help that Christians were followers of someone the Romans had executed as a political threat.

The Roman government became highly suspicious when people gathered in large groups, and Christianity was growing rapidly. For example, when Pliny, the governor of a Roman province, asked the emperor Trajan to allow people to create a fire brigade, Trajan responded: "Whatever name we may give, for whatever reason, to those who gather together for a common purpose, they will turn into political clubs, and that in a short time."[1] Christians were turning into a serious political threat, and their failure to sacrifice further threatened the empire.

Legal problems aside, people had a low opinion of these followers of the Christ. The writer Celsus wrote that "only foolish and low individuals, and persons devoid of perception, and slaves, and women, and children"[2] could be attracted to Christianity. Celsus's statement effectively captures the popular view of Christians at the time.

Ironically, Christians also were often charged with atheism. People saw the gods and their powers as a regular part of daily life, and when Christians refused to acknowledge these gods, they seemed to be denying the very foundation of spiritual belief. This same refusal led them to be charged with hatred of the human race, since the gods were the ones whose good will sustained humanity.

The list of accusations against Christians goes on: sexual misconduct, cannibalism, practicing black magic, arson, and, most importantly, treason. Many believed that all the troubles that almost led to the collapse of the empire during the third century were a direct result of the gods' disapproval of Christians. From this perspective, the empire's very survival depended on suppressing Christianity and getting people to turn back to traditional customs and religion.

So Christians were persecuted, but if anything the persecutions seemed to make this group stronger, and more than a few people were so impressed by the way Christians faced persecution that they themselves became interested in the message of the gospel.

Setting up the Scapegoats

Even without an official policy to seek them out, Christians could always be denounced to local Roman officials. People might do this because they thought Christianity was dangerous, but they might also just want to get rid of them as social, economic, or political rivals. The emperor Hadrian (117–138) recognized this and ruled in 124 that anyone who made false accusations about Christians should be punished.

As time went on, however, the emperors became less tolerant of what they saw as the Christians' refusal to be good citizens. A number of emperors followed a policy of getting rid of Christians whenever possible, but there was nothing widespread or severe until the reign of Septimus Severus (193–211). The boy in the story at the beginning of this chapter, Origen, lived through the persecution of Severus. (Origen wanted to join the ranks of the martyrs. He came close too: he died as a result of wounds he received during Decius's persecution.)

The emperor Gallienus actually granted freedom of worship to Christians and ordered that their confiscated property be restored, but this more generous state of affairs did not last long. In 303, the emperor Diocletian decided after almost twenty years in office that it was his duty as protector of the Roman people to get rid of Christianity.

We are not sure what caused this change in Diocletian's attitude toward Christians since the ancient historians give a couple of different explanations. What we do know is that during the Persian war in 296, some Christians had refused military service and were executed because it was a capital offense to refuse to take the oath of service. Other Christians already in the military refused to participate in some ceremonial events that involved sacrifice. This indicated to Diocletian and his military leaders that if a major war broke out, the Christians could not be counted on as loyal citizens.

The Great Persecution under Diocletian was the most serious and longest lasting of all Roman persecutions of Christianity. Diocletian ordered his officials throughout the empire to destroy churches, make Christians hand over their sacred books to be burnt, and fire Christians in public service. Upper-class Christians lost many of their privileges of wealth and birth, and Christian slaves could no longer be freed. In 305, Diocletian decreed that all church leaders should be imprisoned and that Christians who did not sacrifice were to be tortured and executed.

It was easy enough for Diocletian to give these orders but not so easy for officials to carry them out. Christians were by now in all levels of government; even Diocletian's wife and daughter seem to have been Christian sympathizers. Still, the persecution kept going until 313, when the two new leaders in the East, Licinius and Constantine, issued the Edict of Milan that granted religious liberty to all. This was the end of persecution and the start of a new era for the Church.

A Certificate of Sacrifice

In 250, the emperor Decius ordered every man, woman, and child in the Empire to sacrifice to the gods. Those who complied got a certificate; those who did not faced the death penalty. This certificate found in Egypt was typical for the time:

> To The Commissioners for Sacrifices in the Village of Alexander's Island, from Aurelius Diogenes, Son of Satabus of the Village of Alexander's Island, Aged 72; Scar on Right Eyebrow.
>
> I have always sacrificed to the gods, and now in your presence, in accordance with the terms of the edict, I have done sacrifice and poured libations and tasted the sacrifices, and I request you to certify to this effect. Farewell
>
> Presented By Me, Aurelius Diogenes
> I Certifiy That I Witnessed His Sacrifice, Aurelius Syrus.
>
> Dated this first year of the Emperor Caesar Gaius Messius Quintus Trajanus Decius, Pius, Felix, Augustus, the second of Epiph. [June 26, 250 CE][3]

Focus On
Perpetua

One of the most famous martyrs of the early Church was Perpetua, killed at about age 20 in Carthage in 203 CE. Married and with a baby, Perpetua did not let family obligations stop her from proclaiming her Christian beliefs. She wrote about her experiences, and an admirer finished the story after her death. Let's listen to her words:

> While I was still with the police authorities . . . my father out of love for me tried to dissuade me from my resolution. "Father," I said, "do you see [this vase]?" "I see it," he said. "Can it be named anything else than what it really is?" I asked, and he said, "No." "So I also cannot be called anything else than what I am, a Christian." Enraged by my words my father came at me as though to tear out my eyes . . .
>
> For a few days my father stayed away. . . At this time we were baptized and the Spirit instructed me not to request anything from the baptismal waters except endurance of physical suffering.
>
> A few days later we were imprisoned. I was terrified because never before had I experienced such darkness . . . My condition was aggravated by my anxiety for my baby . . . I spoke to my mother about him, tried to console my brother, and asked that they care for my son. I suffered intensely because I sensed their agony on my account. These were the trials I had to endure for many days. Then I was granted the privilege of having my son remain with me in prison. Being relieved of anxiety and concern for the infant, I immediately regained my strength. Suddenly the prison became my palace, and I loved being there rather than any other place . . .
>
> A few days later there was a rumor that our case was to be heard. My father, completely exhausted from his anxiety, came from the city to see me, with the intention of weakening my faith. "Daughter," he said, "have pity on my grey head. Have pity on your father if I have the honor to be called father by you, if with these hands I have brought you to the prime of your life, and if I have always favored you above your brothers, do not abandon me to the reproach of men. Consider your brothers; consider your mother and your aunt; consider your son who cannot live without you. Give up your stubbornness before you destroy all of us." . . .
>
> These were the things my father said out of love, kissing my hands and throwing himself at my feet . . . I was very upset because of my father's condition. He was the only member of my family who would find no reason for joy in my suffering. I tried to comfort him saying, "Whatever God wants at this tribunal will happen, for remember that our power comes not from ourselves but from God." But utterly dejected, my father left me . . .

The case of Perpetua and the others with her was heard, and all were condemned to fight the beasts in the Arena.

> We were overjoyed as we went back to the prison cell . . .
>
> As the day of the games drew near, my father, overwhelmed with grief, came again to see me

continued on page 50

continued from page 49

. . . Falling on his face before me, he cursed his old age, repeating such things as would move all creation. And I grieved because of his old age.

Perpetua was brought out to face a mad cow. Her admirer wrote the rest of her story.

Perpetua was tossed first and fell on her back. She sat up, and being more concerned with her sense of modesty than with her pain, covered her thighs with her gown which had been torn down one side. Then finding her hair-clip which had fallen out, she pinned back her loose hair thinking it not proper for a martyr to suffer with disheveled hair; it might seem that she was mourning in her hour of triumph . . . [Finally the martyrs were put to death with a sword, and Perpetua] took the gladiator's trembling hand and guided it to her throat.[4] ("The Martyrdom of Perpetua and Felicitas")

Perpetua could easily have evaded her martyrdom, but she decided that being a Christian was more important than being a daughter, wife, or mother. She has been honored for centuries because of it. ■

Making Peace and Making Enemies

Christian writers of the second and third centuries dealt with the issues raised by the persecutions in two ways: by trying to explain Christianity to others or by rejecting the world that persecuted them. A number of early Christians wrote what are called *apologies*, a term with its roots in a Greek word meaning "justification" or "defense." The writers were not saying they were sorry to be Christians but were instead creating literary defenses of the Christian faith. They wrote partly to show that Christians are good, law-abiding citizens and not a threat to the state, but they also wrote to share the Christian message.

The earliest complete apology that we have is from a man named Justin, who wrote in Rome around 155. Justin Martyr, as he is known in history, was well educated but felt unfulfilled by the philosophies he had studied. He saw how strong the Christian martyrs were, how they faced their deaths without changing their beliefs, and this inspired him to join the Christian community around 130. He started a school for Christians in Rome and for many years was left in peace, but in 165, he was martyred.

In his *Apology*, Justin pointed out that Christians were being punished on the basis of a name rather than for any wrongdoing:

Neither reward nor punishment should follow from a name unless something admirable or evil can actually be shown about it . . . Among yourselves you do not penalize the accused before conviction; but with us you take the name as proof . . . What can all this mean? You do not make judicial inquiries in our case, though we are bound [not] to commit crimes.[5]

Some Christian authors wrote to share their belief that the persecutions were signs that the end of the world was coming. These authors saw Christian beliefs and the world as radically opposed. The Revelation to John reflects this view and shows that many in the Church expected persecution. One only had to look at the story of Jesus to see how the world dealt with those who spread the good news.

Origen thought martyrdom for Christ's sake was noble, and in a work called *Exhortation to Martyrdom*, he explains that persecution is not so much an evil as a call to deeper faith and an opportunity to witness to the truth. A writer named Tertullian went a step further and described martyrdom as the only sure road to salvation, as well as an inspiration to others: "We multiply whenever we are mown down by you: the blood of Christians is seed" (*Apology*, 50.13). Tertullian and others like him thought Christians should jump at the chance for martyrdom.

Others disagreed. Two influential writers, Clement of Alexandria and Cyprian, believed that martyrdom was necessary when the only other choice was to deny one's faith but that people who turned themselves in as Christians in the hopes of being martyred—like Origen had wanted to do—were in the wrong because this made them accomplices to their own murder.

All of this persecution may have made good political sense, but it is hard to reconcile with what the Christians were actually up to in their everyday lives and worship services. Like many Roman governors, Pliny had Christians executed, but unlike most, he took time to try and understand Christians and to report his findings to the emperor Trajan:

They affirmed [that] the whole of their guilt . . . was that they were in the habit of meeting on a certain day before it was light, when they sang in alternate verses songs to Christ, as to a god, and bound themselves by solemn oath, not to commit any wicked deeds, fraud, theft, or adultery, never to falsify their word, nor deny a trust when they

should be called upon to deliver it up. After which it was their custom
. . . to partake of food.[6]

A few decades later, Justin Martyr explained more about Christian worship rituals to the pagan audience for whom his *Apology* was intended.

[O]n the day called Sunday there is a meeting in one place of those
who live in cities or the country, and the memoirs of the apostles or the
writings of the prophets are read as long as time permits. When the
reader has finished, the [presider] in a discourse urges and invites [us]
to the imitation of these noble things. Then we all stand up together
and offer prayers . . . [W]hen we have finished the prayer, bread is
brought, and wine and water, and the [presider] similarly sends up
prayers and thanksgivings to the best of his ability, and the congregation assents, saying the Amen; the distribution, and reception of the
consecrated [elements] by each one, takes place and they are sent
to the absent by the deacons. Those who prosper, and who so wish,
contribute, each one as much as he chooses.[7]

Justin Martyr and others tried their best to convince the Roman world
that Christianity was not a threat but without much success. Christians were
forced to face the ultimate test of their beliefs and were called upon to make
the ultimate sacrifice for them.

Wisdom and Knowledge: Christianity, Philosophy, and Gnostic Thought

All the while, there was plenty of controversy going on within the Christian
world. With Christian communities scattered around the Mediterranean in
different cultures and societies, different groups of Christians were coming
to different understandings about their faith. Greek philosophy was the intellectual bedrock of the world in which Christianity developed, so for some
Christian thinkers it made perfect sense to use philosophy's insights as a way
of exploring Christian faith. Others were sure that this was a path to heresy
and destruction.

Clement of Alexandria (150–211) tells us that "the multitude are scared
of Greek philosophy, as children are of masks, fearing that it will lead them

astray,"[8] but Clement did not think the pursuit of knowledge ran in any way counter to Christian faith. In his work, he drew constantly on the Greek philosophers, believing they showed one of the ways in which God has chosen to reveal himself to humanity. Moreover, he was not afraid to let reason be a guide in matters of faith: "If our faith . . . is such that it is destroyed by force of argument, then let it be destroyed; for it will have been proved that we do not possess the truth."[9] His student Origen could not have agreed with him more. Origen wrote: "If every man could abandon the business of life and devote his time to philosophy, no other course ought to be followed but this alone."[10] Origen told his student Gregory to "extract from the philosophy of the Greeks what may serve as a course of study or a preparation for Christianity."[11] Origen felt that the apostles had given to the Church all the teaching that was needful for salvation but that they had left questions on less-central issues for those interested in pursuing philosophical thought.

Tertullian (155–230), on the other hand, felt that philosophical studies were pointless for Christians. Brilliant and well educated, Tertullian was the first great Christian writer in Latin. He rejected the more reasoned approach of philosophy, however; his style was to motivate people to act and to stir up emotions. Tertullian studied law before his conversion to Christianity and ordination as a priest, and we see that rigorous legalistic thinking in his works. In fact, in his later life he decided the Church was too liberal and lenient, and he left to join a group called the Montanists that the Church held to be heretical.

Tertullian wrote passionate defenses of Christian belief in the face of widespread misunderstanding. He also wrote a great deal against other heretical Christian movements, especially against the Gnostic groups who believed Christ's role was to bring knowledge to humans rather than to die for their salvation—in effect, Gnotstics saw Christ as revealing a philosophy rather than as performing an act.

Tertullian felt there was a great divide between the intellectualism of philosophic debate and the universality of the Christian message, and he was deeply concerned that philosophy would lead people to embrace false doctrines. In fact, he referred to philosophers as "those patriarchs of heretics" and wondered ironically if the problem with Christian doctrine "lies in its springing from Judaea rather than from Greece. Christ made a mistake, too, in sending forth fishermen to preach, rather than the sophist."[12] In another work, he famously asks, "What has Jerusalem to do with Athens, the Church with the Academy [of Aristotle], the Christian with the heretic? . . . After Jesus Christ we have no need of speculation, after the Gospel no need of research."[13] ("The Prescriptions Against Heretics," chap. 7)

The Hidden Knowledge: Gnosticism

Tertullian's disapproval did not keep people from turning to philosophy as a path in their quest for meaning and truth, and the Church's disapproval did not keep people from joining one of the many Gnostic groups for the same reason. *Gnostic* comes from the Greek word *gnosis*, meaning "knowledge"; these groups believed the goal of life was to gain knowledge about your true nature so you could escape the material world at death. Some Gnostic groups looked to Jewish Wisdom literature as the source of this knowledge, but many more focused on Christ as the revealer.

For centuries, if people wanted to know about Gnostic ideas, they had to read the works of Christian authors trying to show how Gnostics got things wrong—not exactly unbiased sources. Once Christians gained power in the empire, they did their best to destroy every Gnostic writing they could find, and they did such a fine job that for about sixteen centuries it was next to impossible to find anything written by the Gnostics themselves. But in the middle of the twentieth century, at a place called Nag Hammadi in Egypt, a local villager found some manuscripts that included the largest collection of Gnostic writings ever discovered. For the first time, modern people could see what Gnostics truly thought.

There were many different Gnostic groups with many different sets of beliefs. However, there were also many common themes, and we can create a big picture of Christian Gnostic belief that will more or less fit with the majority of these different systems.

Gnostics believed that God is spirit and good and that matter is evil, so it is clear that God did not create the material world. That was the work of a secondary divine being called the Demiurge, who is comparable to a fallen angel, like Lucifer. However, since the Demiurge was not God, he could not create life. So he trapped sparks of the divine (other angels, or at least other elements belonging to God) in bodies, which sort of "drugged" them into not realizing what was happening. When the bodies died, the sparks still did not know how to escape and return to their home, so they just got trapped in new bodies. Humans, then, are elements of good imprisoned in bodies that keep them from realizing their true nature. The Demiurge even got these beings to think he was God, as most Christian Gnostics saw the God of the Hebrew Bible as the Demiurge.

This is where Christ comes in: Christ revealed to humans the truth about God and their own nature. He showed humans how to break free from the Demiurge's grasp and return to their true home. Gnostics believed Christ was not really a human being—he was divine, so he could not have one of the Demiurge's material bodies. Instead, Christ came down and took over the body of Jesus, using it to get the word out and then leaving before it suffered and died. Thus, Christ is the Savior not because of his death and resurrection but because he revealed how the system works and how humans can get clear of it.

Gnosticism had something in common with those mystery religions discussed in chapter 2. It was all about secret knowledge, who got it, and who gave it. In the Christian versions, it was Jesus who gave it, and the Gnostics had only to look at scriptures like Matthew 13:11 to see this: when the disciples ask Jesus why he speaks to the people in parables, he tells them, "Because knowledge of the mysteries of the kingdom of heaven has been granted to you, but to them it has not been granted." The Christian Scriptures also explained their heavenly origins, such as in John 17:16 when Jesus says his followers "do not belong to the world any more than I belong to the world."

Gnostic beliefs caused much tension within the Christian community because they tore apart what many Christians saw as their basic beliefs. They made the God of the Jews into a being that was at the very least deluded, and they made creation a bad thing. By tossing out the idea that Jesus' death leads to salvation, they overturned the traditional Christian understanding of the gospel stories. Finally, they had the tendency to change the Christian story into the sort of myth found in all those mystery religions.

The leaders of the Christian communities decided they needed to deal with these tensions before they became more widespread. This was the impetus for trying to work out which of the many writings about Jesus should be included in the canon and for using creeds to ensure that everyone in the Church agreed on the basics of faith.

Some Christian writers who felt the threat of Gnosticism to their communities tried to lay out exactly where Gnostic understandings and Christian beliefs diverged. One of the first such writers was Irenaeus, bishop of Lyons in France. In the late second century, Irenaeus wrote a work called *Against Heresies* that described heresies of his time and why they were wrong. Irenaeus confronted the Gnostics head on, saying that the God of the Old Testament (OT), the God of the gospels, and the God that the philosophers came to know through reason were the same. Jesus, he said, was both fully human (not just a body used by Christ) and fully divine (not just a teacher). In becoming human, the Son of God did not leave his divinity behind; he brought it with him, joining human and divine in such a way that humanity was forever changed and redemption was made possible.

Irenaeus disagreed with the Gnostics on philosophical grounds, but his main weapons against them were quite concrete: apostolic succession and the canon of Scriptures. Many Christian Gnostic groups claimed that Christ passed along secret teachings to certain of his Apostles, giving them the true (Gnostic) understanding of his purpose—and as we saw in the passage from Matthew, it was not necessarily a big jump. But Irenaeus was not buying it.

> [W]e are in a position to reckon up those who were by the apostles instituted bishops in the Churches, and [to demonstrate] the succession of these men to our own times; those who neither taught nor knew of anything like what these [heretics] rave about. For if the apostles had known hidden mysteries . . . they would have delivered them especially to those to whom they were also committing the Churches themselves.[14]

In another section of *Against Heresies*, we see Irenaeus claiming as inspired most of the writings that would wind up in the New Testament (NT), effectively dismissing all those other writings and gospel stories so beloved of the Gnostics.

Clement agreed with Irenaeus that the God of the Christians and the God of the philosophers were the same. A pagan philosopher before his conversion to Christianity, Clement traveled all over the Mediterranean, studying and deepening his thought with different teachers. He finally settled in Alexandria, which was both a center of Christian thought and a hotbed of Gnosticism. When Clement turned his attention to the problem of Gnosticism, he started with the understanding that true wisdom and true knowledge are both to be found in Christ. He believed the philosophical path did indeed lead to God, but only the intelligent and educated could follow it. So God in his mercy had sent Christ to open the way to all. God had made faith accessible to everyone, but the educated Christian was the "true Gnostic" because he or she was led to look deeper into the mysteries God had placed before humanity. Those who claimed to be Gnostics apart from Christian faith were misguided, Clement said, and he used a lot of ink refuting the claims of various Gnostic writers.

There was never really any question about whether Gnostic beliefs would replace those traditionally associated with Christianity; after all, the greatest appeal of Christianity was that it opened the door of salvation to everyone, while Gnostic beliefs restricted access to only those who could attain a certain level of knowledge. Nonetheless, these beliefs did appeal to many educated Christians in the early centuries of the Church.

Facing the Test

As Christians of the second and third centuries faced conflict both within their communities and with the society around them, they drew on every resource available to them. When they were called upon to face death as the ultimate test of their faith, they could reflect on the biblical stories of faithful witness. The history of Eleazar and the seven sons, found in 2 Maccabees, tells of Jews who refused to break God's laws during a time when foreigners occupied their land. Acts 7 tells the story of Stephen, who, around the year 37 CE, became the first follower of Christ to be killed for his beliefs. The Revelation to John honors "those who had been slaughtered because of the witness they bore to the word of God" (6:9). Most important was the witness of Jesus, whose execution at the hands of the Romans the Christian martyrs surely held in their hearts as they went to meet their deaths.

It is good to remember, however, that the average Christian was unlikely to be called to the witness of martyrdom. During the Great Persecution, around five thousand people may have been put to death out of the millions of Christians then living. Many thousands more were imprisoned or otherwise harassed, but we can see that while all Christians may have had to deal with the idea of persecution, the majority did not have to experience it personally.

In many ways though, the numbers were less important than the effect the idea of persecution had on the Christian community: The whole Church saw itself as following in the footsteps of the martyrs.

Some Stood Firm . . . and Some Fell Fast

Not all who held Christian beliefs were able to face up to the prospect of torture and death. In a letter to the bishop of Antioch, a bishop of Alexandria named Dionysius explained what happened during the Decletian persecution. When the order came that everyone had to sacrifice,

> . . . all cowered with fear. And of many of the more eminent persons, some came forward immediately through fear, others in public positions were compelled to do so by their business, and others were dragged by those around them . . . But others ran eagerly towards the altars, affirming by their forwardness that they had not been Christians even formerly.[15]

These people are known as *lapsi*, the Latin word meaning "lapsed or failed," because they failed to stand up for their faith.

The *lapsi* included laypeople, priests, bishops, and even a Pope. During the persecution under Diocletian, the Pope Marcellinus handed over copies of the sacred books and offered incense to the gods. The former action made him a *traditor*, Latin for "one who hands over" and the root of the English word *traitor*. Marcellinus either abdicated or was immediately removed from office, but the story goes that he was later martyred after repenting of his actions.

The Church was in a quandary as to what to do with people like Marcellinus; on the one hand, Matthew clearly stated that Christians had to stand up and affirm their faith when it counted most, but on the other, who had the right to turn away someone who came to the Church and admitted to being a sinner? Some people said the *lapsi* should be readmitted; others believed they should be excommunicated for life. Eventually, the Church as a whole came to a decision that those who lapsed needed to do penance but afterwards could once more join the Christian community.

Not everyone agreed, though, and many Christian communities split over the issue. In Rome, the priest Novation decided true Christians should not have anything to do with the *lapsi*; he developed a following, and the group set up separate churches and consecrated their own clergy. The same thing happened in Alexandria, where people followed the bishop Meletius away from communion with the Church. In northern Africa, a group called the Donatists was mainly concerned with the *traditores* that turned over the Scriptures. They thought clergy members who had committed this crime were no longer fit to administer the sacraments.

All of these groups had valid complaints; after all, how would you like it if you had stood firm in the face of imprisonment and possible death, only to find yourself praying next to someone who had caved in and denied his faith? Does that person really deserve the name *Christian* the way you do?

A lot of fear, anger, and pride went into answering these questions, but it comes down to a deeper question of how Christians of the time understood their Church: should it be a gathering of the pure or of broken and sinful people who seek forgiveness? This question surfaces throughout the Church's history.

The Church Then and Now

Modern Martyrs

Persecution and martyrdom are not things of the past. Some argue that more Christians were killed during the twentieth century than in the previous nineteen centuries combined; one study of worldwide persecution claims that the century saw 45 million Christian martyrs.[16] In May 2000, Pope John Paul II led a service honoring more than ten thousand modern martyrs, but the Vatican recognizes that this number is really just a drop in the bucket. As the pope wrote in his 1994 apostolic letter *Tertio Millennio Adveniente*, "The Church has once again become a Church of martyrs."

When we talk about martyrs in the early Church, it is clear we mean people who were killed because they claimed to be Christian, but things get more confusing in our own time. As theologian Leonardo Boff points out, nowadays people rarely run into trouble because they call themselves Christians. "They are persecuted and hated because they commit themselves to [working with the poor] and confess that this commitment comes from their experience of the Gospel and of prayer."[17] Even people who do not claim to be Christians can be "martyrs for the kingdom of God" because they "belong to the cause that was Christ's, the kingdom; they laid down their lives for those values that embody . . . the kingdom, such as truth, justice, love of God and of the poor."[18]

In Latin America, one of the areas hardest hit by persecution in the latter part of the twentieth century, killings took place in countries that were strongly Catholic. In Guatemala, for instance, at least 200,000 people were killed and a million more forced to flee their homes during a civil war that lasted from 1961 to 1996. Most of the killings were done by groups associated with the army, and the list of those who were most at risk is long: human rights activists; the Mayan Indians native to the region; journalists; union members; land reform activists; people involved with the judicial system; teachers; children; and priests, nuns, monks and others working within the context of their Christian faith.

In 1992, I traveled with a group to talk with people who had been affected by the war. In a Guatemalan refugee camp in southern Mexico, we listened to a man describe the destruction of his village: Returning from his fields one day, he saw soldiers and hid. He saw people being herded into a church, which the soldiers locked and set on fire; he could do nothing other than watch helplessly as his wife and children died with the others. We saw this man cry, but we also saw others with similar stories singing and telling us how their faith gave them the strength to work for an end to these horrors. People gathered to talk about the gospel and how to put its message into practice in dealing with their oppressors, whom they recognized as their brothers and sisters in Christ.

Latin America is far from the only area in the twentieth century to have witnessed the blood of the martyrs flowing. More than forty thousand Christians were martyred during the Boxer Rebellion in China; the Spanish Civil War saw the deaths of almost seven thousand members of the clergy and religious orders and thousands more laypeople. Literally hundreds of thousands of Christians lost their lives during persecutions by the Nazis and Communists. We can only hope that someone writing at the end of the twenty-first century will have much less reason to discuss modern Christian martyrs than do we at its beginning.

Questions and Ideas for Understanding

1. If someone you loved continued to proclaim his or her beliefs in spite of facing danger or even death, would you support that person's decision? What if the decision threatened your life as well?

2. In a situation of persecution, which do you think you would choose: trying to explain your views or turning away from a hostile world? Why?

3. In the Roman Empire, religion and government were closely intertwined, but in most modern societies, including the United States, religious activity is separated from the workings of government. Using newspapers, magazines, or the Internet, find a recent event that raises questions about how effective this separation is, either in terms of how well it works or its effects on society. Write a description of the event and an analysis of the pros and cons of separating religion from government.

4. Think about a religion or denomination different from your own about which you have some ideas but not a lot of knowledge. Write a description of a person of that faith based on the ideas that you have. Then do some research and write another description of a person of that faith, this time based on what you have learned.

5. Think about the beliefs you hold and ways in which those beliefs may be threatened in the society in which you live. Write either (1) an apology explaining your beliefs and why you think they are misunderstood or (2) a description of how and why those of your beliefs should reject the views of others.

Notes

[1] In *Pliny: Correspondence with Trajan from Bithynia* (Letter 34), trans. Wynne Williams. Warminster, Wiltshire, England: Aris & Phillips, 1990, p. 33.

[2] Ralph Martin Novak, *Christianity and the Roman Empire: Background Texts*. Harrisburg, PA: Trinity Press International, 2001, p. 81.

[3] Novak, *Christianity*, p. 121.

[4] Novak, *Christianity*, pp. 104-114.

[5] Justin Martyr, *The First Apology*. In Novak, *Christianity*, p. 58.

[6] Pliny the Younger, *Letters of Pliny* 10.96. In Novak, *Christianity*, pp. 47–48.

[7] "The First Apology of Justin Martyr," trans. Edward R. Hardy, *Early Christian Fathers*, in The Library of Christian Classics, Vol. 1. Philadelphia, PA: Westminster Press, 1953, pp. 242–276.

[8] *Alexandrian Christianity,* trans. John E. L. Oulton and Henry Chadwick, The Library of Christian Classics, Vol II, London: SCM Press Ltd. 1954, p. 19.

[9] Novak, *Christianity,* p. 9.

[10] *Against Celsus* I.9. In *Bringing into Captivity Every Thought,* eds. Jacop Klapwijk, Sander Griffoen, and Gerben Groenwould. New York: New York University Press of America, 1991, p. 37.

[11] "A Letter from Origen to Gregory." Retrieved from http://www.ccel.org/fathers2/ANF-04/anf04-52.htm#P7608_1760968 (accessed 10/10/2007).

[12] Tertullian, "A Treatise on the Soul" III.3. In *Ante-Nicene Fathers,* Vol. III, eds. Alexander Robert and James Donaldson. Peabody, MA: Hendrickson Publishers, 1999, p. 183.

[13] Quoted in *Readings in Christian Thought,* ed. Hugh T. Kerr. Nashville, TN: Abingdon Press, 1990, p. 40.

[14] Irenaeus, *Against Heresies* III.3.1. In *Ante-Nicene Fathers,* Vol. I, eds. Alexander Roberts and James Donaldson. Peabody, MA: Hendrickson Publishers, 1999.

[15] Dionysius, *Letter to Fabius.* In Novak, *Christianity,* p. 122.

[16] http:www.gordonconwell.edu/ockenga/globalchristianity/gd/gd16.pdf (accessed 11/26/2007).

[17] Leonardo Boff, "Martyrdom: An Attempt at Systematic Reflection." In *Martyrdom Today,* ed. Marcus Lefebure. New York: Seabury Press, 1983, p. 16.

[18] Boff, "Martyrdom," p. 12.

4

New Understandings
Constantine, Councils, and Creeds

Chapter Overview

In this chapter, we will explore:

▶ A big change in the way the Church and the empire interacted

▶ Different ways of thinking about the relationship between Christ and God the Father

▶ The controversy over Arius's ideas

▶ The Council of Nicea

▶ Other controversies and councils in the fourth and fifth centuries

▶ The Church's creeds

Sabina: What Are These Christians Fighting About?

Working long and working hard, that is your life. You came to work in the palace kitchen forty years ago when your parents died; you were 8 years old and lucky to get this job. First, you cleaned pots, then you moved up to cutting vegetables and carving meat, and now you are one of the main cooks. This is the only life you have ever known, and some of the others working here, like Narisa and Antoninus, are the closest thing you have to a family.

In the last few years, you have seen more and more people turning away from their gods in order to serve the Christian God. Even the great emperor, Constantine, now serves this God. Everyone knows how the Christ of God appeared to Constantine and led him to victory in battle—clearly, this God has great power. That is what got Antoninus interested in the Christians. Narisa was born a Christian. They both talk to you about how Christ came for all people, to set them free. But a kitchen worker? Still, you feel the force of this idea. And each day, although your parents long ago taught you to worship the Great Mother Cybele, you think about serving the Christian God.

Those who serve this God also fight among themselves. Narisa says this Christ *is* God—that they are equal, but Antoninus tells her she is wrong, that Christ is great and glorious but not equal to God. You are not sure why this matters, but the fighting bothers you. The Christians talk about the love this Christ gave, but then they start yelling at each other. This contradiction holds you back from joining them. The worshippers of the Great Mother do not fight like this. What shall you believe, then? You chop a few more onions for the meal this evening and think about asking Narisa to tell you more about her God.

Christian groups found themselves in one conflict after another during the third and fourth centuries, and too often the bonds of what they themselves called "Christian love" were torn apart because of these fights. Nonetheless, the understandings that resulted from these conflicts have influenced how Christians think about Christ and God to the present day. We will talk about some of these conflicts and how they were resolved by bishops meeting together in councils, especially the council of Nicea. We will also see how the creed that grew out of that Council tried to explain Catholic Christian faith. But first, we will look at what was going on in the Roman Empire and how the vision of one emperor completely transformed the way the Church existed within it. ■

Figuring Out Authority in the Empire and the Church

The period from 300 to 500 CE saw big changes in the Church and in the Roman Empire. Many of these changes were about authority—who had it, who lost it, who wanted it, who did not get it. In the midst of these struggles, the Church and the State were developing a new relationship.

In 323, Constantine and Licinius ruled as co-emperors. Licinius believed Constantine wanted to be sole ruler, however, so when Constantine and his army pursued some foreign invaders into Licinius's lands, the co-emperors ended up battling each other. By the following year, Licinius was dead and Constantine was emperor.

Constantine ruled until his death in 337, but before that something unprecedented happened: A Roman emperor became a Christian. Constantine was baptized just before his death, but long before that he had begun to favor the Christian Church above other religions in the empire. He had also moved the center of imperial power from Rome to Byzantium in what is now Turkey. Constantine changed the city's name to Constantinople, a name it kept until 1930, when it was officially changed to Istanbul.

The world was changing, and Rome was no longer its center.

Constantine decreed that after his death, the empire should be divided among his three sons, Constantine II, Constantius II, and Constans I. With an eye to securing their future, immediately after their father's death the three brothers had eight of their male relatives and potential rivals murdered. By 350, his two brothers were dead and only Constantius II remained. Before he died in 361, he appointed his cousin Julian sole emperor.

Like Constantine's children, Julian had been raised a Christian, but the decidedly un-Christian example provided by his own family had entirely soured him on the religion. Instead, Julian decided that the old ways of Roman power were best, so he reinvigorated the practice of pagan worship; this led to Christian history labeling him as Julian the Apostate. Julian granted tolerance for all religions but gave to pagan temples and cults the types of special favors Constantine and his sons had given to Christians. This did not last long, however: when Julian died in 363, only twenty months after taking power, the new emperor Jovian set Christianity back on track to becoming the most important religion in the empire.

Emperor Theodosius took the throne in 379. His reign marked a turning point: not only did he declare Christianity to be the religion of the State, but he was also the last emperor of a united Empire. The Roman Empire had survived insane leaders, political murders, massive infighting, and foreign invaders, but all those struggles had taken their toll, and by the time of Theodosius, the empire was ready to collapse.

Drawing Up the Church-Wide Seating Chart

Nobody in the first century sat down and did corporate planning for the Church. Instead, it evolved, and eventually a well-developed hierarchy became visible. Early on, each city had only one church, led by a bishop, and all the bishops were equal. Soon it became clear that the issues facing bishops in larger cities affected larger areas, so their churches gained "metropolitan" status (*metropolis* means "principle city"). Above the metropolitan churches were three—in Rome, Antioch, and Alexandria—that were honored by all Christians because they had been founded by apostles. Christians across the empire agreed that with their apostolic connections, these churches were unfolding the Christian message with more authority than other churches. They came to be called patriarchal sees, and their bishops were known as patriarchs. The importance of Jerusalem in the Christian story led to it becoming known as a patriarchal see as well, but it was a sign of the changing times when the bishop of Constantinople, the new imperial city, was declared by a fourth-century council to be a patriarch second only to the bishop of Rome.

A fourth-century Christian would have understood the Church's structure as follows: priests and deacons serve their local churches, which are led by bishops, who are under the authority of metropolitan bishops, who in turn recognize the even-greater authority of the patriarchs, with many Christians seeing the bishop of Rome as the highest authority. The Roman Catholic Church is structured similarly today: priests serve parishes that are organized into dioceses led by bishops, archbishops supervise a number of dioceses, and the pope stands at the head of the Church.

Modern Catholics talk a lot about the importance of the bishop of Rome, the pope, and not much about the other patriarchal sees. There are two reasons for this: First, by the middle of the third century, many Christian communities saw Rome as having authority even over the other patriarchal sees, and recognition of that authority continued to grow throughout the Western region. Second, a lot of East–West fighting led eventually to a rupture between the Eastern and Western Christian communities. The pope came to be recognized as the supreme head of the Church in the West, while the Eastern Churches split into different groups centered on either the various patriarchal sees or national communities.

Constantine and a Change in Direction

In 312, when Constantine was still one of three emperors controlling the empire, the last thing on his mind was which bishops should be recognized as patriarchs. He had more immediate concerns—like staying alive. That year, he went out to battle yet another contender for the throne, Maxentius, at the Milvian Bridge just outside Rome. Before the battle, Constantine had his soldiers mark a Christian symbol on their shields; the day ended with Constantine triumphant and Maxentius dead. The battle and its outcome marked a turning point, for this was the moment the Church and the empire stopped being on opposite sides and started coming together.

Ancient historians disagree on the details. Lactantius, writing only five or six years after the battle, simply says that "Constantine was directed in a dream to mark the celestial sign of God on his shields and thus to engage in battle."[1] Eusebius, writing his *Life of Constantine* about twenty-five years later, provides a much more detailed account. According to Eusebius, Constantine thought long and hard about which god to ask for help, deciding finally "to honor his father's God alone."

> He said that about noon, when . . . he saw with his own eyes the trophy of a cross of light in the heavens, above the sun, and bearing the inscription, CONQUER BY THIS . . . [T]hen in his sleep the Christ of God appeared to him with the same sign which he had seen in the heavens, and commanded him to make a likeness of that sign which he had seen in the heavens, and to use it as a safeguard in all engagements with his enemies.[2]

Previously, Constantine had been a worshipper of the Sun God, but soon after this battle it became clear a big change had taken place—now he was following the God of the Christians. That does not mean he was immediately ready to swear off any of the other gods. For years after the Milvian Bridge battle, Constantine's government continued to issue coins showing traditional pagan themes, and Constantine never let go of the title of *pontifex maximus*, chief pagan priest. He had a statue showing himself as the Sun God erected in the center of Constantinople, and this remained a center of cult worship of Constantine for the rest of the century. Nor did Christian morality overtake

Constantine all at once. He had one of his sons and his wife Fausta executed in 326, for reasons unknown.

Despite all this, Constantine in fact did see himself as a devout Christian after his experience at Milvian Bridge. He began doing everything he could to help the Church and place it in a position of strength in the empire. This was not entirely selfless; Constantine believed the best way to unify his empire, and thus maintain his own power, was to bring people together through shared beliefs. Christianity, with its open-door policy of accepting all who came in faith, seemed like the perfect vehicle to bring this about, so Constantine did his best to make Christian beliefs part and parcel of the daily life of people all across his empire.

Funds and gifts. Constantine stopped the practice of using state funds to support pagan worship and transferred the money to churches instead, sometimes seizing the assets of pagan temples and passing them along to the Christians as well. He also gave the Roman Church a palace that was turned into the Basilica of Constantine, as well as some lands that brought in a large income each year.

Exemptions. He exempted priests and other church leaders from having to perform certain public services, and he allowed people to transfer legal cases from the public court system to the bishop's court.

Laws. He enacted laws to restrict pagan worship and encourage people to convert to Christianity. Over time, being a Christian became a big help if you wanted to move up the ranks of government. This, in addition to the exemptions, gave people who had money and/or power strong material incentives to convert to Christianity.

Calendar changes. Constantine reformed the traditional Roman calendar, replacing it with the seven-day week familiar to Jews and Christians. He also made Sunday a legal holiday, a tradition that has continued in most modern Western societies. He also included Christian holy days like Christmas and Easter on the official calendar.

Violence. In a move to point out that not all Christian beliefs were created equal, Constantine allowed the use of violence against those Christian people and churches he considered unorthodox or heretical. These actions may have been unlawful, but they promoted uniformity of belief, which is exactly what Constantine was after.

As Constantine saw it, God had brought him both the Christian faith and an empire to rule. Clearly this meant he was supposed to oversee the development of Christian faith within that empire. This idea that the secular ruler has a divine right to control both the Church and the religious beliefs of people living within his or her realm would be a source of conflict between rulers and the Church for centuries to come.

A Family Fight: Figuring Out the Father and Son

A key theological debate in the early Church concerned the relationship between Jesus and God the Father. Opinions abounded. Gnostics, as we have seen, separated the Creator from the true God and Jesus from the Christ who dwelt within him. Christians who continued in the Jewish tradition usually saw Jesus in Old Testament (OT) terms: as a teacher, prophet, or angel but not divine in the same way as God the Father. Other groups saw Jesus as a human being whom God had "adopted" as his Son so that God came to dwell within Jesus in a special way. Still others thought Jesus was divine, but in his divinity he was not actually a separate being from the Father. In theological terms, this discussion concerns Christology, which simply means the view one takes of Christ and his role.

Many Western theologians of the third and fourth centuries believed Christ was divine in the same way as God the Father but also was distinct from him—not just a name for a different part of the same thing. They believed Jesus' death played a part in God's plan of salvation but working out the details was tricky. If Jesus was just another human, there was no reason to believe his death could have any effect on salvation. The same was true if Jesus was some kind of angel or was inhabited by a divine being—his death would not have any effect on humans' relationship to God.

In the East, Origen led the way in adapting the views of Neoplatonism to a Christian context. Neoplatonism, or "new Platonic thought," began with Plotinus in the mid-third century and quickly became the most important school of philosophical thought in the ancient world. While it derived from Plato's thought, Plotinus did not worry about sticking too closely to the writings of Plato.

In Plotinus's view, three beings are at the heart of the universe: the One, Mind, and Soul. The One is the source of all being and all good, the essential element in the universe. From it arises Mind, the basis of all rational principles (scientific laws plus philosophical concepts). Working through Mind, the One animates existence through the production of Soul, which is the principle of activity in all that exists. To put it simply, the One is the reason why a "hunk of clay" can exist; Mind gives the clay form; and through Soul, the clay is given life and becomes human. The One, Mind, and Soul are totally spirit; things that involve matter, like the world and physical bodies, are not thought of highly. However, humans are a mixture of matter and spirit, and if they focus more on their spirits and less on their bodies, they can come closer to Soul, which means coming closer to the One.

For Origen, God the Father is the eternal One, and Christ his Son is Mind, the being that comes forth from the One and acts always in accordance with it. Origen and other Eastern Christian thinkers talked a lot about how God becoming human in Jesus allowed humans to come into union with the divine. The reasoning was different from that in the West, but the problem was the same: Jesus had to be divine to make the whole scheme work. If Jesus was not God, then he did not bring humans into union with God, only with another created being.

It is easy to think all of this is simply something beyond human knowledge and immaterial to everyday life, but for Christians it is and has always been vital. From the beginnings of Christianity to today, Christians have prayed to Jesus for salvation, believing his life and death made salvation possible. Nevertheless, philosophy and theology traditionally agree that only God never changes. If Jesus is not God, then he can change, and Christians who believe in him can lose their salvation.

The question of Jesus' divinity was hotly debated in the third and fourth centuries. The writer Gregory of Nyssa explained that in Constantinople, you could not get away from people talking about it:

> Every place in the city is full of them: the alleys, the crossroads, the forums, the squares. Garment sellers, money changers, food vendors—they are all at it. If you ask for change, they philosophize for you about generate and ingenerate natures. If you inquire about the price of bread, the answer is that the Father is greater and the Son inferior. If you speak about whether the bath is ready, they express an opinion that the Son was made out of nothing.[3]

The Most Serious Split

All this came to a head with the ideas of Arius. His thinking about Christ was nowhere near the wildest, but its moderation was probably one of the reasons why it sparked major controversy.

Arius started with the idea that God was God and everything else was everything else, and he put Jesus in the "everything-else" category. Arius thought that if God was the beginning of all reality, then there could not have been anything other than God before creation. Arius did not think Christ was just another human, but he did not think Christ was the same thing as God, either. He said that when God decided to make the world, God created the Son out of nothing, so the Son is greater than and before anything else in creation—but there was a time before he came into existence. God's intention was to use the Son to bring salvation to the world, so the Son was born into the body we call Jesus.

This was something new; Arius did not use the language of the OT to talk about the relationship between God the Father and the Son, and he did not turn to Neoplatonic thought. His position came out of his study of the Scriptures; he started with the account of creation in Genesis and then looked at the gospels to understand how Jesus was the Son. He wrote a poem called the *Thalia* expressing his understanding and even put together a song with the chorus, "There was a time when he was not," meaning a time when the Son did not exist, that God had not eternally been a father.

Arius was a priest in the church of Alexandria when he started teaching his views about the Son. His bishop, Alexander, became alarmed when he noticed other clergy members picking up Arius's views, and in 319, he called a council. One hundred bishops attended, and eighty of them voted to excommunicate Arius and his supporters. The Christian Church had a big controversy on its hands.

Arius took off for Palestine, where he was warmly welcomed by bishop Eusebius of Caesarea; he also received support from a number of other bishops. Some of them held their own councils in 320 and 321 that declared Arius's views acceptable; one council even condemned the views of Alexander just as his council had condemned those of Arius. The fight was on.

Eusebius of Caesarea

One of the participants in the Council of Nicea who has left us a record of the proceedings is Eusebius (260–339), bishop of Caesarea. Eusebius is often called the "Father of Christian History" because his most important work, the *Ecclesiastical History*, is the first major source we have about the development of Christianity from the apostolic age until the time in which he lived.

We saw Eusebius earlier welcoming and supporting Arius; a council held early in 325 provisionally excommunicated Eusebius for his trouble. So he came to the Council of Nicea as a bishop on the verge of being thrown out of the Church, but if you read his report, you would never know it. Eusebius said that while everyone was trying to figure out how to proceed, he graciously offered a model creed used in his own church, and the council adapted this into the creed they accepted in the end. He presents his own views as correct and accepted by all. The truth is that he did offer a creed, but it was not so much to help out the council as to prove that he was an orthodox thinker so that he could get the provisional excommunication revoked. He explained later how he could hold the views that he held and still assent to the creed produced at Nicea—his attempt to explain how his understanding differed from that of others.

The Emperor Constantine tried to end the controversy quickly, thinking that all this infighting could jeopardize the favor God showed to the empire. Constantine wrote letters to both Alexander and Arius, pointing out that they agreed on the most important things and declaring that some things were just not knowable to humans. "Having made a careful inquiry into the origin and foundation of these differences, I find the cause to be of a truly insignificant character, and quite unworthy of such fierce contention."[4]

Constantine also explained why he thought the fighting among Christians would jeopardize the empire:

> I consider it absolutely contrary to the divine law that we should overlook quarrels and contentions [among Christians] whereby the Highest Divinity may perhaps be moved to wrath not only against the human race, but also against me, to whose care He has by his celestial will committed the government of all earthly things . . . For I shall really fully be able to feel secure and always to hope for prosperity and happiness from the ready kindness of the most mighty God, only when I see all venerating the most Holy God in the proper cult of the catholic religion with harmonious brotherhood of worship.[5]

Focus On

Finding the Answer: The Council of Nicea

The Council of Nicea is considered the first ecumenical (or worldwide) council of the Church because bishops came from both the eastern and western parts of the world. The vast majority were from the Eastern, Greek-speaking part of the Church, but this made sense; because Arius and his followers were in the East, the Western Church had not really experienced much of the controversy surrounding his ideas. Still, there were Latin speakers present, including the Emperor Constantine.

After the three hundred bishops in attendance were seated, Constantine addressed the assembly:

It was once my chief desire, dearest friends, to en-joy the spectacle of your united presence; and now that this desire is fulfilled, I feel myself bound to render thanks to God the universal King, because, in addition to all his other benefits, he has granted me a blessing higher than all the rest, in permitting me to see you not only all assembled together but all united in a common harmony of sentiment. I pray therefore that no malignant adversary may henceforth interfere to mar our happy state . . . for in my judgment, intestine strife within the Church of God, is far more evil and dangerous than any kind of war or conflict; and these our differences appear to me more grievous than any outward trouble. Accordingly, when, by the will and with the co-operation of God, I had been victorious over my enemies, I thought that nothing more re-mained but to render thanks to him . . . as soon as I heard that intelligence which I had least expected to receive, I mean the news of your dissension, I judged it to be of no secondary importance, but with the earnest desire that a remedy for this evil also might be found through my means, I

immediately sent to require your presence. And now I rejoice in beholding your assembly; but I feel that my desires will be most completely fulfilled when I can see you all united in one judgment, and that common spirit of peace and concord prevailing amongst you all, which becomes you, as consecrated to the service of God, to commend to others.[6]

Constantine's pep talk did little to mollify either side. He reminded the bishops that Christ had instructed them to forgive one another. Then all got to work.

The party against Arius was the stronger. Nonethe-less, both sides mounted arguments from Scripture, essentially canceling each other out. They then began wrangling over terminology for the creed they were attempting to draft. The opponents of Arius wanted to use the term *homoousios*, which means "of the same substance," meaning that God the Father and the Son are not just alike in some way but that they actually share in the same divinity. The Arians wanted to make the smallest possible change, adding one letter to change *homoousios* into *homoiousios*, meaning "of similar substance." But that one small change reopens the whole question. The anti-Arians stood fast, however, defeating this idea and also writing a number of con-demnations of Arius and his positions into the council's canons.

Still the controversy was not over, as it was now time for the bishops to sign the creed. Seventeen remained opposed. Constantine threatened to depose these and send them into exile. This convinced fifteen of the re-maining seventeen to sign, but two stood their ground and were deposed and exiled for their trouble. ■

Still the matter raged, and finally the emperor decided a big gesture was in order. He called the Council of Nicea, possibly the most important council in the history of the Church.

Finishing Up

The Nicene Creed originally was written in Greek, the spoken language for most of the bishops present at Nicea. It took a couple of decades for the creed to become widely known in the Western, Latin-speaking part of the Church.

While the relationship of God the Father and the Son was the most important issue discussed at Nicea, it was not the only one. The bishops also dealt with issues of church discipline and administration. They drew up a list of twenty canons, or regulations, that dealt with (1) the structure of churches; (2) the dignity of the clergy; (3) how to bring the *lapsi*, heretics, and others separated from the Church back into unity; and (4) liturgy.

After three long months, the council had finished its work. The State that had so recently persecuted the Church was now actively promoting and striving to help unify it. The Council of Nicea was not only the triumph of what would become the orthodox interpretation of Christ but also a breathtaking vision of how Church and State could work together. When the bishops headed home with the big job of explaining the council's decisions to the people in their areas, they took with them a deeper understanding of where the Church now stood in the empire that covered almost their entire known world.

That does not mean that Christian unity now reigned supreme. The different sides continued to fight, and Constantine, as well as the emperors following him, went back and forth on which side to support. Each time one group or the other had the favor of an emperor, it tried to get him to use force to suppress the others. All this leads to a terrible statistic: One author estimated that more Christians died at the hands of other Christians in the seventy-five years after Nicea than had died as martyrs during almost three centuries of Roman persecution.[7]

Let's Make a Date: Easter[8]

The early Church struggled to settle on a date for Easter. The gospels were clear that the event celebrated at Easter, the resurrection of Jesus, took place on a Sunday, but exactly *which* Sunday was open to debate. Matthew, Mark, and Luke all indicate that it was the Sunday after Passover, but John names another date. The earliest Christians were not overly concerned about the date because they expected Christ to return and the new world to begin any day; for them, every Sunday was a celebration of the resurrection. When this did not happen, however, they began to see the need for a more formal celebration.

By the time of the Council of Nicea in 325, the dating of Easter had become confusing. For one thing, the Jewish year is based on the lunar rather than the solar calendar. The lunar calendar counts a year as a certain number of full moons, while the solar calendar goes by how long it takes the earth to revolve around the sun. The solar calendar was used by Romans and is the calendar we use today. Some Christian communities celebrated Easter on the Sunday after Passover, some favored setting a date no matter what day of the week it fell on, and some had no particular plan but did not want their Christian holiday based on Jewish calculations of Passover. The Council of Nicea settled the debate. Constantine explained in a letter he wrote to Church leaders not in attendance at Nicea that the bishops had decided to use the solar calendar and that all Christian communities should celebrate Easter on the same day: the first Sunday after Passover that came after the first full moon after the equinox.

A problem remained, however: knowing the date of the equinox. The solar calendar in use at the time was off by eleven minutes per year, meaning they had to stick in extra days every now and then to get things more or less working properly. This meant that over the course of centuries, the date of Easter drifted days and then weeks away from the actual equinox. Plus, there was the East–West split: People in the West counted March 21 as the equinox, while those in the East dated it March 25, and the two groups used different methods of adding days to the calendar to fix it. Most of the time, East and West still came up with the same Sunday for Easter but not always. This difference in dating Easter continues, and Catholic and Protestant churches often celebrate the resurrection on a different day than do Christian communities with their origins in the East.

The Father and the Son: Thinking Through What It All Means

Working through one problem opened the way for others. Those who signed the Nicene Creed could not agree on what it means to say that God the Father and the Son are of the same substance. Some thought "of the same substance" meant that God the Father and the Son share an eternal substance different from everything else; others saw it as meaning that the three persons of the Trinity are without distinction; still others thought it was about the divinity of the Son; and still others were not really clear on any of it but wanted unity in the Church.

Let's take a look at how a few thinkers worked through these issues.

Athanasius

Bishop Athanasius of Alexandria became the strongest defender of the Nicene faith and the most unforgiving of Arius. Even after Arius accepted the decisions of Nicea—and Constantine personally asked that he be forgiven—Athanasius refused to readmit him to communion. Start a heresy, said Athanasius, and you should be permanently excluded from the Church.

Athanasius had a long history of woes during his forty-five years as bishop of Alexandria. Exiled and recalled many times, depending on whether the current ruler was a supporter of the Arians or the Nicene faith, he was accused of immoral conduct, illegally taxing citizens, supporting rebels against the emperor, terrorizing Arians, and even murdering a bishop. He successfully refuted all charges; for the last one, he simply hauled the supposedly dead bishop into court with him.

The way Athanasius saw it, humans were made to be immortal, a perfect reflection of God. People only lost immortality and became imperfect because of sin. Sin is not so much a mistake to be corrected or a debt to be paid as it is the way imperfection and change came into creation. To overcome this, God had to bring about a new creation by entering humanity. Athanasius said that Christ "was made [human] that we might be made god," meaning Christ made it possible for humans to reflect God's image perfectly once again. For Athanasius, then, it is important that Christ is of the very same substance as the Father. His role is not to bridge some gap between humans and God—why would we need this since God created us?—but to participate in humanity so that humans might participate in God's divinity.

Gregory of Nyssa

Gregory of Nyssa agreed with Athanasius that the Son was divine, but he took a different tack in proving it. He did not just want to know if Christ was human or divine; he wanted to truly understand the existence of the Holy Trinity. He believed people often got confused trying to figure out how Christians can talk about Father, Son, and Holy Spirit and still not worship three gods. The key, he felt, was to make a logical and scripturally sound argument to explain the relationship among the members of the Trinity—if you understand how they relate to each other, then you will understand how they are not three different gods.

An admirer of Origen, Gregory used philosophy to develop his theology. In a work called "An Answer to Ablabius," he developed one of the tightest arguments ever created on the subject of the Trinity. He said that God exists in three persons but that all three have one substance or nature. Christian Scripture tells us the Trinity always acts with one accord, but the conclusion Gregory draws from his argument is that this is the result of the three persons sharing one substance, not the cause of it.

Moving Forward: Constantinople and Chalcedon

Theologians kept absorbing the work of the Council of Nicea, but this led them to other thorny questions: Did Christ have only a divine nature, or did he have a human one as well? And what about the Holy Spirit—where did it fit into the picture? Over the next 125 years, the Church tried to untangle these difficult issues.

Years after Nicea, people were still arguing about what it meant to say that the Father and the Son are of the same substance. More local councils were called and more creeds written, but the confusion kept growing. Finally, another council was called, for May of 381 in Constantinople.

The Council of Constantinople is known as the second great ecumenical council of the Church, although "ecumenical" is a bit of a stretch—all 150 bishops attending came from the East. It was certainly eventful, though: the first presiding bishop died just as things got going, the next one had to resign over political issues, and the third was actually a layman who was quickly baptized and consecrated bishop. As for what the council actually did, it is hard to say because the official recordings of the proceedings are lost. It may have revised the Nicene Creed to the form we use today, although there is no mention of this until the Council of Chalcedon in 451, or it may just have restated the importance of the creed. Either way, it definitely held to the Nicene line that the Father and the Son share the same divinity and that those who leaned toward an Arian interpretation of the creed were wrong.

This was not the end of Arianism, though. By the middle of the fourth century, Arian missionaries had already carried their beliefs to some of the Germanic tribes known in history as the barbarians. When these tribes began invasions a few centuries later, they brought their Arian Christian faith with them. The Vandals in North Africa, the Visigoths in Spain, the Lombards in Italy—all established kingdoms with Arian Christianity as their faith of choice. Among the invaders, only the Franks held onto the Nicene faith. However, most of the peoples being conquered by all these invading hordes were orthodox believers. Put this together with the growing power of the Nicene-inclined Franks, and you will see why Arian Christianity eventually died out.

Once they had the relationship of God the Father and Son suitably figured out, theologians started trying to puzzle through what it meant for Christ to be both divine and human. One idea was that Christ had within him two natures, one human and one divine. Nestorius, who became patriarch of Constantinople in 428, took this to a logical extreme. He did not like people calling Mary the *theotokos*, the "bearer of God"; how could this be, he said, since what Mary gave birth to was only the human nature? It is not like God came into being when Jesus was born of Mary. So Mary is the bearer of Jesus but not of God, and to say otherwise is to confuse the two natures. Nestorius said that when the two natures come together, each maintains its ability to exist without the other.

The patriarch of Alexandria, Cyril, thought Nestorius went too far in distinguishing the natures. How can we say that God dwelt among us if we have to figure out whether it was Jesus' divine or human nature acting every time he did something? Cyril argued the two natures cannot be separated, but they exist together as a whole. Mary is the *theotokos* not because the divinity of Christ began in her but because she is mother of the human that exists in union with the divine.

Cyril was also interested in promoting Alexandria as a patriarchal see of greater authority than Constantinople. He convinced the bishop of Rome to support his position, and a synod held in Rome in 430 condemned Nestorius. Cyril sent Nestorius a series of twelve condemnations of his position and told him to sign them or be declared heretical. Nestorius, who had gotten the support of John, the patriarch of Antioch, sent back twelve condemnations of Cyril.

The Western branch of the Church (the patriarchs of Alexandria and Rome) was squaring off against the Eastern branch (the patriarchs of Constantinople and Antioch). A council called in 431 at Ephesus to straighten the situation out just made things worse. Cyril opened the proceedings before any of Nestorius's supporters arrived; because he would not let Nestorius himself speak, the council quickly condemned and deposed Nestorius. When John of Antioch arrived and saw what had happened, he called his own council and deposed Cyril.

Emperor Theodosius III, thinking a crisis was imminent, had Cyril, Nestorius, and John imprisoned. Cyril finally convinced the emperor to bring together a council that could hammer out a solution. Cyril's position was largely accepted, and Nestorius was made to leave Constantinople, eventually ending up in an Egyptian desert monastery.

But the problems did not end there. Many still supported Nestorius's ideas, and even among those who did not, some did not like Cyril's ideas either. Finally, the Council of Chalcedon was called in 451 to hash things out, and this time it worked. The bishops decided Cyril basically had it right: Christ is not some kind of hybrid part God–part human; he is both truly and fully God and truly and fully human.

Nestorius's ideas did not die when they were condemned at the Council of Chalcedon, however. Some of his followers rejected the council's decision and continued to spread his ideas, eventually forming a separate Christian body known as the Nestorian Church. This became the most important Christian group in Persia, and from the end of the fifth century on, they considered themselves officially separate from the Church in communion with Rome.

Nestorian missionaries spread their version of the Christian message as far east as India and China. In the sixteenth century, some Nestorian communities in India rejoined the Roman Catholic Church—these are usually called Chaldean Catholics and are part of the Uniat churches, those that maintain their own traditions while being fully in communion with the Roman Catholic Church. Nestorian churches still exist in Iraq, Iran, parts of India, and even the United States.

After centuries of separation, in 1994 the Nestorian Church and the Catholic Church jointly declared that they recognized how the truth of Christ's mission was continued in both of their traditions.

Church + State = Problems

State support brought much help to the Church, but with the help came problems.

State interference in the Church. Previously, the State had tried to get rid of the Church through persecutions but had stayed out of Church internal affairs. As the State began to support the Church, however, the Church became increasingly dependent on the State. One result was that Church decisions became more and more influenced by a desire to stay on the good side of government.

Mass conversions. Since almost all emperors starting with Constantine favored Christians, great numbers of people began converting for political and social reasons rather than because of their beliefs.

Corrupting power. As their government ties grew stronger, some Church leaders began to get caught up in the trappings of power. This situation grew to a point where a great reformer of the twelfth century, Bernard of Clairvaux, declared that because the apostle Peter had been a humble man, the luxury of the current popes made them "the successor of Constantine, not Peter,"[9] a charge some still echo today.

Use of violence. State-sponsored violence against those whom the Church saw as its enemies was the most disturbing change to follow from greater Church–State cooperation. Often, those "enemies" were other Christians. For instance, when the Church in Carthage found itself at odds with Donatist Christians, Constantine's troops joined a local mob in attacking the Donatist churches in the area and killing some of their members. After Arius's writings were declared heretical, Constantine issued an order that anyone found in possession of Arius's writings would face execution. The reason the Nag Hammadi find was such a boon for modern scholars of Gnosticism was that orthodox Christians, once in power, had made sure to destroy every copy of Gnostic writings that came to light.

Even when Church and State were not actively fighting, they could still interact one of two ways: separate or unified. The West tended to go the separate route; thinkers emphasized that a religious and a civil society co-existed, each with distinct rights and privileges. This meant that Church and State were not to meddle in each other's affairs. In the West, Church and State never became as tight as in the East, where thinkers talked about Church and

State working together to create a unified Christian society. In both parts of the empire, though, determining where the lines should be drawn would be a major struggle for centuries to come.

Constantine himself fell solidly on the "unified" side. He saw himself as having been put by God in the most powerful position in the world; since the Church was part of God's domain, then God had authorized him to govern it and make as many people as possible become Christian. This sounds heavy-handed to modern ears, but it made perfect sense to fourth-century Christians: people had long been forced to worship false gods, so now the true God had changed the situation so people would be forced to worship him instead. This was how Eusebius of Caesarea saw things. He called Constantine "the beloved of God" and wrote that he "receives and bears the image of this Supreme Kingship, and so steers and directs, in imitation of his Superior, the helm of all the affairs of this world."[10] It was this kind of thinking that laid the foundation for the Eastern Church's melding of Church and State.

In the West, we find a history of confrontations between Church and State. One of the earliest came near the end of the fourth century, and in this case it was the Church that wanted to flex its authority. In 388, a local bishop of a small town in Mesopotamia incited a Christian mob to burn down a synagogue. When Emperor Theodosius I ordered that the mob leaders be punished and the bishop and his church pay for the rebuilding of the synagogue, the neighboring Bishop Ambrose of Milan was furious. He argued forcefully that Church funds should not be used to support unbelievers: "Shall a place be provided out of the spoils of the Church for the disbelief of the Jews . . . The Jews will write on the front of their synagogue the inscription: 'The Temple of Impiety, erected from the spoils of the Christians.'"[11] Theodosius tried to compromise, offering to use State funds for the rebuilding, but Ambrose would have none of it. Once the bishop started railing from the pulpit and refusing to perform any worship service if Theodosius was going to attend, the emperor backed down. He could not afford this fight with Ambrose, who was probably the most powerful bishop in the West at the time.

Ambrose and Theodosius clashed again two years later. A mob in Thessalonica killed a military commander, and Theodosius ordered the entire population put to death for the killing. When Theodosius later cooled down and tried to rescind the order, it was too late; seven thousand people had been massacred. Ambrose told him he had committed a terrible sin and must perform public penance. Theodosius did not like the idea of an emperor being treated like everyone else, but ultimately he had to give in and do as Ambrose required.

Theodosius was the last emperor of a unified empire, one that stretched across both East and West. Over the course of the next couple of decades, the empire slowly crumbled. In the West, all semblance of order and government completely collapsed during the next two centuries, but in the East things looked much better. What had been the Roman Empire continued in name there, even though it no longer had any connections to Rome. It eventually evolved into the Byzantine Empire, which held strong for another thousand years until finally falling to the Turks in 1453.

How did all of this affect the Church? As we will see, the breakdown of civil authority left an opening the Church was willing to fill. It became the most stabilizing influence in society, and by the time secular governments once again began to play a major role in the West, the Church was well established as an independent organization that might sometimes work with and sometimes against the State but that would never accept being subject to it.

The Eastern Church, on the other hand, was able to maintain the ideal of a unified Christian society in which Church and State work together under the guidance of a king or emperor. In all practicality, this generally meant that the emperors of the Roman/Byzantine Empire had an easy time maintaining control over the Church. For instance, when John Chrysostom, bishop of Constantinople, tried in 404 to stand up to Emperor Arcadius the way Ambrose had to Theodosius, the other bishops of the area condemned him to exile in the name of the emperor, acknowledging the emperor's right to make decisions about the Church. As it became more subject to imperial power, the Church in the East drifted farther from the Church of Rome.

The Church Then and Now

Creeds

The word *creed* comes from the Latin *credo*, for "I believe." If the gospels are the heart of Christianity, creeds are its brain—works of reason requiring thought as opposed to stories that appeal to emotion. Christians had new members recite creeds as a way of making sure that those joining shared the beliefs of the community, but creeds were also written specifically to exclude certain beliefs.

Let's take a look at two of the creeds most commonly used in Catholic Christianity, the Apostles' Creed and the Nicene Creed, and at one of its most rigorous, the Athanasian Creed.

The Apostles' Creed does not date to the time of the apostles. In the second century, it was standard practice in the Roman Church to ask catechumens a series of questions about their beliefs before they were baptized. By the fourth century, these questions had evolved into the statements in the creed. The exact version of the Apostles' Creed we have today did not come about until the seventh century, but its roots are in the faith professed by the earliest Christians.

The Nicene Creed expresses a much deeper level of theological detail than does the Apostle's Creed. As we have seen, it was created to exclude Arians and other heterodox thinkers from the Church. The creed evolved over time; as more questions arose about the nature of the Trinity and of salvation, Church leaders expanded the creed to cover more ground—and exclude more heresies.

The Athanasian Creed probably was not actually written by Athanasius, but he surely would have approved of its meticulous and absolutist tendencies. In fact, it was probably written somewhere in the Western Church around the year 500, and it was intended to combat a host of heresies. It is repetitive, but every statement is meant to express a precise understanding of the issue being discussed and to absolutely exclude any other understandings. Although not used much by the Western Church these days (and never by the Eastern Church), it is a testament to how intensely Christian thinkers felt the need to parse each thought expressed in a creed so that agreeing to it meant agreeing in entirety with all others who professed it, which is itself a testament to just how difficult it is to get even those who agree on the same words to also share the same meaning.

A side-by-side comparison of the three creeds (see pages 84–85) can help us see how the Church's theology grew and developed over time. By the time even the shortest of these creeds had come into use, Christians had traveled quite far from the simple "I do believe" of Mark 9:24, and it was a journey they could never retrace.

Apostles' Creed	Nicene Creed	Athanasian Creed
		Whosoever will be saved, before all things it is necessary that he hold the catholic faith; which faith except every one do keep whole and undefiled, without doubt he shall perish everlastingly.
I believe in God, the Father almighty, creator of heaven and earth.	We believe in one God, the Father, the Almighty, maker of heaven and earth, of all that is, seen and unseen.	And the catholic faith is this: That we worship one God in Trinity, and Trinity in Unity; neither confounding the persons nor dividing the substance. For there is one person of the Father, another of the Son, and another of the Holy Spirit. But the Godhead of the Father, of the Son, and of the Holy Spirit is all one, the glory equal, the majesty coeternal. Such as the Father is, such is the Son, and such is the Holy Spirit. The Father uncreated, the Son uncreated, and the Holy Spirit uncreated. The Father incomprehensible, the Son incomprehensible, and the Holy Spirit incomprehensible. The Father eternal, the Son eternal, and the Holy Spirit eternal. And yet they are not three eternals but one eternal. As also there are not three uncreated nor three incomprehensible, but one uncreated and one incomprehensible. So likewise the Father is almighty, the Son almighty, and the Holy Spirit almighty. And yet they are not three almighties, but one almighty. So the Father is God, the Son is God, and the Holy Spirit is God; and yet they are not three Gods, but one God.
		So likewise the Father is Lord, the Son Lord, and the Holy Spirit Lord; and yet they are not three Lords but one Lord. For like as we are compelled by the Christian verity to acknowledge every Person by himself to be God and Lord; so are we forbidden by the catholic religion to say; There are three Gods or three Lords. The Father is made of none, neither created nor begotten. The Son is of the Father alone; not made nor created, but begotten. The Holy Spirit is of the Father and of the Son; neither made, nor created, nor begotten, but proceeding. So there is one Father, not three Fathers; one Son, not three Sons; one Holy Spirit, not three Holy Spirits. And in this Trinity none is afore or after another; none is greater or less than another.
		But the whole three persons are coeternal, and coequal. So that in all things, as aforesaid, the Unity in Trinity and the Trinity in Unity is to be worshipped. He therefore that will be saved must thus think of the Trinity.
I believe in Jesus Christ, his only Son, our Lord.	We believe in one Lord, Jesus Christ, the only Son of God, eternally begotten of the Father, God from God, Light from Light, true God from true God, begotten not made, one in Being with the Father Through him all things were made.	Furthermore it is necessary to everlasting salvation that he also believe rightly the incarnation of our Lord Jesus Christ. For the right faith is that we believe and confess that our Lord Jesus Christ, the Son of God, is God and man. God of the substance of the Father, begotten before the worlds; and man of substance of His mother, born in the world. Perfect God and perfect man, of a reasonable soul and human flesh subsisting. Equal to the Father

Apostles' cont.	Nicene cont.	Athanasian cont.
	For us men and for our salvation he came down from heaven:	as touching His Godhead, and inferior to the Father as touching His manhood. Who, although He is God and man, yet He is not two, but one Christ. One, not by conversion of the Godhead into flesh, but by taking of that manhood into God. One altogether, not by confusion of substance, but by unity of person. For as the reasonable soul and flesh is one man, so God and man is one Christ;
He was conceived by the power of the Holy Spirit and born of the Virgin Mary.	by the power of the Holy Spirit he was born of the Virgin Mary, and became man.	
He suffered under Pontius Pilate, was crucified, died and was buried. He descended into hell.	For our sake he was crucified under Pontius Pilate; he suffered, died, and was buried.	who suffered for our salvation, descended into hell,
On the third day he rose again	On the third day he rose again in fulfillment of the Scriptures;	rose again the third day from the dead;
He ascended into heaven and is seated at the right hand of the Father.	he ascended into heaven and is seated at the right hand of the Father.	He ascended into heaven, He sits on the right hand of the Father, God, Almighty;
He will come again to judge the living and the dead.	He will come again in glory to judge the living and the dead, and his kingdom will have no end.	from thence He shall come to judge the quick and the dead. At whose coming all men shall rise again with their bodies; and shall give account of their own works. And they that have done good shall go into life everlasting and they that have done evil into everlasting fire.
I believe in the Holy Spirit,	We believe in the Holy Spirit, the Lord, the giver of life, who proceeds from the Father and the Son. With the Father and the Son he is worshipped and glorified. He has spoken through the prophets.	
the holy catholic Church, the communion of saints,	We believe in one holy catholic and apostolic Church.	
the forgiveness of sins,	We acknowledge one baptism for the forgiveness of sins.	
the resurrection of the body,	We look for the resurrection of the dead,	
and the life everlasting.	and the life of the world to come.	
		This is the catholic faith, which except a man believe faithfully he cannot be saved.
Amen.	Amen.	

Questions and Ideas for Understanding

1. What benefits do you see in the Church's developing a more organized structure? What do you think might have happened to the Church overall if the various Christian communities had not begun to develop these structures of authority?

2. Think for a moment as though you were a Gnostic. How would you go about living in the world? What sorts of things would you think you should or should not do?

3. People still argue over who and what God is and whether or not God exists. Do you think the scientific worldview of modern American society challenges the Christian belief in God? What about the diversity of people and close contact among different faith traditions? If so, in what ways do you see modern Christians responding to these challenges?

4. Think about the ways that Arius, Athanasius, and Gregory of Nyssa understand the relationship of God the Father and the Son. Then make a visual representation—a chart, a graph, a picture, and so on—that explains these different views.

5. Look at the Nicene Creed. Write an essay explaining what is meant by each statement given about God the Father and the Son, including where the creed specifically refutes the ideas of Gnostics and Arians.

Notes

[1] Lactantius, *On the Death of the Persecutors* 44. In Ralph Martin Novak, *Christianity and the Roman Empire: Background Texts*. Harrisburg, PA: Trinity Press International, 2001, p. 156.

[2] Eusebius of Caesarea, *Life of Constantine* 1.27–32. In Novak, *Christianity*, p. 156.

[3] *Oration on the Deity of the Son and the Holy Spirit*. In *Patrologia Graeca*, Vol. 46, ed. J.P. Migne. Paris: Garnier Fratres, 1863, col. 558. Quoted in William C. Placher, *A History of Christian Theology*. Louisville, KY: The Westminster Press, 1983.

[4] Eusebius of Caesarea, *Life of Constantine* 1.27–32. In Novak, *Christianity*, p. 156.

[5] W. H. C. Frend, *Martyrdom and Persecution in the Early Church*. New York: New York University Press, 1967, pp. 399–400.

[6] Eusebius, *Life of Constantine* 1.10. In Novak, *Christianity*, p. 173.

[7] Ramsay MacMullen, *Christianity and Paganism in the Fourth to Eighth Centuries*. New Haven, CT: Yale University Press, 1997, p. 14.

[8] Paraphrased from David Ewing Duncan, *Calendar*. New York: Avon Books, 1998.

[9] Bernard, *De Consideratione*, Book IV, c. III, 6, Rome: Editiones Cistercienses, 1963. p. 453.

[10] Eusebius, *De laudibus Constantini* I.6. In Frend, *Martyrdom*, p. 403.

[11] Ambrose, "Epistle 40 to the Emperor Theodosius." In Novak, *Christianity*, p. 212.

5
Life and Times of a Seeker
Augustine of Hippo

Chapter Overview

In this chapter, we will explore:

▶ Changes in the Roman Empire

▶ Ambrose's allegorical interpretations of Scripture

▶ The life and writings of Augustine

▶ Three heresies that affected Augustine

▶ The idea that salvation is to be found only in the Church

Augustine: Looking for the Truth

As you hold your baby son in your arms, you give thanks for the joy that he brings you. You were not always so happy about becoming a father, but as you see his smile and watch his little fingers curl around yours, you cannot feel anything but love. The child's mother laughs to see you so delighted at holding your baby, and you smile at her. You almost wish you could marry her, but that sort of union would never do. You are only 17, and when the time comes, you will need a rich wife, a well-stationed woman whose money will open doors and provide you with the lifestyle that a professor of rhetoric deserves. Having a lover now is no shame for a man like you; even your Christian mother agreed that it was better to focus your sexual attention on one unmarried woman than to be tempted by a married one.

The thought of your mother stops you cold for a moment. You love her, but she is always wanting to interfere in your life. She expects you to raise your son as a Christian, and she has been pestering you to say the proper prayers over the child each day. But she does not know that you have found Christianity cannot answer all your questions, especially the question of evil. If a good God created a good world, then how do we explain evil? The teaching of the Manicheans seems far superior on this question. The Manicheans say that the good God did not create this world but rather that good has been trapped inside a world that is inherently evil. The more you think about this, the truer it seems. You may join the Manicheans, yet you know this would break your mother's heart.

Ah, but here is your son, Adeodatus. You put these thoughts out of your mind. You will raise a little philosopher, but for now, you just want to enjoy the sweet feeling of holding your child. Your lover comes to sit beside you. Laying her head on your shoulder, she gently touches the child's cheek. For the moment you sit there, quietly content, as the child drifts off to sleep.

Augustine's life at 60 looked nothing like he expected at 17: a bishop rather than a professor, unmarried and committed to poverty rather than husband to a wealthy heiress, and childless because his son Adeodatus died young. The world around him looked even stranger: Rome had fallen, barbarian invasions were underway, and the Church was troubled more by internal threats of heresy than by the external problems of pagan religion and Manichean thought.

We will take a look at all these things as we try to get a vision of Augustine's life and writings, and we will finish by talking about Augustine's idea that salvation is to be found only within the Church. A brilliant and multitalented bishop, theologian, and philosopher, but most of all a seeker, Augustine examined every part of his life for ways to move closer to the divine. In fact, he believed all people are seeking God in everything they do, whether they recognize it or not. As he says to God in *The Confessions*, "Our hearts find no peace until they rest in you."[1] ■

Rome Takes a Nosedive

The late fourth and early fifth centuries were a rough time if you were a Roman citizen. The stories of Rome's glorious history you learned as a child would not have matched up well with what you saw going on around you.

The empire had long been in decline, and in 377, a Germanic tribe, the Goths, attacked the eastern part of the empire. The following year, the emperor Valens battled the Goths at Adrianople in modern Turkey. The fight went poorly as he lost two-thirds of his army—and his life. The Goths advanced to the borders of Constantinople itself before being turned back. Barbarian tribes had been invading various parts of the empire for many years, but this was the first time the world dominated by Rome really had to face a major invasion.

To pay for all this warring, taxes were greatly increased. The poor became desperate, as every coin that went into the government's war chest meant less food for their families. Even the rich began hoarding to protect themselves.

Then the unthinkable happened: another Germanic group, the Visigoths, took Rome itself on August 28, 410. Under the command of their leader, Alaric, the tribe ran killing and plundering through the streets of the city for three days before moving on. Mighty Rome was mighty no more.

In the midst of all this destruction, people wanted to know who to blame. Theodosius had made Christianity the official religion of Rome on the grounds that getting people to worship the true God would strengthen the empire. If the pagans thought their silly gods could put up a good defense, just wait and see what the true God could do! This reasoning backfired spectacularly with the fall of Rome, and pagans seized on it immediately. They said the Christian God had failed to protect Rome, and the pagan gods had let it fall because they were no longer receiving their rightful worship.

It was a terrible situation all around, but Augustine met it head on.

"I Rise by Stages towards the God Who Made Me": Augustine's Life[2]

In 354, Patricius and Monica welcomed their son Augustine to the world in their hometown of Thagaste, part of what is now Algeria. Although Patricius had been raised a pagan and only came to the Church when Augustine was almost grown, Monica was born a Christian. She raised her children—Augustine, his older brother, Navigius, and possibly two sisters—to be Christians as well.

Augustine's parents made his education a priority early on, sending him first to study with a local teacher in Thagaste, then to the much larger city of Carthage. When he was 16, Augustine had to return home for a year, as the family could not afford to pay for his teachers anymore. About this time, he first felt the stirrings of the sexual temptation that would weigh heavily on his mind for years to come. Looking back later, Augustine thought his parents were more concerned about the state of his education than the state of his soul: "I surrendered myself entirely to lust . . . My family made no effort to save me from my fall by marriage. Their only concern was that I should learn how to make a good speech and how to persuade others by my words"[3]—a reference to the career his family had picked out for him as a rhetorician, one whose job is to make forceful and persuasive speeches and to teach others to do the same. Augustine soon started a romantic relationship with a woman that would last for the next fifteen years. Although she became the mother of his son, Adeodatus, and had a big impact on his life, in all his writings, Augustine never tells her name.

Also at about age 17, Augustine experienced the first great intellectual transformation of his life: he discovered philosophy. Certainly he had read some of the great ancient philosophers before, but nothing made a deep impact on him until he read a work by Cicero that held up philosophy as the only path to making life meaningful, specifically contrasting it with the rhetoric Augustine was studying. Augustine says that reading this work made his heart "throb with a bewildering passion for the wisdom of eternal truth,"[4] and so he turned to the God he knew—the Christian God, as presented in the Christian Scriptures.

When Augustine tried to read the Bible seriously, to go more deeply into it rather than sticking with the Sunday school stories he had heard all his life, he decided it was a big disappointment. He found the Scriptures poorly written compared with the great literature he was accustomed to reading, and he was troubled by what he saw as contradictions between various parts of the Scriptures. The Hebrew Bible, with all its animal sacrifices and wars and God telling these people to kill those other people, was particularly difficult for him.

It led him straight to a question that plagued him for a long time: if God is good, how can evil exist?

Not convinced that Christianity offered a valid answer to this question, Augustine began looking around for something that would—and discovered Manicheism. This religion combined elements of Gnosticism, Christianity, Buddhism, and a Persian faith called Zoroastrianism. Its founder, a third-century Persian named Mani, saw the world as a cosmic battle between the Kingdom of Light and the Kingdom of Darkness. Everything in the world, including humans, is a mixture of Light and Darkness, and the work of the Manichean is to free the Light so that it can return to its true home. Manicheans believed the material part of humans has its origin in the Kingdom of Darkness, but the spiritual part is completely good and of the Light.

Augustine found in Manicheism an explanation for why people commit sins: not because they are inherently evil but because the good spiritual part of them is in bondage to the evil material part. God is indeed good, said the Manicheans, but evil exists independently of God. And evil is a physical quality rather than a moral one: The spirit, which is Light, could no more sin than the material body could be good. Manicheans believed Christ had come from the God of the Kingdom of Light to show people the truth about the good within them and how to free it, but they did not see Christ as the only revealer: the Buddha, Zoroaster, Plato, and Mani himself were also sent by God to reveal the truth.

By the time of Augustine, Mani's religion had spread throughout the Roman world and was strong in North Africa where Augustine lived. Manicheans were still growing in numbers during Augustine's time, although there were many laws against them. Persecution led to the end of Manichaeism in the West by the sixth century. In the East, though, it continued to spread, reaching as far as China, where Manicheans continued to exist down to the sixteenth century.

Augustine was 18 when he became a Manichean, a conversion that lasted nine years. His mother, Monica, was so upset by his choice that she banned him from her house. In the end, though, Augustine came to think that Manichean thinking lacked intellectual rigor. He came to believe that Manicheism gave superficial answers to his serious philosophical and theological questions, and in his late 20s, he left the religion of Mani behind. Much of Augustine's writings, however, continued to reflect a world-denying Manichean strain.

Ambrose, Allegory, and a Big Change

At 29, Augustine needed a change. He had been teaching rhetoric in Carthage and decided to head for Rome, thinking he would find better students, better pay, and more prestige. Although no longer the center of the cultural universe, Rome remained impressive. Besides, his boyhood friend Alypius was already there.

Augustine's father had died a number of years earlier. His mother was upset by the thought of him moving so far away and wanted to go with him. Augustine did not like the idea, so when Monica showed up at the port where he was looking for a ship to Rome, he convinced her to spend the night praying at a local shrine for his safety. When she went looking for him the next morning, she discovered he and the ship had already sailed.

Augustine ended up teaching in Milan, and his mother did join him there. She convinced him to send away the mother of his child so that he could make a wealthy marriage. After fifteen years of life together, Augustine's lover returned to Africa, leaving behind Augustine and their child. Augustine wrote that this separation hurt him deeply, yet he felt that it made him a better person because it was designed to lead him to the form of marital love that was pleasing to God.

By this time, Augustine had left behind his interest in Manicheism, but he was still tangled in the philosophical questions that had led him there in the first place. His sense that philosophy was a means of approaching God became much more profound when he discovered Neoplatonic ideas in 386. Augustine said that reading the works of Plotinus and his followers made him feel like he had reached the free air. Even in his later years as a Christian theologian, Augustine always saw Neoplatonic philosophy as taking a person as far as humans could go on their own in approaching God, missing only those things concerning redemption that God had revealed in Christianity alone.

In Milan, Augustine had the opportunity to hear the sermons of Bishop Ambrose, whose rhetorical style was extraordinary. Ambrose was a much-loved bishop and influential theologian in addition to being a shrewd player in Church–State relations. The first person descended from the highest ranks of Roman society to devote his life to the Church, Ambrose had grown up in Rome, where he was able to develop his intellectual nature with a good education.

As a bishop, Ambrose became convinced that while theology and politics both were vitally important, preaching and teaching were the bishop's most important tasks. In his sermons and writings, Ambrose developed an allegorical interpretation of the biblical texts. He looked beyond their literal meaning for a deeper truth. This approach opened a whole new world for Augustine, as stories in the Hebrew Scriptures that had been so difficult for him to accept at face value were rich fodder for Ambrose, who taught that through those stories, God had been preparing people to recognize and accept Christ when he came.

All of this soon led Augustine to the point of conversion, which he describes in this famous passage from his *Confessions*:

> I felt that I was still the captive of my sins, and in my misery I kept crying "How long shall I go on saying 'tomorrow, tomorrow'? . . . Why not make an end of my ugly sins at this moment?"
>
> I was asking myself these questions, weeping all the while with the most bitter sorrow in my heart, when all at once I heard the singing voice of a child in a nearby house . . . again and again it repeated the refrain "Take it and read, take it and read" . . . I stemmed my flood of tears and stood up, telling myself that this could only be a divine command to open my book of Scripture and read the first passage on which my eyes should fall. . . For I had heard the story of Anthony. . .
>
> So I hurried back to the place where Alypius was sitting, for when I stood up to move away I had put down the book containing Paul's Epistles. I seized it and opened it, and in silence I read the first passage on which my eyes fell: "Not in reveling and drunkenness, not in lust and wantonness, not in quarrels and rivalries. Rather, arm yourselves with the Lord Jesus Christ; spend no more thought on nature and nature's appetites." I had no wish to read more and no need to do so. For in an instant, as I came to the end of the sentence, it was as though the light of confidence flooded into my heart and all the darkness of doubt was dispelled.
>
> [Augustine tells Alypius what he is experiencing, and the latter asks to see the book] . . . [H]e read on beyond the text which I had read. I did not know what followed but it was this: "Find room among

The Simple Life: Christian Contemplatives

Augustine was deeply inspired by the life of a third-century Egyptian named Anthony, or Antony. Christian communities had always included people who chose lives of celibacy, poverty and devotion to good works, but Anthony became know far and wide as a saint, thanks in large part to Athanasius's *The Life of Antony*.

Anthony's story goes like this: One Sunday when he was about 20, Anthony walked into a worship service and heard the reading from Matthew where Jesus tells the wealthy young man: "Go, sell what you have and give to [the] poor, and you will have treasure in heaven" (19:21). At that moment, Anthony felt these words were directed at him, so he sold his farm and moved to the edge of the desert to live as a hermit. Eventually his fame as a holy man and miracle worker spread, and others came wanting to follow his example. They formed a community of hermits, each person living alone but all coming together on Sundays for worship.

Anthony died in 356, but his devotion to a simple and solitary life as a path to God lived on. Much of what we know about Anthony comes by way of Athanasius, who met Anthony and was so moved that he wrote *Life of Antony*. Here Athanasius describes Anthony and the fame that came to him:

Antony, as was his custom, would withdraw by himself to his monastic cell, devoting himself to his ascetic discipline: each day he would sigh, reflecting in his heart on the heavenly dwellings, focusing all his desire on them, and contemplating the transitory nature of human life . . . He used to say that it is necessary to give all one's time to the soul rather than to the body, but to concede a little time to the body for its necessities. . .[5]

To all the monks who came to see him he never tired of giving this exhortation: have faith in the Lord and love him, and to keep themselves from

continued on page 95

you for a man of over-delicate conscience." Alypius applied this to himself and told me so. This admonition was enough to give him strength, and without suffering the distress of hesitation he made his resolution and took this good purpose to himself.[6]

On Easter Eve of 387, Augustine, his friend Alypius, and his son Adeodatus were baptized by Ambrose. After Augustine's conversion, he gave up his plans for marriage and a successful career, choosing instead a life studying philosophy and the Christian Scriptures. Augustine was not destined to remain simply a scholar, however. His would be a life of contemplation and action, reading and writing, but also leading and serving.

continued from page 94

all filthy thoughts and the pleasures of the flesh and, as it is written in Proverbs, 'not to be deceived by filling the belly,' to flee false pride and to pray without ceasing, to say the psalms before going to sleep and after arising from sleep, to learn by heart the precepts in the Scriptures, and to remember the works of the saints and with them zealously train the soul to be mindful of the command-ments.[7]

Another Egyptian, a younger contemporary of Anthony's named Pachomius, also was living the solitary life. Pachomius's path to the contemplative life was indi-rect. Raised a pagan, Pachomius was quite young when he became a soldier and fought in one of Rome's many wars. During that time he met some Christians, and their devotion to charity and kindness so impressed him that he decided to become a Christian when his service as a soldier was done. Soon after he joined the Christian community, he decided to leave it again but this time so that he could devote himself entirely to pursuing holi-ness as a hermit. But the lonely path, it turned out, was not his destiny; when the call came to him, Pachomius began to build a life devoted to the divine but lived in community with others. And his monastic vision was not limited to men: He founded a house for women as well, and his sister took on the role of superior. By the time of his death in 346, Pachomius had founded a number of monastic houses for men and women.

Anthony valued solitude and came together with others only for worship, while Pachomius brought people together in a communal life; both men, however, worked from the same desire to find holiness by leaving behind the routine cares of home and family. These two men and the people who gathered around them were not the only Christians seeking lives of service and sim-plicity, but as their stories spread they inspired others throughout the world to follow their example—among them Augustine.

The Bishop Years

Augustine and those around him decided it was time to return to their home in Thagaste. They were on the road waiting for a ship to Africa when Monica became ill and died, leaving a hole in Augustine's life that would never be filled. Although an uneducated woman who did not share her son's concern for philosophical questions, Monica had a singular effect on Augustine's life and thinking. Hers was the voice in his head calling him to look beyond fame and fortune, beyond even intellectual pursuits, to a faith that would sustain him. It is only in Augustine's writings that we know about her, but that was enough for the Church to declare Monica not just the parent of a great man but a great woman and a saint in her own right.

A New Life in Christ[8]

Even though he was raised in a Christian household, Augustine was not baptized as a child. In his time, it was still common for people to wait until they were adults and ready to make a commitment to the Christian life before they received the sacrament of baptism.

The word *baptism* comes from a Greek word meaning "to immerse." In Jesus' time, converts to Judaism were baptized to represent the crossing of the Red Sea; in this way, the convert ritually shared in the trials and blessings of being a Jew. John, who baptized Jesus, used the ritual a little differently: as a symbol of a person's moral conversion and desire to lead a more godly life. Among Christians, baptism was the way a person became part of the community of believers. Paul saw baptism as breaking the power of sin and bringing a person into the blessings of Jesus' death and resurrection. For him, the act of being plunged into water and then raised from it was a symbol of the death of a person's old life of unbelief and rising to a new life in Christ.

During the second century, baptism became more elaborate. People were not baptized immediately after coming to belief; first, they received some instruction in the Christian way of life. During this time of preparation when they prayed and fasted, the people wanting to be baptized were known as *catechumens,* from the Greek word for "instruction." There was some secrecy about this process; as protection against persecution, catechumens were not told about all of the Christian rituals and meeting places until they had been baptized.

The Church had been baptizing children and infants since the second century, but in Augustine's day, theologians were still struggling to understand exactly what the ritual meant in that case. Surely an infant had not sinned, so how could baptism break sin's power? Some theologians looked beyond what a person had done during his or her lifetime and talked about original sin, the guilt of Adam that had been passed down to all people. Augustine took this view, explaining that original sin was transmitted through sexual passion—and since every child is born of a sexual union, every child receives the weight of this sin at conception. Therefore, baptizing an infant meant bringing the child into the life of Christ by freeing him or her of original sin rather than the sins he or she had personally committed. As the practice of infant baptism became more widespread, the phase of being a catechumen died out; all the instruction in Christian living and beliefs would come after baptism, as the child was growing, rather than before as a prelude to acceptance by the community.

Throughout the Middle Ages, people thought of baptism primarily in Augustine's terms of freeing a person from original sin, but now the Church understands the sacrament more in terms of welcoming a person into the life of Christ as lived in the Christian community. At Vatican II, the bishops revised the rite of baptism for children to reflect this, and they instituted the Rite of Christian Initiation for Adults (RCIA). RCIA revives the custom of instructing people in Catholic doctrine and practice before they formally join the Church through receiving the sacraments. However, not all parts of the practice have been revived; nowadays no one has any concerns about letting catechumens know anything and everything about where Catholics gather to worship.

Once he was back in Thagaste, other sorrows soon found Augustine: His dear friend Nebridius and his beloved son Adeodatus both died. Having lost so many of the people closest to him, Augustine felt himself at loose ends, so he threw himself into the Church ministries that he and Alypius had begun. Alypius soon became bishop of Thagaste.

In 391, Augustine made a fateful trip to the nearby town of Hippo. There, Augustine attended a worship service led by that town's bishop, Valerius. When some people noticed Augustine in attendance, they dragged him to the front, demanding that he be ordained a priest. Augustine later wrote that this distressed him greatly, as he feared priesthood would take him away from the life of contemplation he craved. However, he accepted what he saw as God's command. Five years later, Valerius had Augustine consecrated as his joint bishop, and Augustine took over the task fully when Valerius died.

Augustine served as bishop of Hippo for thirty-five years, and he took his work seriously. He was expected to look after the Catholic population of the town in ways that may seem strange to us today. He visited the jails not just to comfort prisoners but also to protect them from ill treatment. One of his most important functions as a community leader was to arbitrate lawsuits. Acting as a judge was a job Augustine particularly disliked but which he did particularly well—so well, in fact, that pagans and others who had reason to dislike his theology still streamed through his door in search of his help as an arbitrator in their disputes. But what Augustine saw as most important in his work as bishop was preaching, teaching, and leading souls to Christ. He once said in a sermon:

> [W]hat do I desire? Why do I give sermons? Why am I seated here in my cathedral? What is the purpose of my life? My only purpose is that we should live together in Christ. This is my desire, my honor, my riches, this is my joy and my glory. But if you do not listen to me, since I have not kept silence, I shall save my soul. However, I do not wish to be saved without you.[9]

When Augustine came to Hippo, the Donatists, those Christians who had split from the Church during the time of persecution over how to deal with clergy members who were *traditores,* formed a larger group in the town than did Catholics, but during Augustine's years as bishop, the Catholic minority became the majority. We will discuss how this happened, and Augustine's role in the change, later.

Seeing the church in Hippo grow during his time there must have pleased Augustine, but toward the end of his life, he also saw the destruction of much of what he had built. Just as the Visigoths had overtaken Rome, another Germanic tribe, the Vandals, overran the area around Hippo in 429–430. Augustine did his best to care for the refugees who came to Hippo, going so far as to have the golden objects in his church melted down and used as money to get supplies. Finally, however, the Vandals laid siege to Hippo itself. During the third month of this military action, Augustine became ill. He died on August 28, 430, at age 75.

Right Love, Right Will: The Writings of Augustine

The case might be made that Augustine's writings have had a greater impact on Christianity in general and on Catholicism in particular than have any other writings outside the Scriptures. Augustine wrote about virtually everything. Looking back over the body of his work late in his life, Augustine counted that he had published no less than ninety-three texts, and he actually forgot some. He wrote so much that his student and first biographer, Possidius, said that he thought it nearly impossible for any one person to read them all.

Often Augustine was responding to a question that had been put to him, sometimes writing about an issue facing his congregation or the Church as a whole; rarely did he sit down and write something that did not come directly out of the work at hand. Where other writers were methodical in their writings, trying to create a coherent system of thought, Augustine's works can seem haphazard, but he was always trying to understand spiritual truths, usually in philosophical terms. Augustine did not distinguish between philosophy and theology—nobody did until the Middle Ages. He saw himself as simply trying to understand the truth that God had revealed.

Given the extraordinary number and breadth of Augustine's writings, it is hard to find the common thread running through them, but we might find it in his belief that the final goal of all love is God. As Augustine saw it, whatever a person loves, what the person really wants to find is the love of God. He saw this as both the deepest motivation of all human activity and its highest goal. Every human action is based in love; the only question for Augustine is to what that love is given. If it is given to something wrong, then evil will result from the action; if it is given to something good, then in reality it is given to God. When we love things rightly, we love them as a vehicle moving us toward God.

In fact, Augustine's whole theology can be summed up in his famous phrase, "Love and do what you will." If you act with true love, love ordered toward God, then your actions will always be right: "Let love be rooted in you, and from this root nothing but good can grow."[10]

"To Know and Understand": *The Confessions*

One easy-to-read and enjoyable work of Augustine is his *The Confessions*. In this spiritual autobiography, he uses his experiences as jumping-off points to describe what was going on in his inner world. To really understand what Augustine intended, we have to think of the word *confessions* as it was used in the Latin Bible he read: as praise of God and witness to him, as well as descriptions of sin. Written in the form of a prayer, *The Confessions* has two distinct parts: a biographical part that goes up to the time just before Augustine returns to Africa and a section where he uses the first chapters of Genesis to talk about the blessedness of being in God's presence.

In *The Confessions*, Augustine wanted to make clear that anything good in him was God's work, not his own. As he described his sins, he tried to show how a defect of his will led to them. This defect of the will made him want to do what he knew he should not, sometimes *because* he knew he should not. For instance, he writes about how he and some other boys stole pears from a tree just to throw them to the pigs. Augustine did not think that taking pears was so terrible, but this desire to sin just for the sake of sinning was. If what you love is not the thing you get but the act of sinning itself, how can you ever hope to be good? This desire seemed to Augustine something humans could never overcome on their own; it required the help of God. Getting that message out is why he wrote the book in the first place: "When others read of those past sins of mine . . . their hearts are stirred so that they no longer lie listless in despair. . . Instead their hearts are roused by the love of [God's] mercy."[11]

Why, then, does it matter to me whether men should hear what I have to confess, as though it were they who were to cure all the evil that is in me? They are an inquisitive race, always anxious to pry into other men's lives but never ready to correct their own. Why do they wish to hear from me what sort of man I am, though they will not listen to you when you tell them what they are? . . .

I confess not only to you but also to the believers among men, all who share my joy and all who, like me, are doomed to die; all who are my fellows in your kingdom and all who accompany me on this pilgrimage, whether they have gone before or are still to come or are with me as I make my way through life. They are your servants and my brothers. You have chosen them to be your sons. You have named them as the masters whom I am to serve if I wish to live with you and in your grace. . .

My love of you, O Lord, is not some vague feeling: it is positive and certain. Your word struck into my heart and from that moment I loved you. . . But what do I love when I love my God? Not material beauty or beauty of a temporal order; not the brilliance of earthly light, so welcome to our eyes; not the sweet melody of harmony and song; not the fragrance of flowers, perfumes and spices; not manna or honey; not limbs such as the body delights to embrace. It is not these that I love when I love my God. And yet, when I love him, it is true that I love a light of a certain kind, a voice, a perfume, a food, an embrace; but they are of the kind that I love in my inner self, when my soul is bathed in light that is not bound by space; when it listens to sound that never dies away; when it breathes fragrance that is not borne away on the wind; when it tastes food that is never consumed by eating; when it clings to an embrace from which it is not severed by fulfillment of desire. This is what I love when I love my God.[12]

Citizens of a New City: *The City of God*

Augustine looked inward to write *The Confessions,* but he also looked at the world around him in order to understand it from a Christian perspective—and with the empire crumbling less than a century after it had come to be ruled by Christians, the world needed some explaining. Why would a just and power-ful God allow the empire to fall? Why would a good God favor the barbarians over those who served him? Augustine tackles these and other questions head on in *The City of God*.

In dealing with the pagan argument that the Christian God was to blame for the fall of Rome, Augustine went the unlikely route of accepting full responsibility. God, he said, could easily have protected Rome if he had wanted; if he let it fall, then that was part of his divine plan. Augustine mocked the pagans who refused to blame their own gods for all kinds of catastrophes in Rome's past when those gods were still being worshipped "while they hold Christ responsible for the disasters of modern times."[13] In addition, he took to task the Christians who looked to the heavens for a material benefit like protection from invasion; that sort of security, he said, is not what believing is about.

Augustine was able to make a case for how Christianity led people to be better rulers and better citizens than was possible for pagans. He said that worshipping many gods who were always fighting among themselves led pagans to do the same; Christians, on the other hand, joined together to worship the one true God, so they experienced a natural unity. While this unity was helpful to the State, the most important work of Christianity was to lead people to salvation as citizens of the City of God.

For Augustine, there exists an invisible city in which Christians are the citizens and God is the ruler; the Church is the form this city takes on earth. This spiritual city coexists with the city of the world, which for Augustine was represented by Rome and its empire. The worldly city is part of God's creation and essential to God's plan for humanity. The fact that people feel such love and patriotism for their homelands, reasoned Augustine, allows them to see "what love they should have towards the City on high, in view of life eternal, if the earthly city had received such devotion from her citizens."[14] In Augustine's view, all you have to do is open your eyes to understand that everything good in the worldly city points to the one true God and leads people on their way to salvation.

For Augustine, this is especially true of the virtues that Rome upheld as ideal and the Greek philosophy that supported those ideals. These things, he believed, were great goods, given by God to help lead humans in the right direction, but they were undermined by the polytheism that was so much a part of Roman culture. Augustine had seen the end of Roman polytheism during his lifetime, and he could not have been happier when Roman emperors sent generals to destroy the pagan temples in Carthage. In fact, the decline of Rome seemed in some ways less important to him than did the decline of Roman religion. When Christian author Jerome, living near Bethlehem but with the memory of his years in Rome burning in his mind, heard of the Eternal City's fall, he wrote, "Rome has been taken by assault. My voice is still, and sobs disturb my every utterance,"[15] and "With this City, the whole world is, in a way, faced with annihilation."[16] Augustine, by contrast, saw the current troubles as "lighter afflictions" than those the empire had seen during its civil wars. He scoffed at those who "demand the restoration of the worship of th[e] gods . . . although the worshippers in days of old were not spared those heavier catastrophes."[17]

The Lover, the Beloved, and Love Itself: *On the Trinity*

Augustine wrote many treatises that were polemical, meaning they were intended to attack a particular person or belief, but in one particular treatise, he aimed to work out the philosophical implications of the nature of the Trinity. Beginning with the completely orthodox understanding that "[t]he Father is not greater in divinity than the Son; nor together are the Father and the Son greater than the Holy Spirit; nor is any single Person of the three anything less than the Trinity itself,"[18] Augustine argues that spirit by its very nature is triune, meaning it is three-pointed. If I look at my own mind, he says, I discover that it is composed of three things: memory, understanding, and will. If I look more deeply at how my mind works, I will see that I experience three things: myself as a thinker, the act of thinking, and the thought itself. Love is also three-part: "There we have three things: the lover, that which is loved, and love. Love itself is only a kind of life which unites together or tries to unite two beings, the lover and the beloved."[19]

We can see trinities all around and within us, but what about within God? Augustine begins by declaring that God and God's attributes are one and the same thing. A human being and that human's goodness are two different things; the human can exhibit the goodness but may also choose not to. Not so with God, according to Augustine: We cannot talk about God's mercy, God's justice, God's power separate from God himself, because there is never a time when God is not being these qualities. And the qualities are not separate from each other; God's power and God's justice are simply two ways that we think about God, not two separate things in God. Similarly, when we talk about the Trinity, we are speaking about things that do not exist apart from one another. God is Father because God is also Son; a father cannot be a father unless he has a child, and a son cannot be a son without a father. Therefore, when we talk about God as Father, Son, and Spirit, we are talking about relationships within a whole, not three separate beings. We are back to an understanding of love here: God the Father is the lover, God the Son is the beloved, and the Holy Spirit is the love (sometimes translated as "charity") that they share.

> [A]ll and each possess all three characters in their proper nature; and . . . in them the three are not separate . . . but that there is one single potency for them all, such as wisdom itself, so possessed in the nature of each several Person that he who possesses it is that which he possesses, i.e., the form of a changeless and incomposite substance.[20]

Augustine's work was the most influential understanding of the Trinity all through the Middle Ages, and it remains the foundation of Catholic and much Protestant thought on this difficult subject to this day. His ability to start with biblical verses and illuminate them in such a way that an entire philosophical theology is drawn out of what seem to be simple phrases is brilliantly displayed in *On the Trinity,* and it is at the heart of why even fifteen centuries later, Augustine is still one of the Church's most important thinkers.

Putting Down Heresies: Donatism and Pelagianism

In the course of his massive writing, Augustine made a catalogue of all the heresies he had seen or heard about. Hundreds of years later, his descriptions were still used by Church writers to understand ideas and beliefs arising in their own times that contradicted Church teaching. Augustine wrote against his former friends, the Manicheans, but two other heresies received much of his attention as well: Donatism and Pelagianism.

Donatism

By the time of Augustine, the Donatists were a major influence in North Africa. They had their own churches, bishops, and priests, and they believed themselves to be the true representatives of Christ's Church; to them, Catholics were the ones who had fallen into heresy. When Augustine came to Hippo, Donatists far outnumbered Catholic Christians in the area, so dealing with them and refuting their teachings was one of his major concerns. He was convinced that people were endangering their souls by following the Donatists in being separated from the Church. The fact that the Donatists worshipped the same God, believed in the same Christ, and performed the same sacraments as Catholic Christians was not enough to ensure their salvation; that could only come through the Church, God's instrument for bringing salvation to the world. As Augustine wrote, "Whoever is separated from this Catholic Church, by this single sin of being separated from the unity of Christ, no matter how estimable a life he may imagine he is living, shall not have life, but the wrath of God rests upon him."[21] Students of Christianity have long debated whether the Apostle Paul changed the focus of Christian belief from right action (working for the kingdom of God in the world) to right faith (believing in Christ). But for Augustine, we might say, the central focus was right affiliation—being in communion with the Church as a mediator of God's grace.

Augustine fought the Donatists on many fronts. He engaged in public debates with Donatist leaders, where he put his rhetorical training to good use. In his many writings against the Donatists, Augustine essentially made the case that the group was "throwing the baby out with the bathwater" when they rejected the sacraments of priests who had not stood firm during the persecutions. We know these priests are not perfect, Augustine said, but how can you know that any priest is? If the priest you think is righteous really has committed some terrible sin, then according to Donatist thinking, people baptized by him are still unbaptized, people married by him are living in sin, and so on. In essence, the Donatists were making the validity of the sacrament dependent on the righteousness of the person performing it. Wrong, said Augustine. The validity of the sacrament comes through the Church that has received its authority through apostolic succession. The priest is merely a conduit; if he is in communion with that Church, then he is fully able to transmit the grace that God has entrusted to it. Donatist priests and bishops, on the other hand, no matter their good intentions or good deeds, since they were not in the line of apostolic succession, did not have that grace to transmit, and their sacraments were meaningless.

Although they argued for years, Augustine and others like him never made any headway in convincing Donatists to rejoin the Catholic Church.

Still worried about all these people excluded from salvation, Augustine finally came to believe that even using violence to shut down Donatist churches and to force people to rejoin Catholicism was acceptable. Augustine wanted the civil authorities to use every means in their power to get rid of the Donatists, and they were more than happy to comply. Edicts had been issued in individual cities against the Donatists before, but in 405, Emperor Honorius outlawed Donatism and gave all Donatist property to the Catholic bishops. As this edict was enforced, horror stories emerged about Donatist congregations putting up suicidal defenses of their churches against the troops that came to take them over, and much blood was shed between Donatists and Catholics. Augustine regretted this use of force but believed it was necessary.

Augustine's thinking about the use of force to stop heresy took on a life of its own. Time and again, the Church would encourage the State to use violent means when peaceful ones were unsuccessful in turning people away from heresy. From Augustine onward, these instigators of violence in the service of religion truly believed they were doing what was necessary to bring people to salvation. Everything else was secondary: individual rights, a person's conscience, even human life—none of these mattered in the face of certain damnation. Over the centuries, this belief has led to unbelievable horrors and terrible tragedies that the Church is still trying to repair.

Pelagianism: Taking Good Ideas to a Bad End

Augustine also tried refuting another great heresy of his time: Pelagianism. An English monk named Pelagius saw that people were using Christianity as a sort of magic charm to rescue them. Since humans are basically sinful, these Christians thought, there is no point in fighting it too much; instead you should just depend on God's mercy to save you from the consequences of your bad actions. Pelagius believed people were using God's saving grace as an excuse to do what they knew they should not. He said that God gives us the possibility of doing either good or evil, and which one we choose depends on how we use our will. We might wish that God had given us a will that would only incline toward the good, but we cannot blame our bad actions on God because we ourselves make the choice to do evil.

While there is much common sense in encouraging people to do what they know is right, from a Christian perspective, Pelagius's ideas led ultimately to a theological dead end. For if humans just need to act better, then where does God's grace enter in? What is Christ's role if his action did not free humanity from the consequences of sin? If we can be good just by the strength of our will, then when we do sin, how can we ever be forgiven?

Pelagius thought human weakness leading to sin was unpardonable, but Augustine saw it as simply a sign of the fallen human condition. He said that Pelagius had missed a key point: Our wills were damaged by original sin, and just deciding to do good does not change that.

In the biblical book of Genesis, Adam and Eve eat fruit from a tree that God has specifically prohibited, and God responds by tossing them out of the Garden of Eden. As Augustine saw it, Adam had used his free will to sin, and even though after that first sin his will remained technically free, it was always inclined toward evil. Since Adam was the first human and all others would eventually spring forth from him, Adam's actions affect us all. We are all born in a state of original sin, meaning we carry the burden of an inclination toward sin and the guilt of that first sin already committed. God's grace helps us overcome this inclination toward sin and choose the good instead.

We are back to Paul here, who came to believe that he could not fulfill the Law and that Christ's death and resurrection meant that faith was more important than Law. Augustine continues this argument, saying that we paint ourselves into a corner if we try to depend totally on our will without recognizing our need for God's help. The Church has always taught that sins can be forgiven, and on this Augustine stands firm: Humans may be deliberately disobedient, but forgiveness is written as fully into the equation as is a disordered will.

The Church Then and Now

No Salvation outside the Church?[22]

Augustine made no bones about the need to be in communion with the Church:

> Outside the Catholic Church there can be everything except salvation. He can hold office, he can have sacraments, he can sing "alleluia," he can respond "amen," he can hold to the gospel, he can have

faith and preach in the name of the Father and Son and Holy Spirit. But never except in the Catholic Church can he find salvation.[23]

Yet Augustine did not mean only people who called themselves Catholics could be saved. As he saw it, even before the time of Jesus, salvation had always been available to people worthy of it and had always come through Christ even though the people receiving salvation did not know it. Augustine stood with many thinkers from the early Church in teaching this. For instance, Justin Martyr and others who valued philosophy as a revelation from God thought that people who lived according to reason were really following Christ without knowing it. Others did not place much value in philosophy and reason but were sure that God had always provided ways for people to follow Him.

Almost all of these early writers agreed that once the gospel had been preached, those other ways became obsolete. They talked about there being "no salvation outside the Church," as Cyprian put it, to explain why heretics and others who consciously broke away from the Church were rejecting salvation, but it is not until the fourth century that we see Christian writers using this phrase to say that salvation is denied to Jews, pagans, and those of other faiths. Christians really thought that by then the gospel had been preached everywhere, so anyone who had not accepted Christianity was consciously rejecting the truth and so was justly condemned.

This understanding prevailed throughout the medieval period. Theologians continued to believe that God always offers salvation to all people but that the only way for people to accept that offer was to be in communion with the Church. Augustine's understanding of original sin permeated Christian thought, so it seemed clear that all those who did not receive the grace of God through the sacraments had no way to be anything other than sinful and no way to have those sins forgiven. Thomas Aquinas wrote:

> [T]he unity of the church primarily depends on its unity of faith, for the church is nothing other than the congregation of the faithful. Since it is impossible to please God without faith, there can be no place of salvation other than in the church. Furthermore, the salvation of the faithful is consummated through the sacraments of the church, in which the power of Christ's passion is operative.[24]

Aquinas did not shut the door on salvation for those who were not Catholic, though. He said that while salvation always comes through the Church and especially through the sacraments, sometimes these do not come to a person in a visible or physical way. Someone may have true faith in God and work to live that faith in his or her life without knowing about Christ; true faith brings with it an implicit faith in Christ. Therefore, this person who has never heard of Jesus but who lives a good and moral life, intending to do the will of God, attains salvation through the Church and the sacraments even without knowing anything about them. This did not apply to heretics or others who consciously reject Christ or his Church but rather to those who had no knowledge whatsoever.

Still, theologians continued to struggle with what it means to say that someone "knew" the gospel in such a way that not accepting it could make one guilty of rejecting the truth. A sixteenth-century writer named Albert Pigge came to the conclusion that people of other religions may have heard of Christ without understanding the truth of Christianity, which means they were not consciously rejecting the true faith. He said that non-Christians could still be saved by their sincere faith in God through practicing their own religions. Catholics would eventually embrace this understanding of salvation.

Twentieth-century theologian Karl Rahner expanded on Aquinas's and Pigge's thinking when he talked about "anonymous Christians" who are saved through faith even though they do not consciously accept Christ or the need for communion with the Catholic Church. He said that God grants grace to all people and that humans experience this grace as the call of their consciences. When people act according to their consciences, they are unknowingly accepting that God is the source of the call and the reason for following it. Whether or not these people know or accept anything about God, they have faith in truth, a faith that has its roots in Christ. So, while they may not consider themselves to be Christians, it is ultimately through faith in Christ, even though they would not recognize it as such, that they are saved; they are spiritually in communion with the Church.

Rahner's way of thinking about this issue came strikingly into focus at Vatican II. In a document called *Lumen Gentium*, the bishops restate the Church's traditional teaching that it is the fullest expression of the means of salvation and that all people are called by God to salvation. Not only do the bishops talk about the salvation of people of other faiths, and of those who have no faith, but they also say that in order to be outside of salvation, a person must know that the Church is necessary for salvation and consciously reject it. The

Church still teaches that it is necessary for the salvation of all peoples, but we have come a long way from the idea that only Catholics can be saved.

So how can the Church get from condemning anyone who is not Catholic to understanding the Church as a sign of the grace God uses in calling all people to him? Through the deeply held belief that while the faith the Church expresses stays the same, the way it expresses that faith changes and grows with the times. As the post-Vatican II document *Mysterium Ecclesiae* explains, truth can be expressed in a less perfect way at one point in history and more perfectly later; the truth does not change, but the expression does. To the Church's way of thinking, its understanding of salvation now reflects God's truth better than ever, but in the future, God may grant the Church the grace to express that truth even more perfectly.

Questions and Ideas for Understanding

1. Some people see times of national sorrow, such as the fall of Rome or the terrorist attacks on the United States in 2001, as ways that God punishes a nation for its actions; others think such times are God's way of testing the faith of a nation's citizens; still others think the responsibility rests with other humans rather than with God. What do you think?

2. The Manicheans were dualists because they believed in two main forces at work in the universe. Christians, on the other hand, see God as being the source of all. Think about this idea that the universe is a battle between equally matched good and evil. In what ways does this idea make sense of the world as you know it? In what ways does it cause problems?

3. Modern governments sometimes use force to protect their citizens from others who want to harm them. Augustine and those around them endorsed using force because they believed that the Donatists were doing greater harm to people than a warlike nation ever could. Do you agree with the use of force in these situations? Why or why not?

4. The main ideas behind Manicheism, Donatism, and Pelagianism have all arisen at various times in the history of the Church. For instance, the Manichean idea of the world as a battleground for good and evil was later part of the belief system of a medieval group called the Cathars.

Choose one of these groups and find out more about it and why it was considered a threat to the Church. Then look at later expressions of its main idea, and write a short essay explaining the connection between the idea as presented in Augustine's day and the way it is presented later.

Notes

[1] Augustine, *The Confessions* I.1, trans. R. S. Pine-Coffin. New York: Penguin, 1961. All quotations from *The Confessions* are from this version.

[2] *The Confessions* X.8.

[3] *The Confessions* II.2.

[4] *The Confessions* III.4.

[5] Athanasius of Alexandria, *The Life of Antony* 45.1 5–6, trans. Tim Vivian and Apostolos N. Athanassakis. Kalamazoo, MI: Cistercian Publications, 2003.

[6] *The Confessions* VIII.12.

[7] *The Life of Antony* 55.1–3.

[8] Paraphrased from Joseph Martos, *Doors to the Sacred.* Tarrytown, NY: Triumph Books, 1991.

[9] Augustine, *Sermon* 17:2. In *Augustine of Hippo: Selected Writings*, trans. Mary T. Clark. New York: Paulist Press, 1984, p. 265.

[10] Augustine, "Homily on the First Epistle of St. John" 8. In *Augustine of Hippo*, p. 305.

[11] *The Confessions* X.3.

[12] *The Confessions* X.3, 4, 6.

[13] Augustine, *The City of God* III.30, trans. Henry Bettenson. New York: Penguin Books, 1972, p. 131.

[14] *The City of God* V.16.

[15] Jerome, *Epistle* 127.12. In *Palanque*, Jean-Remy, "St. Jerome and the Barbarians," in *A Monument to St. Jerome*, ed. Francis X. Murphy, C.SS.R. New York: Sheed & Ward, 1952, pp. 171–200, p. 192.

[16] Jerome, *Ezech* I. In *Palanque*, pp. 171–200, p. 191.

[17] *The City of God* III.31.

[18] Augustine, *On the Trinity* VIII, preface. In *Augustine of Hippo*, p. 313.

[19] *On the Trinity* VIII.10, p. 330.

[20] *On the Trinity* XV.28.

[21] Augustine, *Letters* 141:5. Retrieved from http://www.catholic.com/library/Salvation_Outside_the_Church.asp (accessed 12/11/2007).

[22] This section draws heavily from Francis A. Sullivan, SJ, *Salvation outside the Church?* New York: Paulist Press, 1992.

[23] Augustine, "Sermon to the People of Caesaria," *Sermo ad Caesariensis Ecclesiae Plebem*, trans. Jean Goodwin. Retrieved from http://www.public.iastate.edu/~goodwin/sermo.html (accessed 9/28/2007).

[24] Thomas Aquinas, *I Decret.* ed. Parma 16:305. In Sullivan, *Salvation*, p. 47.

6

Missionaries, Artists, and Servants of God

Monks and Nuns in the Early Middle Ages

Chapter Overview

In this chapter, we will explore:

▶ What was going on in the Frankish kingdom

▶ The growth of the monastic movement

▶ Christianity as it developed in Celtic lands

▶ The Book of Kells

▶ The way the Church understands the pope's authority

Brendan: A Living Offering

You remember taking your vows at 15; while it moved you deeply to say the words, you had been living the life since your parents sent you to the monastery when you were 7. It was hard in the first years, but you came to enjoy the daily routine of praying and working. There is a peace in this life that you do not think you could have known on the outside.

The year before you were born, a missionary came to your home village urging people to leave behind their pagan gods and Druid priests and worship the Christian God. He baptized your parents and older brothers, and your family tried to learn his Christian ways before he left. They did not see another preacher of the Word for five years, when a priest began coming to the village a few times a year to say Mass, marry people, and baptize children. This was when you received the sacrament. You remember watching the priest all during the ritual; you did not understand his words, and he kept looking in a book—something you had never even seen before! You were sure it was all some kind of magic, and you still thought that three years later when your parents sent you off with that priest back to his monastery. Your parents wanted to offer thanks to God for a rich harvest after two years of meager crops, and you were their offering.

You wonder how your older brothers are doing. Both are married with grown children, and at 42, the eldest is now a grandfather as well. The little sister who was just a baby when you left—her you never really knew, although you do your duty and pray for her every day. You cannot say that you miss any of them too much— you left them so young that your memories are scarce, and the monks of the monastery long ago became your true family.

But you do wonder sometimes what your life would have been like if you had stayed in the village and one of your older brothers had been chosen for the monastery instead. You would not have learned to read, that is certain, and you cannot imagine the idea of life without the written word! You give thanks every day that you sit down in the scriptorium to copy the manuscripts; you are humbled that God will use your work to spread the true teachings to other monks like yourself in far-off lands. But now it is time for manual labor, as the sainted Benedict ordered for his monks, so you resolutely turn your mind to prayer and pick up a hoe as you head out to work in the garden.

A man like Brendan would have been right in the middle of one of the most important developments in the Church during the fifth through eighth centuries: the monastic movement. Monks led the way in preaching the word as missionaries and in teaching it as educators. They created beautiful manuscripts of the Bible and other writings, works we now see as the greatest artistic achievements of their time. And they did all this in chaotic times, as Germanic tribes took control of much of Western Europe, and in wild lands like Ireland, which was then about as remote a spot as anyone could imagine. We will look at all these changes and at how two popes who oversaw the development of the monasteries also laid claim to a level of authority that has been influential down to the present day. ■

Changing of the Guard: Germanic Tribes Take Control

In the last chapter, we left Rome in chaos after having been overrun by the Visigoths. That chaos spread as other barbarian tribes surged through Western Europe. *Barbarian* did not then have the bad connotation it does today. It comes from a Greek word that simply means "foreigner," but it is what the Romans called the Germanic tribes, and you can get a sense of how bad things went for Rome and its territories that the word comes down to us meaning someone who is uncivilized and cruel.

By the year 500, the European world looked quite different than it had just a century before. England was in the hands of the Anglos, Saxons, and Jutes. The Ostrogoths had established a kingdom in Italy that eventually fell to imperial troops, but this left northern Italy so defenseless that soon another group, the Lombards, swept down and easily established their own kingdom. The Franks entered the Roman province of Gaul (which included modern France, Belgium, the Netherlands, Luxembourg, and parts of Switzerland and Germany) in the late fifth century and by 534 had conquered it all. By the sixth century, the Roman structure of government was just a memory—there was no civil service, no standing army, no legal code, no public court system, and no method of taxation. The only person who could still administer any form of justice or get public works started was usually the local bishop.

Popes took on even more public responsibilities. In 452, Attila the Hun was tearing up northern Italy and getting ready to head south to Rome, but Pope Leo I saved the city by persuading him to turn back. Three years later, Leo tried the same thing when Rome was under attack by the Vandals and their king, Gaiseric; Leo could not get Gaiseric to withdraw, but he did persuade him not to torch the city or massacre its inhabitants. Pope Gregory I got even more involved in governmental affairs when Lombards were threatening Rome in 592. The emperor's viceroy was unable to stop them, so Gregory took the lead and got a truce established. When the viceroy broke the truce and Lombards again threatened Rome, Gregory bribed them to leave. At this point, Gregory became Rome's de facto political as well as religious leader—not only did he direct the affairs of the Church but he also negotiated treaties, paid troops, and appointed generals and governors.

The Merovingians and Carolingians

The Church's influence on politics went even farther than stopping invasions. The Franks arrived in Gaul as pagans, but in 496, their king, Clovis, gained ground with his formerly Roman subjects by converting to Catholic Christianity and hauling his Frankish followers along with him. Conversion turned out to be a smart political move for Clovis; almost all of Gaul was under his control by the time of his death in 511, and sharing a faith gave conquerors and conquered some common ground.

Clovis was first in a line of kings known as the Merovingians. Often when a Merovingian king died, a bloody battle would ensue to determine his successor. Regardless of outcome, the rivals for power would still end up splitting the kingdom into pieces. Finally, by the start of the eighth century, the role of king had been so weakened that the mayors of the palace were the real power behind the throne. In 723, Mayor Charles Martel led an army that defeated Muslim troops invading from Spain, a battle that halted Islam's expansion into the West. Charles gave his name to a new dynasty, the Carolingians, whose first king was his son Pepin the Short, crowned with papal approval in 751 after the last Merovingian king, Childeric III, was bundled off to a monastery.

The collaboration of Church and State had reached a new high. Since Constantine, emperors had been claiming control over the Church and the Church had been claiming the right to tell emperors what to do, but now we have a pope approving the removal of one king and putting another in his place. In 755 and 756, Pepin showed his gratitude by marching into Italy to fight the Lombards, who were then threatening Rome. Pepin then turned the government of the areas he conquered over to the pope—the beginning of the Papal States, territories over which the pope had control until the nineteenth century. As we will see in the next chapter, this was a turning point for the Church: The pope had turned for help to the "barbarian" West because he could no longer rely on the empire as it continued to exist in the East. The gap between East and West widened.

The most famous Carolingian king was Charlemagne, who ruled from 768 to 814. By 800, Charlemagne had expanded his kingdom to Central Europe. To Pope Leo III, this sounded like an empire, and on Christmas Day in 800, he crowned Charlemagne as emperor of a revived Roman Empire. The new empire did not look anything like the old one, and Leo's actions did not win

Charlemagne any friends at the court in Constantinople, where the old Roman Empire remained strong. The revived empire barely outlasted Charlemagne himself, but it eventually led to the creation of the Holy Roman Empire by Otto I of Germany in 962.

The political situation in Western Europe stabilized enough under Charlemagne that he could turn his attention to cultural affairs. He wanted to encourage serious learning in his realm, but he ran into a serious problem: It was next to impossible to find any real scholars in his empire. Undaunted, Charlemagne set about importing scholars from everywhere. These scholars engaged in editing and copying many of the era's basic sources of wisdom: the Bible, the works of classical authors, and writings from the early Christian Church. Thanks to them, these works were preserved for future generations.

Seeking Perfection: The Growth of Monasticism

In the last chapter, we met Anthony and Pachomius, both of whom went into the Egyptian desert to live monastic lives. *Monasticism* means the way of life of monks and nuns, and it comes from a Greek word meaning "to live alone," which applied especially well to Anthony's hermit lifestyle. In fact, Athanasius's *Life of Anthony* was one of the most influential works in getting people interested in monasticism, but it was being read in translation in the Western part of the Church because it, and all the other earliest writings about the monastic life, had been written in Greek. Another of these influential Greek writings was a work of Basil of Caesarea (330–379) called a Rule, which is a recipe for daily life and routine for those living the monastic life. Anthony and Pachomius both left society for the desert, but Basil had a different idea: He thought monks should be living lives of service in the heart of the Christian community, and the monastery he founded included a hospital and a poorhouse where those who had no other place to go could come to live.

The first writings in Latin about the monastic life that have survived come from Augustine. In the previous chapter, we saw how the story of Anthony affected Augustine deeply, and when he became a priest in Hippo, he started his own small monastery. He laid down guidelines for the life there, eventually writing three different Rules for his community. Augustine wanted his monks to lead simple, prayerful lives: all property was to be held in common, the people were to dress modestly and live chastely, no one was to leave the house alone, and everyone was to come together seven times a day for common prayer. All of this could be modified if necessary, said Augustine, with the exception of one rule: everyone had to live in poverty.

Augustine was not the only one in the West thinking through what a monk's life should look like. A contemporary of his named John Cassian knew early on that he wanted to be a monk.

Born somewhere in the eastern part of the Roman Empire, Cassian traveled to Bethlehem and Egypt searching for the life he was to lead. Later he headed west, eventually founding a monastery for men and another for women in Marseilles, in modern France. When a nearby bishop wanted to start a monastery in his city, he asked Cassian to write a description of how Egyptian monasteries were organized. Writing this work, called *Institutes,* helped Cassian realize that monks and nuns needed more than just a list of rules and regulations—they needed an explanation of the theological foundations of the monastic life. So he wrote a second work, *Conferences,* in which he tried to show how the rules were just a means to an end; the real goal was to bring the soul into perfect uniformity with God. "Everything we do, our every objective, must be undertaken for the sake of . . . purity of heart. This is why we take on loneliness, fasting, vigils, work, nakedness . . . [W]e do so to trap and to hold our hearts free of the harm of every dangerous passion and in order to rise step by step to the high point of love."[1]

Another fourth-century influence on the growing world of monasticism was Martin of Tours. Born into a pagan family in modern-day Hungary, Martin served in the military as a young man, converted to Christianity, and eventually left the military and became a hermit. When his friend and mentor, Hilary of Poitiers, returned from exile in 361, however, Martin joined him and set up a monastery near Poitiers in modern-day France. A decade later, Martin became bishop of the town of Tours, although a number of the bishops consecrating him were unhappy at having a monk for a colleague. Monks were considered wild-eyed ascetics, while bishops tended to be law-and-order types, but Martin saw no problem with serving the Church as a bishop while also living a monastic life. In fact, he founded another monastery near Tours after he became bishop there.

Augustine, Martin of Tours, and a number of others in Western Europe established monasteries in the fourth century, but most of these dwindled soon after the deaths of their founders. The only ones with lasting influence were on the islands near Marseilles that are now called Saint-Honorat and Sainte Marguerite. They were founded by a man named Honoratus, a nobleman from Gaul who became a monk. The monks who gathered around him followed a model influenced by the writings of Cassian, with most of the monks living a communal life and only the most advanced living in separate cells. As late as the sixth century, people were still coming from all over Gaul to these islands to learn about the monastic life. Soon, however, monasteries would be springing up everywhere.

Laying the Foundation: The Two Benedicts

Open an encyclopedia to *monasticism,* and you will likely see a picture of Benedict of Nursia. Born around 480 in the Italian city of Nursia, Benedict felt called to the contemplative life and so settled in a cave. When followers began to gather around him, he formed them into a community; eventually so many wanted to join that eleven more communities were founded. Benedict's guidance of these communities brought him into conflict with a local priest, so he moved with a few of his closest associates to the mountain town of Cassino, where he died in 547.

These are the bare details of Benedict's life, but it is the Rule that he wrote that has made him so influential in the development of Western monasticism. Benedict knew Augustine's Rule and used parts of it, but he described in much greater detail what a monk's life should be. What it should not be, Benedict thought, was a hermit's life. Benedict believed that living day in and day out with others in community was the best teacher of humility and compassion. He wanted the rhythm of the community's life to be guided by eight daily worship services, with the monks also performing manual labor and having time for reading. This three-part focus on physical work, study, and prayer became the basis for the Benedictine way of life.

While the hermit in the Egyptian desert practiced extraordinary asceticism—little food, little sleep, little clothing or warmth, little contact with other humans—Benedict's Rule was decidedly different. Benedictine life was all about order and balance. Benedict believed in moderation in everything; while his monks should not overindulge or have luxuries, they needed enough of the necessities that they could come before God with quiet minds ready for contemplation. The life Benedict laid out was much more achievable than that of the ascetic hermit, which is part of what made it attractive to so many and eventually so influential in Western monasticism.

Pope Gregory I, born three years before Benedict's death, later made Benedict the central figure in a collection of stories about the lives and miracles of some early saints. Called *Dialogues,* Gregory's work did not say much about the Rule, but it did show Benedict as a holy figure whose life was full of miracles. *Dialogues* established Benedict as a model for monks, which led to greater interest in the Rule he wrote.

With Benedict's death, however, the communities he founded either dwindled or were destroyed by invaders. Although his Rule lived on, it was not strictly kept.

Then in the eighth century, a Visigothic nobleman named Witiza became a monk and took the name Benedict. Witiza made it his mission to revive interest in the Rule of the first Benedict. He founded a community at Aniane (in modern France) that observed the Rule much more strictly than did most of the monastic houses of the time. The community attracted a good deal of attention, and in 792, Charlemagne took it under his wing. Charlemagne liked this Benedict's idea of making the Rule the foundation for all monasteries, so in 802, he ordered all religious communities in his empire to follow it. Due to his widespread influence on European monastic life, Witiza has come to be known as the Second Benedict.

Let's Not Forget the Women

While the earliest Christian communities offered women roles in service and ministry that the rest of society denied to them, as Christians became more entrenched in mainstream society, women's roles diminished. The role of nun, however, remained open to women, and while it pulled them from the community rather than immersing them in its service, the role still gave them meaning, purpose, and a freedom they could not experience elsewhere.

The lives of some of these women are recorded in the writings and sayings of those known as the Desert Mothers. Like the Desert Fathers, these women decided to leave society and head into the wilderness of the desert, especially in the area of Egypt. Many lived alone, many others gathered followers, all gave themselves entirely to the service of God, and most have been overlooked by Christian history.

Voices from the Past
The Rule of St. Benedict

▶ Author: Benedict of Nursia
▶ Written: Early 6th century
▶ Audience: Monks of his monastery

The Rule of St. Benedict was written by Benedict of Nursia in the early sixth century to the monks of his monastery. In addition to laying down specific regulations about everything from the clothes monks should wear to how services should be performed differently on weekdays and feast days, Benedict also explained how a person entering the monastery should understand the life he had chosen. Here are a few examples of these descriptions.

The Purpose of the Rule

This message of mine is for you, then, whoever you may be, who, giving up your own will in order to serve under the true king, Christ the Lord, take up the strong and noble weapons of obedience... We must therefore establish a school for the Lord's service. In drawing up its regulations, we hope to set down nothing harsh, nothing burdensome... Never swerving from his instructions, then, but persevering in observing his teaching in the monastery until death, we shall through patience share in the suffering of Christ that we may deserve also to share in his kingdom.[2]

Sleeping Arrangements

If possible, all are to sleep in one room. Should their number preclude this, they will sleep in groups of ten or twenty... They shall sleep clothed and girded with belts or cords... so that the monks will always be ready and that when the signal is given they will arise without delay, each hastening to arrive at the work of God before the others, yet with all seriousness and decorum.[3]

Personal Property

Above all, this vice must be uprooted and removed from the monastery: let no one presume to give or receive anything without permission from the abbot, nor to retain anything as his own, not one single thing—neither book, tablet nor stylus—in short, absolutely nothing, since they are not even entitled to have their bodies or their wills at their own disposal.[4]

Manual Labor

Idleness is the enemy of the soul. Therefore the brothers must be busy with manual labor at specified times, and also with divine reading at specified hours... for they are really monks when they live by the labor of their hands, as our fathers and the Apostles did. Yet, all things are to be done with moderation.[5] ■

In the West, most women who wanted to follow a life of prayer and service did so in their homes because few women's monasteries existed. These women were usually widows or unmarried, living in cities, and they did works of charity and prayed for the community. However, cities declined as Western Europe fell into chaos, and as more monasteries for women were founded, it became the norm for men and women who wanted the contemplative life to follow the same path to the monastery.

By the sixth century, many Rules had been written for men, but the first one in the West designed specifically for women was written by Bishop Caesarius of Arles, who founded a community of nuns in his diocese in 512. In most ways, this Rule is like those written for men but with one significant difference: Nuns were not to leave the monastery for any reason. We are talking not just about a lifelong commitment but about not setting foot outside the gates of the monastery. Known as enclosure, this practice became a far more important part of the women's monastic experience than it ever was for men.

Caesarius was neither the first nor the last to talk about the necessity of enclosure. Pope Gregory I, for instance, wanted nuns to be enclosed so that they would "no longer suggest any evil suspicion to the minds of the faithful."[6] A ninth-century work for nuns tells them to "let your convent become your tomb: there you will be dead and buried with Christ, until rising with him you will appear in his glory."[7] Rules for men usually discuss reasons why they might need to leave the monastery, and abbots had final say about when this might happen. Women's Rules, on the other hand, tended to stress that they must never leave, and abbesses were supposed to get the approval of their bishop before even they could leave the cloister.

Not all nuns were so strictly enclosed. In fact, some became quite famous for their works within the wider society. Brigid of Kildare, one of Ireland's patron saints, in about 468 started a women's monastery at Kildare—the first formal religious community known in Ireland. She convinced a group of solitary monks living nearby to move their community next door to hers so that a priest would be present to celebrate the sacraments in her church. This quickly became what is known as a "double monastery," a monastery where men and women lived separately but came together for worship and followed the same Rule. Brigid also started other monastic communities for women, and her influence was strong enough that in a time when men usually took the lead on all Church matters, Brigid met with bishops and abbots to discuss issues of doctrine and practice.

Three centuries after Brigid, an Englishwoman named Leoba took the veil as a nun and rose to some prominence. At a time when few men and even fewer women could read, Leoba was renowned for having studied the Hebrew Scriptures and New Testament (NT), the writings of the Church Fathers, council decrees, and ecclesiastical law. When the monk Boniface asked her to accompany him on a mission to Germany, Leoba happily complied. There she founded a monastery, and soon German recruits were flooding in. Her fame spread to the ears of Charlemagne, who summoned her to court to speak with him. Charlemagne's queen, Hiltigard, loved Leoba dearly, but Leoba hated life at court, preferring to spend her time instructing the various convents of nuns that by this time had come under her guidance.

Brigid and Leoba are unique; few women were given such opportunities, and fewer still would find their accomplishments listed in history books many centuries later. We will never know the names or stories of most of the women who took the veil in those times, but we do know they were there. Their lives were more restricted and their activities less discussed, but it is clear that in the fourth through eighth centuries, increasing numbers of women as well as men felt the call to the contemplative life and answered that call by entering monasteries.

Teaching and the Word: Monasteries as Learning Centers

During the Middle Ages, only 5 percent of the population could read, and fewer could write. Most who could read were connected to the Church as clerks, priests, monks, or nuns. Most came from the upper classes, although farther down the societal ladder you would find clerks with these skills hired by merchants to record their business dealings. By this time, Latin was no longer the language of the common people, even in Rome, but it was still used in the king's court and in education. Thus, even those who had the good fortune to learn to read almost certainly did not do it in the language they spoke.

Secular schools existed here and there down through the seventh century. There were some scattered throughout Gaul, and at least a few continued to exist in Italy throughout the Middle Ages. Still, almost everyone, layperson or cleric, who learned to read did so in a church-sponsored school. In 789, Charlemagne began a big education push, ordering every monastery in his kingdom to set up a school that taught the Psalms, music, singing, arithmetic, and grammar. With the system of monasteries growing, they became the new centers of education in the Western world. Since monasteries allowed children to enter at a young age, schools had long been necessary there; the monasteries had to have a way to educate their future monks or nuns. But many monasteries also had schools open to others as a kind of boarding school, usually with a secular clerk rather than one of their monks as the instructor.

Just as importantly, monasteries made learning available to others by being the premiere centers for the copying of manuscripts. If you have ever seen a surviving work from the early Middle Ages, most likely it was copied by a monk.

Christianity in Celtic Lands

Hear the word *Celt* and you might think of people in Ireland and Scotland. Go back far enough in history, though, and you will discover that England, Wales, Scotland, Ireland, France, and Spain were all originally peopled by Celtic tribes.

The Celts were polytheistic, meaning they had more than one god. Their priests, the Druids, went through twelve years of training in traditional lore. Besides performing religious rites, the Druids also served as political advisors and teachers of science and ethics. By the end of the first century, the Druids were outlawed in the Roman Empire, which after 43 CE included England, Wales, and shifting parts of southern Scotland. Ireland, though, was never part of the empire; only the coming of Christianity ended the influence of Druids there. In fact, many of the stories about early Irish saints like Patrick and Columba have them in showdowns with Druids—always winning, of course.

While the Celts in what are now France and Spain received missionary attention early on, this was not the case off the European mainland. By the middle of the fourth century, we hear about British bishops attending synods on the European continent, but for the most part, news of Christian activity in what is now the United Kingdom was scant.

Ireland was still a religious backwater where Christianity was concerned until about the mid-fifth century, when missionaries from Gaul and Britain as well as scholars fleeing the chaos in Gaul began to appear. In 431, Pope Celestine sent Bishop Palladius to serve Christians in Ireland, but Christianity only really took off when the most famous missionary to Ireland, Patrick, showed up around 460.

Patrick began to found monasteries in Ireland. He saw these as being under the bishop's authority just as they were in other Christian areas. However, Ireland was not like those other areas, and it soon became the custom for

"Patrick, yes a sinner, and the simplest of peasants . . ."[8]

Catholics celebrate Patrick's feast day with green clothes and symbols of Ireland, so it may surprise some that Patrick actually was born in Scotland in 387.

Born into a respectable family, Patrick was 16 when he was kidnapped by marauders and carried off to Ireland, where he was sold as a slave to a local chieftain. He spent six years tending sheep for the chieftain; with just himself and the animals out in the fields, Patrick had plenty of time for praying, and he felt that in this time he drew closer to God. One day he heard a voice telling him that a ship to take him home was in a port about two hundred miles away. Patrick escaped and walked the length of Ireland to get to that ship.

Safely back in Scotland, Patrick felt Ireland calling him back; he came to believe that God intended to convert the whole country through his efforts, so he entered a monastery in Gaul and waited for his chance. After being ordained a priest and spending some time as a missionary in Britain, he was consecrated Bishop of the Irish and sent back to the land that had once been his prison.

Patrick traveled up and down the northern part of Ireland spreading the gospel message. He met with serious danger in his work and went to the most remote places that he and his contemporaries could imag-ine, but he ended up baptizing thousands, including many young people. He tells us that "many sons and daughters of the kings of the Irish are now proud to be counted monks and virgins of Christ . . . Not that their fathers agree with their decision; more often than not, they gladly suffer persecution. . . Yet, in spite of all, their numbers grow more and more."[9]

Only two writings have survived from Patrick's own hand: a letter he wrote protesting the capture of some young converts who were carried into slavery by a gang of pirates, and his *Confession*. Patrick wrote the *Confession* late in his life with two purposes in mind: to justify his mission to the Irish, since it was being questioned by some British bishops; and to thank God for the road he had traveled. As he tells us:

I began life more rustic than any man you care to name: an exile, unschooled . . . yet I am sure in my mind of one thing: that before I was brought low, I was like some great stone lying deep in mud, until "He who is power" came and "in his mercy" lifted me up. . . And so, because of that, I must shout out loud to the Lord in order to give back some small thing for all his gifts that are so great both here and in eternity. The mere mind of men can never plumb such gifts as these.[10]

Irish bishops to live in monasteries and be subject to their abbots. It is hard to say why this arrangement occurred. Maybe the fact that the Irish were still organized in tribes had something to do with it. Also, whereas dioceses with bishops at their head were organized around large towns in other areas, such towns just did not exist in Ireland, so there was no natural place of authority for the bishop.

There were other differences between Celtic and other European church-es. The Celtic Church focused strongly on Scripture and did not trust any the-ology that could not be proven by Scripture. This did not bode well for papal or council decrees. This biblical focus also led the Celtic Church to maintain a Sabbath separate from the Lord's Day. In fact, many Christian communities had done this throughout the first five centuries of the Church's history, until a series of councils in the sixth century declared that the Sabbath, on which no work could be performed, and the Lord's Day, on which Christians wor-shipped their God, were to be one and the same. The Celtic Church, how-ever, continued to observe both days. These sorts of differences in practice would soon cause conflicts between the Celts and their brothers and sisters on the European mainland.

Monks on the Move

The Irish took to monastery life like fish to water. In the sixth century, monastic communities were popping up all over the island. In fact, it is entirely pos-sible that a larger percentage of people entered monasteries in Ireland than in any other area. These monastics did not just stay put, either; they wanted to spread the word. In the sixth and seventh centuries, the Irish started send-ing missionaries all over the place, including to the countries that had origi-nally sent missionaries to Ireland. Irish monks became the leading missionaries of the time, carrying their ideals across Europe, and where they carried the Christian message, they carried their monastic ways. Monasteries founded by Irish monks turned up not only in England, Scotland, Belgium, and parts of France but also in Switzerland, Germany, and even Italy. All these Irish mis-sionaries kept in close contact with their home monasteries, and the abbots of the founding houses maintained authority over these far-flung monastic communities.

The Irish missionary monks focused on the peasants in the areas they entered, sharing their lives and work as a way of spreading the gospel. The monks cleared forests and put land that had been devastated in the barbarian raids back into cultivation. They also gave new significance to much of the old peasant culture: peasants living close to the earth had always revered certain wells, trees, and stones as sacred, but the Irish monks led them to associate these sacred places with Christian saints rather than with local deities. Their efforts went a long way toward Christianizing the daily lives of the people among whom they lived. This kind of syncretism sometimes gets a bad rap in theological circles, but it is as old as Christianity itself.

As these Irish monks moved around, they came into contact with older churches and traditions as well as the latest theology, doctrine, and liturgical forms. Because of their continued contact with Ireland, this enhanced the contact of the Irish Church with the religious and cultural ideas of the early medieval world. While Irish Christianity developed in some ways that differed from what was going on in the rest of the Church in the West, by bringing the Irish into closer contact with the wider Church, the missionary activity of the Irish monks eventually led to a more unified Church.

The spread of Irish monasticism around Europe owes much to a monk named Columba. Born in 521, Columba turned his back on an aristocratic lifestyle—tradition says he was in line to be chieftain—in favor of becoming a priest and a monk. At age 42, political trouble forced him to leave Ireland. He went to Britain and eventually Scotland, where the son of a local king gave him the island of Iona so that he could start a monastic community there.

Columba's monastic vision did not have a lot in common with Benedict's desire for communal living and moderation. Columba's monks did divide their time between manual labor, reading and study, and prayer, but off in the wilds of Iona they lived a severely austere life. They got by on as little sleep as possible (Columba is supposed to have used a rock for a pillow) and kept silence most or all of the time. They ate little, fasted a lot, and engaged in various other forms of penance. Despite its severity, Columba's monastery drew people from all over Britain, Scotland, and Ireland. He and his monks soon began setting up monasteries in the countries around Iona that became centers of learning and missionary activity. Columba died in 597, but the group of monasteries he founded became one of the most influential monastic networks of the early Middle Ages.

New Missions, Old Conflicts

The same year that Columba died, Augustine of Canterbury landed on the English shore. He and the forty monks accompanying him had been sent by Pope Gregory as missionaries to the Anglo-Saxons. Celtic monasteries had already established missions with these groups, but Gregory wanted priests there who were loyal to Roman, not Irish, ways of doing things. Augustine set up bishops at Canterbury, London, and Rochester and worked at making con-

Focus On

Illuminating the Word: The Book of Kells

Columba's monasteries were known as centers of learning, but two of the most famous written documents to come from them are not works of scholarship but of beauty: the intricately decorated Gospel books known as the Lindisfarne Gospel and the Book of Kells.

Lindisfarne is a monastery of the Columban network, situated in England. The Gospel produced there near the end of the seventh century is astounding for the radiance of the colors used in its illustrations. The Book of Kells was probably begun in Columba's own Iona, but when the monks had to flee in 804 because of Viking raids, they headed to another Columban monastery, Kells in Ireland, carrying the book with them and continuing work on it once they were settled.

Books like the Kells or Lindisfarne Gospels are not made for a little bedtime religious reading. These are big volumes, with pages that are easy to see from a distance, something that would be quite useful if the books were carried in processions or used on the altar during Mass. The typical person from the eighth or ninth century would have seen few, if any, paintings. Imagine the jaw-dropping experience of seeing these illustrations for the first time. However, these pictures were more than just pretty; they were significant. The average person could not read, so the pictures told the story.

Both books are amazing, but the elaborate Book of Kells has become the more famous. The text in the Book of Kells is a modified version of the Vulgate Gospels, but a poor one with many inaccuracies. The illustrations, however, are stunning. Color and decoration are everywhere, with patterns around the page edges and oversized, ornate beginning letters.

What made the Book of Kells famous, though, are its full-page pictures. The artistry is astounding, and it reflects its world. The illustrations are a mixture of Celtic design and the Mediterranean religious art that the Irish monks probably saw on their travels and in the books they brought back with them. Scholars have also drawn parallels to Byzantine, Coptic, Assyrian, and Armenian art.

What was it like to produce something as magnificent as the entirely handmade Book of Kells? Labor intensive! The book is written on vellum, a parchment made from calfskin. To make vellum, the calfskin first was soaked in water. Next, chemicals were applied, the hair scraped off, and the skin stretched on a frame to dry. When it was finally ready for use, the vellum was taken to a scriptorium, the place in a monastery where monks worked on manuscripts. Here, the scribes who wrote the text—scholars think there were three of them—would make ink, crushing oak apples with iron sulfate to make the brown and soot to make the black, for example. We might picture one of these brothers hunching over a table, dipping his goose-feather quill pen into the cow's horn that held the ink. In addition, since the scribe could not just erase, he would keep a small knife beside him to use in scraping off mistakes.

Then the illustrators would have taken over; most likely there were at least two. These monks would have needed a bit of room just for their tools: brushes of many thicknesses, compasses for circular drawings and rulers for straight sides, templates for intricate images. And let's not forget the paints, those beautiful colors that bring the images to life: blues made from the

continued on page 127

continued from page 126

indigo plant, white from chalk, green from copper, and many more. Many of the pigments for the paint were not readily available to the monks, either; they would have been imported from all over Europe. Most amazing of all is the brilliant ultramarine blue made from lapis lazuli, which at the time was known to come from only one mine in modern-day Afghanistan. The lapis was rare and expensive, but the monks clearly believed that you cannot put a price on the word of God.

Nor can you rush it. The writing would have taken months; the illustrations, likely years. A magnifying glass must be used to see the intricate, lavish detail in some of the paintings. There is a great deal of fill-in illustration, including the Celtic knots so popular in modern times.

However, the larger pictures are all about symbolism. For instance, the artist painted Christ in the garden of Gethsemane with his arms raised on either side of him in prayer, in just the same position the monks used when praying the vigil of the cross during Lent. Christ has apostles at his side, and the olive trees painted above their heads show them to be on the Mount of Olives. This Christ is clearly Celtic—blond hair, red beard, and eyes as blue as the sea. The drawings needed to be symbolic because they were meant to be educational; like the stained-glass windows that would become so popular a few centuries later, each picture is designed to tell a tale that will bring the viewer closer to the heart of God.

The thirteenth-century historian Giraldus Cambrensis called the Book of Kells the work of angels rather than men.[11] A more recent observer, novelist Umberto Eco, gave a rather less-flattering appraisal, calling it "the product of a cold-blooded hallucination."[12]

Angelic or disturbing, the Book of Kells is beautiful, complex, and a testament to the faith of some Irish monks all those centuries ago. ■

versions among the political and social elite—a top-down approach that has a long history in Christianity of being quite effective from a social perspective and quite problematic from a theological one.

It was probably inevitable that Augustine's mission from the Roman Church would come into conflict with the Celtic traditions of Columba's monks. The conflict came to a head at the Synod of Whitby in 664. The way Celtic monks were tonsured, the way Celtic priests practiced the rite of baptism, and the way Celtic bishops were consecrated all differed from Roman practices, and all were discussed at the Synod.

The main issue, however, was how to calculate the date of Easter, specifically whether to follow the Christian practices from the local Celtic monastery of Lindisfarne or those practiced by the monasteries started by Augustine of Canterbury. King Oswiu of Northumbria called together monks from both sides and listened to their arguments. The Celtic monks explained that they had received their method of calculation from Columba, while the Roman side argued that as the successor of Peter, the pope had greater authority. The latter argument convinced Oswiu, who decreed that in his lands, Easter would be calculated by the Roman method. This decision eventually prompted the Columban monks to leave Lindisfarne, which made way for the Benedictine Rule to become the norm there and eventually throughout Britain. Over time, their contact with Britain and the churches on the European mainland led the Irish to accept the Roman ways of doing things, too.

The Church Then and Now

The Pope's Power

When Pope Gregory I sent Augustine of Canterbury to England as a bishop who would support the Roman, not the Irish, way of doing things, he was concerned not only about Christian unity but also about asserting his authority. So just what is the role and authority of the papacy? A historically contentious issue, for one thing. A few popes during the fifth through seventh centuries weighed in on this issue of papal power with considerable and lasting influence.

Leo I was elected pope in 440. While he was certainly not campaigning for the job (Leo was a deacon on a diplomatic mission to Gaul when the election was held), once in office, he had a big effect on how the Church understood the power of the papacy.

Previous popes had understood themselves to follow in Peter's footsteps: Leo went a step further and claimed that he was Peter's heir. This claim had its basis in Roman law: an heir had all the rights and powers of the person from whom he inherited. In effect, Leo was saying that he did not just get Peter's position, he inherited his authority—a big claim, given Peter's closeness to Jesus and role as leader of the apostles. In fact, Leo was claiming an absolute authority that trumps the authority of other patriarchs. (Not surprisingly, that claim did not go over well in the East, where the other patriarchs now lived.) In his twenty-one years as pope, Leo put his claims to good use: he took control of the bishops of Italy, corrected abuses, resolved disputes, and united people in their church practices.

Fifty years later, Pope Gelasius I (492–496) took Peter's throne. He shared Leo's interest in papal power and found just the right argument for it in the theory of the "two swords." According to this idea, God has appointed two powers on earth, a spiritual one centered in the pope and a secular one that the emperor wields. These "two swords" are independent, but as Gelasius made clear in a letter to Emperor Anastasius, the spiritual power is greater. "You are . . . aware, dear son, that while you are permitted honorably to rule over human kind, yet in things divine you bow your head humbly before the leaders of the clergy and await from their hands the means of your salvation."[13] Gelasius's theory of the two swords got a lot of repeat play during the rest of the Middle Ages.

Pope Gregory I asserted papal authority in several areas. He took over as the real political power in Rome, sent Augustine of Canterbury on his mission to England, wrote about the life of Benedict, reformed the liturgy (Gregorian chant bears his name), strengthened the monastic movement, and even organized the distribution of food to people who were starving during all those troubles with the barbarians. Moreover, he did it all with the firm conviction that God had given him authority over the whole Church. This meant that the other patriarchal sees should be subject to Rome and that when councils or synods issued decrees, the pope could authorize or annul those decrees as he wished.

We will see in coming chapters how later popes exercised the authority claimed by Leo, Gelasius, and Gregory, but let's jump forward to the Church of today. In the Vatican II document *Lumen Gentium,* the bishops acknowledge that the pope "has full, supreme and universal power over the whole Church" (22), but they talk about the Church's structure with the pope at its head as a ministry of service and not domination. They see the pope's authority as communal: the pope and the bishops are "related with and united to one another" (22). In addition, since he is a bishop himself, the pope is part of the community of bishops, with the added role of being its leader. The bishops also see papal authority as uniting and not dividing Christians; they describe the pope as the "visible source and foundation of the unity both of the bishops and of the whole company of the faithful" (23). For many Christian groups not in communion with the Roman Catholic Church, however, this same papal authority remains a serious wedge between them and the Catholic Church.

Questions and Ideas for Understanding

1. To what extent do you feel a religious organization should be involved in politics? How do your own religious beliefs affect your thinking on this?

2. We have seen time and again the Church's drive to create uniformity of action as a way of ensuring uniformity of belief, including Rome's dealings with Christianity in Celtic lands. In what ways is it helpful to have everyone in a worldwide Church doing the same things? In what ways is it problematic?

3. Think more about Gelasius's theory of the "two swords." In what ways is it akin to the modern understanding of separation of Church and State? How does it differ? Is there a problem with the fact that religious power is referred to as a sword in this theory?

4. Research a modern-day monastery for either men or women and write a short essay describing the daily routine of activities and overarching philosophy of that life. In what ways do the modern monks or nuns resemble their ancient counterparts? In what ways are they different?

Notes

[1] John Cassian, *Conferences* I.7, trans. Colm Luibheid. New York: Paulist Press, 1985, p. 41.

[2] From the Rule of Benedict. In Adalbert de Vogue, *Reading Saint Benedict,* trans. Colette Friedlander, OCSO. Kalamazoo, MI: Cistercian Publications, 1994, Prologue, 3, 45, 50.

[3] Rule of Benedict, Section 22.

[4] Rule of Benedict, Section 33.

[5] Rule of Benedict, Section 48.

[6] Quoted in Jane Tibbetts Schulenburg, "Strict Active Enclosure and Its Effects on the Female Monastic Experience (ca. 500–1100)." In *Medieval Religious Women*, Vol.I: *Distant Echoes*, eds. John A. Nichols and Lillian Thomas Shank. Kalamazoo, MI: Cistercian Publications, 1984, pp. 51–86 at p. 53.

[7] Quoted in Schulenburg, "Strict," p. 60.

[8] *The Confession of Saint Patrick and Letter to Coroticus,* trans. and notes John Skinner. New York: Image Books Doubleday, 1998, p. 26.

[9] *Confession*, p. 61.

[10] *Confession*, p. 35.

[11] Quoted in Bernard Meehan, *The Book of Kells.* New York: Thames and Hudson, 1997, p. 9.

[12] Meehan, *Kells*, p. 9.

[13] Gelasius, "Letter to Emperor Anastasius." Retrieved from http://www.fordham.edu/halsall/source/gelasius1.html (accessed 9/28/2007).

7

Across a Great Divide
The Eastern Church

Chapter Overview

In this chapter, we will explore:

▶ What was happening in the Eastern Empire

▶ The rule of Justinian and Theodora

▶ The Hagia Sophia

▶ The East–West split of the Church

▶ Eastern Orthodox Christianity

▶ Bringing together the Church and other Christian groups

Zoe: Going to the Great Church

You live in a small village about six days outside of Constantinople; never before have you made this trip yourself. When would you have had time? Six children, your husband's weaving business, keeping the house, growing and cooking the food—for most of your life you barely had time to fall into an exhausted sleep for a few hours each night before it was time to get up and begin the morning meal.

But all that is behind you. You are an old woman now, able to sit back and let the wife of your oldest son do the work. You help her, of course, but since falling ill last winter, you have barely been able to get out of bed. As a matter of fact, that illness is why you are on this journey. Your second son, Basil, made a vow that if God would spare your life, he would take you on a pilgrimage to the Great Church. He hoped that God would be pleased to finally make you well if you went to worship him there.

You are tired, sore, and a little motion sick from the constant bumping of the cart, but you do not mind. Basil has been telling you about his business trips to Constantinople, and especially about the Great Church, the Hagia Sophia. The first time he walked in, he could only think, "This must be where God lives!" All your life you have longed to go, but you never imagined that you really would. That kind of travel is just not a woman's way.

Now you have entered the city, and it is all just too much. Everywhere there are shopkeepers and street vendors selling things you did not even know existed. The smells of food, leather, metal, and animals make you long for the country air. Never in your life have you seen so many people or heard such noise! They rush past the cart without even noticing you. Still, you are so excited you can hardly breathe.

And then you see it, the Sophia, and everything around you is forgotten. You do not know how God will choose to answer your prayer for health, but for right now, all you can do is whisper thanks that God has allowed you to see this magnificent church!

Today, the distance between a village like Zoe's and Constantinople might be a couple of hours of travel, but in her time, the two were worlds apart. The Churches in the East and the West seemed to be worlds apart too and eventually split entirely. We will see what led up to this split and get a glimpse of the Eastern Church as it is today. But first, we must look in on the Eastern Empire and stop for a moment to admire one of the empire's greatest marvels, the Hagia Sophia. Finally, we will look at how the modern Catholic Church is working to overcome this and other divisions that have developed over the course of Christian history. ■

Continuing the (Not So) Roman Empire in the East

The empire in the West collapsed as Germanic tribes swarmed over Europe and set up their own kingdoms, but things were looking much brighter in the East. The empire centered in Constantinople still considered itself the "Roman" Empire, even though it had little or nothing to do with Rome. In a way, this made sense: Constantine had moved the capital of the Roman Empire to Constantinople in the first part of the fourth century, and there was a straight line from Constantine to the emperors of the sixth and later centuries. Essentially, the Roman Empire had become the "Byzantine" Empire. It was even centered in Byzantium, an old name for Constantinople.

Why did the Eastern Empire remain strong while the West collapsed? For a couple of reasons: By the fifth century, the bulk of the population—and the wealth—fell in the Eastern part, so they were better prepared to face hard times. In addition, the area we call the East also extended south, which buffered it from the northern areas where the Germanic tribes got their start.

The Germanic presence did have some effect on the East. Essentially, it is what divided East from West. The Western emperor's power slipped away as Germanic troops steadily carved off pieces of his territory for themselves. Part of Italy, at least in theory, remained under Western control until 489. That year, the Byzantine emperor, Zeno, sent the Germanic Ostrogoths to Italy, supposedly to get it firmly under Eastern control. Actually, Zeno wanted the Ostrogoths and their leader Theodoric out of his hair. He understood that once Theodoric and his people got to Italy, they would establish their kingdom there, with just a nod back to the emperor. What in name solidified Emperor Zeno's control over part of the West actually limited his power to the East, but in the process it eliminated a threatening Germanic presence in the East.

Less than fifty years later, an Eastern emperor would try to restore unity between East and West. When Justinian came to power in 527, he dreamed of uniting the empire under his rule. He set his general, Belisarius, to work, and by 540, all of Italy up to the borders of the Frankish kingdom, plus parts of Spain and North Africa, were under his control. This reunion did not last long, however, as the Eastern Empire began losing these lands almost immediately after Justinian's death. This time, there would be no going back. By the begin-

The Life and Times of a Really Big City

Constantinople was not just the capital of the empire; it was the biggest city in the medieval world. With half a million people, Constantinople was huge for its time.

Many in the city had some connection to government service, such as those working at the imperial court or in government administration and, less directly, those employed maintaining and repairing the palace and other official buildings. The city had a fair number of wealthy with money to spend, which meant a large population of skilled craftsmen—workers in gold, silver, jewels, ivory, mosaics, cloth, and sculpture—eager to give them a way to spend it. Now throw in all the people in support services, like supplying food or household goods such as lamps and pots, plus street vendors selling their wares, and you have a loud, bustling place.

Constantinople benefited from all the city planning and technology available at the time. This included aqueducts and sewer systems, as well as a primitive sort of street lighting, since shopkeepers were required to keep lights burning in front of their stores all night. Churches were everywhere, hundreds of them, and lots of monasteries, too. While many of these places helped care for the poor and sick, there were also government-run hospitals with qualified physicians.

To help ensure the general good, cheap (and sometimes free) bread was distributed to all registered households in the city. The government even had a system to control inflation and keep other basic food items affordable. This was a government that paid attention—a big part of why Constantinople remained strong for so long.

ning of the seventh century, the East and the West would be totally separate, at least politically.

Justinian and Theodora

Especially early on, Church history can seem a story about men. We just do not hear much about women—not that women were simply staying at home minding their manners. While the socially accepted roles of the time may have meant it was less common for women to get out into the public realm, plenty of women were busily teaching the Christian message, following the monastic path, acting as patrons for monasteries, and generally acting in ways just as important to the daily workings of Christian society. In fact, since the mother was by far the parent with the most active control over the upbringing of children, we might even say that women had at least as profound an influence on the work of Christianizing society as did the men.

For all that, though, women's words, thoughts, and actions were recorded far less often than men's, which is what makes exceptions like Theodora, the wife of the Emperor Justinian, so rare. This strong and forceful woman not only seemed to have a charmed life, but she was also a real leader alongside her husband. Together they ruled the empire, weathered daunting political storms, and dealt with conflicts in religion that were pulling Christians apart.

Justinian grew up in a poor farm family, hardly anyone's pick for future emperor. His uncle, Justin, also born to peasants, had traveled to Constantinople, where he entered the palace guard. Eventually, Justin brought his nephew to live with him there, making sure the boy got a good education and was able to become a soldier himself. Justin, meanwhile, rose through the ranks and eventually was selected to become the emperor in 518. Shortly before his death in 527, Justin had his capable nephew crowned co-emperor. Justinian did not stand alone that day. Theodora was at his side, receiving her crown as his consort. When Justin died a few months later, Justinian and Theodora together had complete control over the empire.

Theodora was an even less likely person to wear an imperial crown than was Justinian. She came from a family of entertainers, and she herself was an actress, which made her part of the lowest level of society. Beautiful, cultured, and quick-witted, she had quite a life before she met Justinian. She had many lovers and at least one child out of wedlock. Theodora became the mistress of a high-ranking government official and traveled with him to his new job as governor of a region far from Constantinople. When the two of them quarreled, she was left to make the thousand-mile journey back home alone. The idea of this trip must have seemed overwhelming at first, but it was destined to change her forever: on the way back, Theodora stopped in Alexandria and was converted to the Christian life.

Justinian met Theodora and quickly fell in love with her; they were married a couple of years later. The two made a good pair. He was an intellectual who could get overly emotional about things, and she was the epitome of social grace and never lost her head in a crisis. They ruled as a team; regional governors took their oaths of loyalty to both Justinian and Theodora. Laws were enacted in Justinian's name alone but usually first had the approval of both husband and wife. Justinian referred to Theodora in those laws as the partner sent to him by God.

Theodora's ability to keep cool in a tight spot served her and her husband well, especially during riots that almost toppled them from their throne in 532. When Justinian ordered the execution of the leaders of two rival groups, the groups joined together to revolt. Rioting ensued, and part of the city was set on fire. Justinian and his counselors wanted to flee, but Theodora told Justinian to take control and make the hard decisions. By this time, most of the rioters had gathered in the Hippodrome, the big arena where sporting events were held. Justinian sent his troops in, and historians from that time report that when the troops had finished their bloody work, more than 30,000 corpses littered the floor. It was a brutal suppression of dissent, but it worked, and it kept Justinian and Theodora in power.

Compiling the Code

Justinian has special significance in contemporary law. The emperor ordered the creation of a Latin code of law, called the Justinian Code. The code had three parts: a collection of all the Roman laws up to that time, a compilation of opinions from the great Roman legal scholars, and a textbook for law students that included extracts from the other two works. What made the code remarkable was that it gathered into one orderly system laws and opinions that often contradicted each other, thus allowing legal experts to work through the contradictions. This idea of getting everything to fit together was a turning point in the history of Roman law and, through it, laws in the Western world to the present day.

Fighting about Faith

Justinian thought of himself as fulfilling a divine mission and thought one of his responsibilities as emperor was to bring unity to the Church as well as to the empire. Among other things, this meant tackling head-on a doctrine called Monophysitism that was threatening the unity of both.

Monophysitism is the belief that Christ had only a divine nature and that the human nature of Jesus either dissolved into the Christ nature or that the divine nature had taken the place of what might be called Jesus' mind. The Council of Chalcedon in 451 had dealt directly with the question of Christ's

Healing the Spirit

Healing was a major aspect of Jesus' ministry. He usually brought about healing by laying his hands on the people being cured. Jesus taught those who followed him to do the same, so praying for healing through touch has been a part of Christian practice for as long as Christians have been practicing. People soon began using oil for healing and blessing, although the first clear reference to its use comes in a letter written by Pope Innocent I in 416: when a bishop asked him about healing the sick, Innocent replied that in Rome they performed a sacrament using blessed oil. The practice spread to Alexandria and Antioch and was common in some parts of France by the sixth century. At this point, and for centuries after, the oil was generally blessed by priests but used by laypeople for every kind of mental, physical, and spiritual difficulty and for the strength to face these difficulties as they occurred.

Along the way, though, Catholics came to a different understanding of this ritual: rather than being for illness, it became more and more a sacrament for the dying, which is how it came to be part of what was known as the "last rites." As the Church began to recognize it as a sacrament, it also became a blessing that only priests could perform, although this understanding emerged in a backdoor kind of way. When Charlemagne had the Roman sacramental books copied and distributed throughout his empire, the theologian helping him put the books in order added some prayers and rituals that were lacking in the books they had received from Rome. In the new books, the section containing the priestly anointing of the dying also contained prayers for anointing the sick. Out went the books to bishops throughout Charlemagne's realm, and when many of them read this section, they understood it to mean that in Rome only the priests anointed the sick, so they began prohibiting the laity from performing the ritual themselves. In Rome, meanwhile, the sacramental books did not contain any anointing ceremony at all, but when liturgical books were sent back to Rome in the tenth century, last rites officially became a sacrament performed in the Roman Church as well.

In the 1950s, scholars and theologians began questioning the way the sacrament had come to be used only for the dying. They helped make their case by looking to the Orthodox Church, which continued to use the ritual for illness. When the bishops gathered at Vatican II, they agreed that the ritual should go back to its roots as a sacrament for the sick and ordered that the way it was performed and the prayers that were said should reflect this understanding.

Today the sacrament of anointing the sick emphasizes healing and strengthening rather than the forgiveness of sins, and priests are encouraged to perform the ritual for all people who are seriously ill. Most modern Catholics probably do not expect physical healing when they are anointed by their priests in a time of illness or when they lay near death, but they assuredly do hope to experience renewed strength and support to face the difficult road that lies before them.

Focus On
The Hagia Sophia

Justinian's desire to unify the Church led him even into the area of architecture. One of the greatest achievements of his reign was the creation of an incredible basilica in Constantinople called the Hagia Sophia. The site of the Hagia Sophia—Greek for "Holy Wisdom"—had been holy ground long before Justinian arrived. A church called the Hagia Irene had already been there for many years when the Emperor Constantius decided around 350 to build another church, the Hagia Sophia, right next to it and put a big wall around both, effectively making one giant church. At first people just called it the Great Church, but eventually it became known as the Hagia Sophia.

The Hagia Sophia had been damaged by fire in 404, repaired and rededicated in 415, then finally burned to the ground during the rioting in 532. Justinian wasted no time; within forty days, construction on a new church was underway. The emperor did not want to just put back up what had already been there; he wanted something new that would bring glory to God—and to himself. He had in mind something that would visually capture the idea of the church as the place where God's eternity and human reality come together—a place that stands on the edge of another world.

Justinian poured money into the project, spending around 23 million gold soldi on the work—about half a billion dollars in today's currency. His two main architects supervised one hundred master builders and more than ten thousand masons, sculptors, and other workers. If you lived somewhere in the empire and had needed skills, you likely ended up in Constantinople during that time. In just under six years, the Hagia Sophia was finished. Compare this with the rebuilding of St. Peter's in Rome at the beginning of the fifteenth century—a project that took more than a hundred years to complete.

The new and greatly improved Hagia Sophia was dedicated in 537, and the ceremony was something to see—and probably to smell. Justinian had massive sacrifices performed that day: 1,000 oxen, 6,000 sheep, 600 stags, 1,000 pigs, and 20,000 birds. He also gave 30,000 bushels of meal to the poor. When Justinian walked into the church that day, he threw his arms toward heaven and cried that in fulfilling such a work, he had surpassed even Solomon.

This grand building sat in the middle of a city destined for hard times in the form of wars, conquests, and the rise and fall of empires. The Hagia Sophia was built as an offering to God by an emperor yearning for unity, but it became a symbol of conflict: the conflict of the Church in East and West (more on this shortly), and later the conflict between the Christian East and the Islamic invasion that overwhelmed it.

The year 1453 saw the creation of the Ottoman Empire when the Turks conquered Constantinople and renamed it Istanbul. They converted the Hagia Sophia into a mosque, which must have been a bitter pill for the city's inhabitants to swallow; they had to watch the beloved symbol of their city and their Christian faith changed into a symbol of the conqueror's power. A mosque it stayed for five centuries, until Mustafa Kemal Ataturk brought the new Republic of Turkey into being in 1923. Ataturk wanted to unify the Turkish people after a long period of conflict and war, so in 1935, he changed the Hagia Sophia from a symbol of conflict as first a church and then a mosque into a symbol of unity as a museum celebrating all its past under the Byzantine and Ottoman empires. And so it remains today. ■

human and divine natures, but its decision that Christ is both fully human and fully divine was not accepted everywhere. All over the East, particularly in Egypt and Syria, people had other ideas. Also, a host of emperors in the East supported the Monophysite idea that Christ had only a divine nature.

Justin and Justinian, however, stood firmly on the side of Chalcedon, which meant they were firmly on the side of Rome. This placed them in a bind. On the one hand, they wanted the support of Rome, which led Justin to force the Patriarch of Constantinople to get rid of all the bishops under his authority who supported Monophysitism. On the other hand, they needed to keep Egypt happy because it was from Egypt that they got the bulk of their grain supply. Therefore, the bishops of Egypt were exempted from this requirement.

Justinian tried to find some middle ground, but the fighting was simply too fierce on both sides. Theodora, too, tried to find a compromise. She approached things differently than her husband: her conversion at Alexandria was to a Monophysite brand of Christianity, and despite her loyalty to Rome and to Church unity, she was always seen as a strong supporter for the Monophysite cause. Neither husband nor wife, however, had much success. Still, they usually managed to keep tension on this issue at a low simmer rather than the full boil that it threatened to bring about.

Breaking Up Is Hard to Do: The Church Splits

Looking back over the first 1500 years of Church history, the picture is not one of perfect harmony. Political conflicts, religious controversies, invasions, destructions, hatreds, and condemnations tore the Church apart bit by bit, so that what once was the Church of all Christians slowly became something much more confined. Churches in individual areas had broken from communion with Rome before, but between the ninth and thirteenth centuries, the situation between the Eastern and Western parts of the Church went from bad to worse to awful. Let's take a look at some of the signposts along the way.

They spoke different languages. Throughout the Church's early history, people in individual areas spoke their own languages but wrote things in common languages: Greek in the East and Latin in the West. This had always been something of a problem, but as the gap grew greater and travel became more difficult due to all the invasions, it became less common for scholars of either area to read the language of the other. This meant that East and West, they were not using the same books or developing the same ideas as their brethren on the other side of the Church.

They thought differently about political issues. As we have seen, the empire prospered in the East but collapsed in the West. While the emperor remained strong in the East, the lack of someone who could hold things together in the West more or less forced the pope to assume that role. The pope became a political ruler in a way that the Eastern patriarchs never dreamed, and when Charlemagne came along in 800 and had himself crowned emperor—with the pope's approval—people in the East saw him as trying to take the throne that rightfully belonged to their own emperor.

They thought differently about theological issues. We have already seen that perhaps the most basic Christian theological question—what did Christ do for humans?—was answered very differently in the East and West. Eastern theologians talked about Christ giving humans a way to become divine once again, while Western scholars thought more in terms of Christ saving humanity from the consequences of their sins. This and other differences led the Eastern and Western churches to different conclusions about whether priests could marry, when Christians should fast, what sort of bread (leavened or unleavened) should be used in the Eucharist, what the liturgy should look and sound like, and any number of other small but important issues. Then there was the completely different understanding of where authority should rest in the Church. The West said that the pope was head of the whole Church and had authority over all matters within it, while the East saw the pope simply as first among equals of the ancient patriarchal sees. The East has always believed that the Church's highest authority lay in the works of councils, not in the decrees of popes or patriarchs.

The Eastern and Western parts of the Church had lost much of their common ground without most people even noticing, but a few big controversies brought the split to the point of no return.

Ironically, the beginning of the end came when Bulgaria, an area that lies nicely between East and West, converted to Christianity. The Bulgarians had first received missionaries from the East, but in 865, their leader, Boris, transferred allegiance to Rome over a political scuffle, and the pope appointed a bishop for the Bulgarians. This put a Roman Church right on the doorstep of Constantinople and the areas that its patriarch considered to be under his jurisdiction. In 867, the patriarch of Constantinople declared the pope heretical and broke communion with the Roman Church. Not long after, Boris changed allegiance again, and the Bulgarians were once more allied with the patriarch of Constantinople. Meanwhile, the damage to East–West unity had been done.

In the eleventh century, another pope and another patriarch of Constantinople locked horns. By this time, the liturgies were different in the East and West, and the patriarch ordered all the churches in his area—including churches faithful to Rome—to follow the Eastern liturgy or be shut down. In the West, Pope Leo IX was already unhappy with the Eastern Church because of some of their practices. The two sides tried to work things out, and in 1054, the pope sent representatives to Constantinople in an attempt at diplomacy. When it became clear that this was not going to work, the pope's representatives walked into the Hagia Sophia during a worship service, laid a letter excommunicating the patriarch on the altar, and walked out. For his part, the patriarch wasted no time in calling a council and excommunicating the papal representatives.

The bad blood between the East and the West was not at all helped by two great controversies during these centuries—iconoclasm and the filioque.

Iconoclasm

Icons are pictures of Christ, Mary, and the saints. Today, we usually associate them with Eastern Orthodox Christianity, and in fact, a major debate over icons took place in the East, although the Pope did get involved.

The argument centered over whether it is wrong to make any art that portrays God or humans, a position called *iconoclasm*. That was the stance taken by Emperor Leo III in 726. He ordered all churches in the empire to get rid of icons, saying that people were worshipping these pictures rather than understanding them as signs of the divine. Leo also thought having icons in churches hurt efforts to convert Jews and Muslims, both of whom believe that using "graven images" is against God's commandments.

The next year, Pope Gregory II called a synod that denounced iconoclasm. This was more than just a fight about art: Gregory and others like him thought that icons actually helped people understand the Incarnation properly—there is no way to represent God eternal, but Christ made himself visible when he took human form, and icons help us remember that. Those on this side of the argument, called *iconodules,* thought the iconoclasts were moving dangerously close to thinking that things of the spirit are good but that things of matter (like icons) are bad.

Angered at Gregory's position, Emperor Leo confiscated papal estates in Italy and Sicily and took some archbishoprics that had previously been under the jurisdiction of the pope and placed them under the patriarch of Constantinople. In effect, Rome was cut off from the empire and the Eastern Church, and after this, popes who needed political help knew they could not turn to the East to get it.

Iconoclasm continued as a policy in the empire until 780, when the empress Irene put a stop to it. Just thirty-five years later, Emperor Leo V renewed the attack on icons, but in 843, another empress ordered the return of icons to the churches, and this time they stayed. This final victory over iconoclasm is celebrated in the Orthodox Churches on the first Sunday of Lent as the "Triumph of Orthodoxy."

The Filioque

One thing you will not see in a Latin translation of the original Nicene Creed, in the section where it talks about the Holy Spirit, is the Latin word *filioque,* meaning "and the Son." Instead, the creed just says that the Holy Spirit proceeds from the Father. *Filioque* was added to the creed in the sixth century as a protection against Arianism. The filioque puts the Son on a level with the Father, which is exactly what Arians rejected. The creed with filioque became the form popular throughout France and Spain, and the form known to Charlemagne. In 792, he sent a letter to the pope charging, among other things, that the emperor in Constantinople was a heretic because he said that only the Holy Spirit proceeded from the Father. In other words, Charlemagne called the emperor and the Eastern Church heretics for continuing to use the Nicene Creed as originally written—something the Eastern Church still does to this day.

The pope did not use the filioque either, however. Popes Hadrian (772–795) and Leo III (795–816) thought that Charlemagne had the right idea but did not want to change the wording of the original creed. The filioque did not become part of the Roman liturgy until 1014, when the German emperor, Henry II, came to Rome to be crowned by Pope Benedict VII and asked the pope to use the liturgy common in Germany, which included the filioque. Five years earlier, though, Pope Sergius IV had sent a statement of faith to Constantinople that included the filioque, so it had already been accepted, although it was not used in the Mass.

The Eastern part of the Church had a number of objections to adding the filioque. First, they did not think it was theologically sound: they saw the Father as sending both Son and Spirit into the world, and changing that gives a different understanding of how God works. Second, they thought that since the creed belongs to the whole Church, the West was wrong to make this kind of change on its own. Finally, Church councils had clearly stated that the creed was not to be altered, so the East was displeased that the West in general and the pope in particular thought they could override this. The filioque controversy solidified the Eastern Church's belief that the Roman bishop was trying to overstep his authority.

The Final Break

The final straw between East and West came in 1204, with the disaster of the Fourth Crusade. Crusaders from the West were supposed to be on their way to the Holy Land to fight Muslims for control of the area, but they were persuaded to stop in Constantinople to help a Byzantine emperor who had been tossed off his throne regain power. The Crusaders ended up attacking and conquering the city. For three days, they ran through Constantinople, stealing its treasures and terrorizing the citizens. They even sacked the Hagia Sophia. To top it off, they installed a Westerner as patriarch of Constantinople, with the approval of Pope Innocent III.

Between its founding and the Fourth Crusade, Constantinople had withstood seventeen sieges from groups on every side, but it finally fell to Christian troops attacking a Christian city and patriarchal see. The city was recaptured and the Westerners expelled in 1261, but there was no going back; the Church of the East officially broke communion with the Church of the West. This wound has not healed, even after eight centuries. While the two sides at times have tried to come together again, they have never been able to bridge the gap between them.

Dating Christmas

Ancient calendars were not always precise, so throughout the East and West, December 25 was celebrated as the winter solstice, the longest night of the year. It was a big party, and some of the traditions might sound familiar: People lit candles, hung greenery, and exchanged gifts. Around the middle of the fourth century, Roman bishops began celebrating the birth of Christ on this day as a way of drawing people away from the pagan ritual. Before that, most Christian communities did not celebrate Christ's birth, and the date varied from place to place for those that did. However, many communities did celebrate Jesus' baptism on January 6, and in the East, people had started celebrating the birth on the next day. When Christians in the East heard about the Roman practice of celebrating the birth on the (supposed) solstice, they were horrified that the West was using a pagan holiday as the basis for a Christian celebration. Each side stuck to its guns and continued celebrating Christ's birth on their chosen day. In the last century, some Eastern Orthodox Churches began celebrating Christmas on the same day as Catholics and Protestants, but most hold to the older tradition of celebrating it on January 7.

How It Looks Today: Eastern Orthodox Christianity

Today we talk about Eastern Orthodox Christianity as if it were one Church, but really this is a name given to a number of national churches that share basic beliefs and traditions. Russian, Greek, Romanian, Serbian, Bulgarian, Albanian—these nationalities and many more are represented within the Eastern Orthodox Church. Orthodox communities also exist in many areas of the United States.

Those who are Orthodox often call their communion "The Church of the Seven Councils" because they look to the first seven ecumenical councils as the foundation for their beliefs. In these councils, they believe, the Holy Spirit guided imperfect people to a perfect understanding of Christian faith. The Catholic Church agrees, but Catholics also see this process continuing in later councils.

The various Orthodox churches use different languages in their liturgies and have some differences in their practices and calendars, but the beliefs they share bind them together. Each is self-governing and falls under the authority of one of the ancient patriarchates, but they share a high regard for the patriarch of Constantinople. The patriarch is not an Orthodox equivalent of the pope, though; he has certain rights and privileges that the other patriarchs do not share, but he is not understood to have supreme authority in the Orthodox Church, nor is he likely to ever get it because the issue of the pope's authority remains a critical one in the separation of the Catholic and Orthodox churches.

The Church Then and Now

"That They May All Be One" (John 17:21)

Drive down the main street where you live, and you will probably see any number of churches: Methodist, Baptist, Episcopal, Catholic, maybe others. So what is more important: the Christian beliefs these groups share or the beliefs that separate them? For centuries, Catholics and most other Christians would have voted for the latter. But as we saw in chapter 5, while the Church still understands itself as the sacrament of salvation for all people, today it also recognizes the value and validity of other Christian communities and even other religions.

Getting from point A to point B took centuries, but when the change started happening in the twentieth century, it happened quickly. In 1919, Christians from a variety of churches organized a meeting to promote ecumenism, or unity among Christians. Pope Benedict XV was asked to send Catholic representatives, but he believed the idea went against the Church's teaching that the only road to Christian unity was for non-Catholics to come into the Church. In 1928, Pope Pius XI continued that position when he forbade Catholics to participate in the ecumenical movement. By the 1950s, however, the Church was beginning to open to the idea: Catholics were allowed to participate in dialogues with other Christian groups as long as their discussions stayed within the Catholic understanding of what it means to be Church.

Things really picked up speed in 1960 when Pope John XXIII established a Vatican office devoted to promoting unity with other Christian groups. Moreover, unity was on the minds of the bishops that John called together two years later for Vatican II; not only were representatives from other Christian groups asked to be observers, but the council published a *Decree on Ecumenism* highlighting the unity that already existed among Christians due to their

Eastern Monks

One of the differences between the Eastern and Western churches is how their monks live the monastic life. Unlike Catholic monks who join particular orders like the Benedictines or the Franciscans, Orthodox monks are attached to a particular monastic house but are understood to be part of one great whole. Western writers sometimes call them Basilian monks because they honor the Rule laid down by St. Basil, but Orthodox monks do not refer to themselves this way.

In the West, many orders of monks and nuns work in missions and Christian communities, but Orthodox monasticism has generally followed the older model of having monks and nuns separate themselves completely from the rest of society. This tendency to seclusion came in handy for Orthodox monasteries during times of invasion, allowing them to keep functioning and maintain much of their Christian and national cultures.

This means that even though Orthodox monks and nuns are not usually involved in a day-to-day way with the laity, they have had a profound influence on the cultures in which they live.

At least two Orthodox monasteries have unbroken histories from the sixth century to the present: St. Sabbas in the Jordan Valley and the Monastery of St. Catherine at Mount Sinai. Since the tenth century, though, the heart of Orthodox monasticism has been at Mount Athos in northern Greece. Mount Athos—the "Holy Mountain"—has twenty large monasteries and many smaller ones, along with the cells of individual hermits. They say that at its peak, more than forty thousand monks lived there, but times have changed, and today only about two thousand monks live at the site. No women are allowed on the mount, not even as pilgrims or visitors.

shared beliefs in the Trinity. In 1963, the Church began participating in the World Council of Churches, a fellowship of churches from around the globe that seeks to promote unity among Christians.

By the 1970s, the Church had committed itself to the cause of Christian unity. It began dialogues with a number of Christian communities in the hopes of finding common ground, among them Lutheran, Reformed, Methodist, Disciples of Christ, Baptist, Pentecostal, Evangelical, Anglican, and Orthodox. At the local level, Catholic communities are encouraged to collaborate with other Christians in prayer, worship, and Bible study; in sharing resources; and in providing pastoral care, education, and health care.

In January 2002, Pope John Paul II hosted spiritual leaders from many religious traditions at a gathering in Assisi, Italy, to pray for world peace. More than two hundred spiritual leaders attended, representing Christian, Muslim, Jewish, Buddhist, Shinto, Jainist, Sikh, Hindu, Zoroastrian, Confucian, Tenri,

The Ark of the Covenant in Africa

One of the oldest national Christian churches in the world is in Ethiopia. This was a pagan place until the fourth century, when two missionaries on their way to India were shipwrecked near what was then called Abyssinia. The missionaries were taken in as the king's servants: One became his cupbearer and the other the tutor of his son. The missionaries took this as a sign from God and started teaching the son and others at court about the Christian God. When the son became king, he and his nobles all converted, and Christianity was declared the official religion of the state.

There is an Ethiopian legend that claims a longer history with the Judeo-Christian God. It is said that when the Queen of Sheba (another name for Ethiopia) visited Solomon's court, the two were married; after the Queen returned home, she gave birth to a son, Menelik I of Ethiopia. Menelik later visited his father, then returned to Ethiopia with the Ark of the Covenant in tow, which is said to still be stored in a church in the city of Axum.

What became known as the Ethiopian Orthodox Church separated from Catholic Christianity at the time of the Council of Chalcedon in 451. They continued to affirm that Christ has only one nature, whereas Catholic Christians follow Chalcedon's teaching that Christ had both a human and a divine nature. For centuries, Ethiopian Christians were cut off from the rest of the Christian world by invasions, and it is perhaps this that allowed them to maintain customs that have more in common with traditional Judaism than is true of most Christian churches. For example, the Ethiopian Church celebrates Saturday as the Sabbath, they observe many dietary laws, and their priests still sacrifice animals.

The Ethiopian Church was the official state religion until a Marxist revolution overthrew their emperor in 1974. The country has gone through many governments in its history—even the communist government set up after the revolution is long gone—but the Church has remained strong throughout. Protestant and Catholic missionaries have made some headway in the country, but some 60 percent of its 55 million citizens remain members of the Ethiopian Orthodox Church.

and traditional African religions. The leaders recognized that religion is often a source of conflict in the world, and they prayed that it would become instead a source of hope and healing. They signed a Peace Pledge, committing themselves to proclaiming peace in the face of violence, promoting changes in the political and economic spheres that will help break down the divisions between people, and fostering dialogue and forgiveness between their various groups.

This is the heart of the Church's vision for its relationship with other Christians and other religions at the beginning of the twenty-first century: respecting the diversity of beliefs while striving for a unity based on the understanding that the divine is open to all people.

Questions and Ideas for Understanding

1. When modern people talk about the healing power of touch, they usually are referring to a psychological benefit that promotes physical well-being rather than to an instantaneous cure. Still, many people claim to have the gift of healing through faith, and many others claim to have experienced it. How do you think the Church's response to such claims has changed over the centuries? How would you expect it or other Christian religious bodies to respond now?

2. Given the centuries of separation, do you think the Eastern and Western churches could reunite if they were able to overcome their theological difficulties, or would cultural differences keep them apart? If they could reunite, what would that look like?

3. Look more deeply into Monophysitism and the questions about Christ's nature. Explain in a few paragraphs why this issue mattered enough to people to break communion with the established Church over it.

4. Describe an experience in which you sensed the deep power of a particular place, perhaps a religious building, a seat of government, or a beautiful natural space. How would you explain the source of your feeling during that experience?

8

Shaking Things Up
The Church Reforms Inside and Out

Chapter Overview

In this chapter, we will explore:

▶ Invasions and a new way of structuring society in Europe

▶ Relations between the State and the Church

▶ A far-reaching Church reform

▶ A new way of setting up monasteries

▶ How and why the Church and Catholics are involved in politics

William: Living Up to the Call

As you eat your morning bread, you think about how you came to be bishop: your uncle, a cardinal, got you elected to your hometown diocese. "Just keeping things in the family," he said, and you felt lucky to have such a powerful relative. After all, how many 15-year-olds find themselves set for life? Okay, so you were not always sure that you wanted to be a churchman, but as the second son of a minor nobleman, there was not a lot you could do: Your brother would inherit the land, and outside the Church you would always be in his shadow. But in the six years since you took your vows, you have come to realize that you have an important position and a good income, and you can help your family. What could be better? At least, that is how you saw things before you went to the synod a few weeks ago.

Adalbero, a bishop from a nearby diocese, had been to Rome on business just before the synod, and he was afire with talk of reform. "The Pope is trying to get the message out that the Church must be purer and more spiritual. Our priests must dedicate themselves to living for God—they should not be married or have concubines, and it's up to us to put a stop to it. It's a scandal that people buy and sell Church offices or arrange for their relatives to be in powerful positions." Your cheeks flushed as he gave you a sideways glance. Why was he picking on you? Your uncle was just looking out for his family, like everyone does.

On the ride back to your own diocese, though, you couldn't stop thinking about what Adalbero had said about the Holy Spirit calling the Church to renew and reform—and about your own position as bishop. Much as you had not wanted to admit it, you couldn't help feeling that what he said about people doing favors for relatives was true. But what could you do about it now?

Over the next few days, a sense of purpose grew inside you. In the years since your quick ordination as

priest and consecration as bishop, you had been going through the motions, doing only what you had to do and otherwise just enjoying yourself. After all, you had thought, it was not like you had a real calling to this life, so why put yourself out? But you came to realize that however you got here, the Lord was now calling you to be a good priest and a reforming bishop.

You take a bite of bread, turning your thoughts to the hard day ahead. You have called your priests together today to tell them they must separate from their wives and concubines. You expect many of them will want to dismiss what you say. Who does a man of 21 years think he is, telling them what to do! You may be young, but you are also a successor of the apostles—and you plan on making your voice heard for the rest of the time that you serve the people of God.

Young men of William's age did not become bishops often, but it did happen, usually because they had powerful relatives. Getting relatives a position within the Church is an abuse of power, and such abuses led some popes during the ninth through eleventh centuries to be great reformers. They worked hard to pull the Church toward greater dedication to its ideals, and they demanded that priests and bishops show a renewed commitment to their duties. These popes decided that their best bet for reforming the Church was to strengthen papal power, which meant making kings and the nobility stay out of the Church's business.

Many changes were going on inside the Church, and lots outside, too. Europe was once again under attack from invasions, and societies were struggling toward new ways of setting up social and political structures. Politics is a theme that runs throughout this chapter, and we will finish by exploring how the modern Church understands its presence in the political sphere. ∎

Fighting and Feuding in a Feudal World

Europe in the early Middle Ages was under siege. Remember all those invasions in the fourth and fifth centuries? Now Europe was being invaded again, only the invaders had changed. These ongoing threats led to a new way of organizing society, called feudalism.

For the better part of the ninth and tenth centuries, Europe lived in a state of constant threat. A nomadic tribe from central Asia called the Magyars got a vice grip on Eastern Europe, until they were finally defeated by Otto I of Saxony in 955. A group of Scandinavian tribes known together as the Vikings were easily the best shipbuilders and sailors of the time, which gave them a way to invade not only Western Europe but also Russia, down to Constantinople, and as far away as what would later be known as North America. One Viking tribe, the Danes, had so much success in England that in 878, the English king Alfred the Great decided to give them part of the country, hoping they would leave everybody else alone. Nearly the same thing happened in France, with King Charles giving the Normans, yet another Viking tribe, the area that became known as Normandy. And the Saracens—a collection of Muslim groups including the Arabs, Berbers, and Moors—terrorized southern Europe, setting up camp in Spain, raiding deep into southern France, conquering Sicily, and foraging in Italy. They held onto Sicily until the eleventh century, and the last Moorish king was driven out of southern Spain only in 1492.

What was the result of all this invading? A big decline in population as people were killed off or forced out; a bad time for agriculture—lost crops plus fewer people to plant and harvest; increased poverty; and great destruction of property. The raids also contributed to the collapse of Charlemagne's empire and helped break apart political alliances in Germany. On the upside, Otto's defeat of the Magyars set him up as savior of the Western Christian world and a favorite of the Pope. Otto was able to bring much of Western Europe under his control, and in 962, Pope John XII crowned him head of the new Holy Roman Empire.

Lords and Knights and Peasants, Oh My!

With all the invasions and the disintegration of Charlemagne's empire, Western Europe was lacking a solid central government, so people looked to their local leaders for direction. These tended to be landowners, who incidentally were also the ones trained as warriors. By about the mid-eighth century, cavalry was becoming important in the way war was fought, but a horse and gear were expensive, and typically the only ones who could afford them were landowners. So these warriors, or knights, were either wealthy themselves or got help from someone who was.

Despite the popular image of knights today, they rarely fought on their own. Usually they owed allegiance to a lord, who as often as not was fighting with some other lord—private war was a fact of life in those days. The lord gave the knight financial help, and in return, the knight owed the lord military service. In this situation, the knight was called a vassal. Interestingly, the lord himself was often the vassal of some other, more powerful lord, so when a lord wanted his vassal to provide military service, that vassal in turn might call his knights into service. Pretty much the entire system was built around the possibility of war.

All this worked reasonably well if you were a lord or knight, but for peasants, it was another story. Peasants, or serfs as they were called, worked the land, tended the animals, and provided the food. They were more or less the property of the lord who owned the land and had to turn over most of what they grew to the lord, with barely enough left over to feed their families. In return, in addition to the right to farm, they received protection from the hostile intentions of other lords. It was a tough way to live.

This way of organizing society is called feudalism, although that word did not appear in English until the seventeenth century. Feudalism got its start in France in the ninth and tenth centuries and spread quickly throughout Europe. To people of the time (at least to the ones in power), it seemed to make good sense, and it did help move things forward politically. With the local landowners owing allegiance to the more powerful lords, and those lords to the king, a structure was in place that began to have the outline of a nation. The idea that vassals had rights as well as duties had an impact, too. It took awhile, but eventually this led to the idea that all citizens have certain rights and liberties.

The feudal system affected the Church as well. Churchmen such as bishops and abbots were part of that landed class; they might have their own land, they might have control of Church lands, or they might have both, but in any case, they often found themselves vassals of some lord, a problematic relationship, as we will soon see. But the Church had an impact on feudalism,

Making Life a Little Easier

Around the tenth century, some new inventions had a big impact on how people worked. For instance, when they needed horses or mules to pull their plows, people had traditionally harnessed them with flexible straps around the animal's neck that nearly asphyxiated the poor creatures if they pulled heavy loads. But around this time, people started using a rigid collar that let the animals breathe while pulling up to ten times as much as before—better for the animals and faster for the farmer trying to plow the field. The wheelbarrow came on the scene about this time, as did the spinning wheel. People started shoeing their horses, too, and using stirrups, which helped riders keep from falling off their mounts.

A new kind of rudder (a device that helps guide ships) came into use that made it possible to build larger ships, and larger ships could make longer sea voyages. This eventually enhanced trade, but even more quickly it helped ferry Crusaders. As a result of their adventures, Crusaders brought back a variety of new crops: different kinds of fruit trees, maize, buckwheat, potatoes, and tobacco made their way back west, along with new dyes and silkworms.

too. The lord and the vassal were understood to be involved in a sacred trust in their duties toward each other, and the vassal even took an oath to God to perform his duties properly.

Fighting for Control: Problems between Church and State

So far in its history, the Church had been ignored by the State, then persecuted by it, and finally joined with it under Constantine. Now another chapter opened in Western Church–State relations: fighting for control. We have seen that in all the chaos following the fourth- and fifth-century invasions, Church leaders were often the only ones able to exert any kind of social control. As you might expect, they were not always happy to hand back control to secular governments once those governments had regained their footing. This was especially true because kings and nobility often wanted their sphere of influence to cover the Church within their lands.

Popes were having a rough time of it. Politics and alliances worked out in such a way that the papacy was almost completely dominated by people on the outside, mainly German kings and a few powerful Roman families. The party in power could appoint and depose popes on a whim, or worse; we read stories about popes from this era being blinded, mutilated, imprisoned, and murdered by outside forces. It was a bad scene, and the popes had good reason to want the situation changed.

Pope John XII may have entertained such hopes when he crowned Otto I as Holy Roman Emperor in 962, but such was not to be the case. Otto expected obedience from his bishops, including the pope, and he eventually kicked John out of office for conspiring against him, putting a more easily controlled pope in his place. (Not that John being deposed was any great loss for the Church: Elected at 18, John had used his power in selling church offices, gambling, bedding many women, and even castrating and killing a cardinal.)

Church–State problems did not end at the top. As centralized control fell apart, local lords began taking control of the clergy in their lands. Some lords stole Church property or demanded "protection" money, but most just wanted the right to decide who would be the priest or bishop in areas they controlled. This did not seem at all unreasonable to them: the lords owned the land on which the churches were built, and they had control over who managed other parts of their property, so why should the churches and Church lands be any different? However, in the Church's view, this made a bad situation worse; it was hard enough dealing with the outside interference of kings and emperors. Add the local lords, and you've got an awful lot of fingers in the pie.

Who Decides? The Investiture Controversy

All these problems came to a head over what is called *investiture*. In this ceremony, vassals pledged obedience to their lords, and in return, the lords gave them some symbol of the land they were receiving. This was only a problem when the vassal happened to be a churchman, especially a bishop, and it went right to the heart of determining who would control the appointment of bishops: the lord from whom the bishop had control of the land or the Church through which he received his spiritual authority.

In 1075, King Henry IV of Germany, head of the renewed Holy Roman Empire, appointed a new archbishop of Milan when the post opened up. At the same time, Pope Gregory VII also appointed a new archbishop. Gregory told Henry to pull his appointee, but Henry felt justified in that even popes were being appointed by kings. Henry assembled a synod of bishops to depose Gregory, who responded by excommunicating Henry and releasing

Henry's subjects from their oath of fealty—in effect, telling them they did not owe allegiance to Henry anymore. All this was just the opening needed by a group of German nobles who were plotting to get Henry out of the way. Soon, King Henry had open rebellion on his hands. Henry decided the best way out of the situation was to publicly say that Gregory had been right all along. He showed up where the pope was staying and stood outside in the snow for three days, barefoot, asking to be readmitted to communion. Gregory could hardly ignore this very public penance, so he absolved Henry and revoked his excommunication—which also put those oaths of fealty back in place.

As Henry expected, his little display gave him a political advantage; not only had he shown himself to be a good son of the Church, but he was also in the perfect position to go home and quell the rebellion there. When Gregory excommunicated Henry again over another matter three years later, Henry simply deposed Gregory again and installed a new pope. The issue of two popes running around went unresolved until Gregory died in 1085.

Gregory's successors kept up the fight to keep lay lords from appointing bishops, with mixed results. Things settled down some with the Concordat of Worms in 1122, which gave rulers the right to be present at the election of bishops and even to decide in the event of a dispute; so while the rulers retained some power, the Church was given more of a free hand in dealing with appointments. Nevertheless, the whole issue continued to be a problem in many areas, including England, and we still hear talk of it as late as the fourteenth century.

Cleaning House: Reform in the Church

As we have seen, during the ninth through eleventh centuries, it was not uncommon for kings to appoint popes, and as you might expect, it did not always result in the holiest of men being chosen for this holiest of offices. For instance, in 1032, Benedict IX ascended the papal throne at around age 18 because his father, the count of a region not far from Rome, was able to get it for him. Benedict was so corrupt and thoroughly hated by the Romans that they ran him out of town and put another man, Sylvester III, on the papal throne. Benedict excommunicated Sylvester and managed to fight his way back to the papacy but got tired of the whole situation and six weeks later sold the office to Gregory VI. At this point, Emperor Henry III stepped in; threw

Serving the People

Priests have played a central role throughout most of Church history, so it might seem surprising that exactly what that role should be has not always been clear. In the early Church, priests were the Jewish men offering sacrifices in the Temple. Catholics today may understand Jesus as the ultimate priest who sacrificed himself for his people, but Jesus and his apostles were certainly not priests in the traditional Jewish sense. What they were, though, were ministers.

We tend to think of ministers as clergy members, but the word really refers to any person who serves the community. Many different ministries developed in the early Church, such as proclaiming the word, helping the poor, and administering community resources. One group of ministers, called presbyters, acted as a sort of advisory board for Christian communities. Later, it was decided to have one presbyter head up the others; this person came to be called the bishop. The bishop usually led the worship services, and by the end of the third century, people were seeing the bishop's role as a priestly one because he offered the sacrifice of the Eucharist just as the Temple priests had offered the sacrifice of animals.

When Christian communities started growing too large for one person to always preside at the Eucharist and perform baptisms, presbyters took on some of these functions. This meant that presbyters, like bishops, were playing a priestly role. Soon the words *priest* and *presbyter* were being used interchangeably.

By the Middle Ages, people tended to think of priests as those who celebrated the sacraments rather than as those who helped the community through ministry. Theologians were trying to understand what it really meant to be a priest, but their focus was more on working out what made priests and bishops different. Why could priests celebrate some sacraments such as baptizing and forgiving sins, but only bishops could do other things like ordain priests? They decided it was because bishops were priests in a fuller sense. Bishops were the successors of the apostles, which meant they rightly celebrated all the sacraments. "Presbyter" priests, on the other hand, were ordained as helpers for bishops and did not have the same level of authority.

During the Reformation, Luther and others called the whole idea of priesthood into question. All Christians are called to be a holy people, so why should some be set apart through a special sacrament? Catholics responded by defending the sacramental nature of the priesthood, but they also sought to improve the way priests lived and worked. Seminaries were established to better educate priests in theology and canon law, and rules were laid down for celebrating the sacraments. All this resulted in a better-educated and more committed priesthood.

Vatican II took a deep look at the history of the priesthood and its role in the community. The bishops reaffirmed that priests are helpers of bishops and that their primary duties relate to the sacraments, especially the Eucharist, but they also emphasized that priests should be ministers in service to the community. Since many ministries associated with the priesthood had been performed in the early Church by laypeople, Vatican II opened up many ministries to the laity and once again began talking about ministry as something to which all Christians are called. In modern Catholic understanding, the liturgical and sacramental functions of priests are still vital, but priests work together *with* the rest of the community rather than simply *for* it.

Benedict, Sylvester, and Gregory all out of office; and proceeded to appoint the next four popes.

Throughout the ninth through eleventh centuries, popes were accused, often with good reason, of simony (buying or selling Church offices), nepotism (appointing relatives to powerful offices), having concubines, and living large. At least one pope ordered murders of rivals; another was elected after twice having been kicked out of the priesthood. Not all the popes in this period were bad—far from it. However, those who were made a deep impression, as did the ill behavior of other churchmen during this time.

Eventually, it became clear the status quo was unworkable, and Gregory VII, the one who had battled Emperor Henry IV over investitures, took on the task of cleaning up the Church. He gave his name to a series of changes called the Gregorian reform. Actually, though, Pope Leo IX had begun the reforms about twenty-five years earlier. Appointed pope by Holy Roman Emperor Henry III, Leo went on to tackle the policies of Henry and his successors head-on. In fact, he is the one who first challenged lay investiture.

In his five years as pope, Leo only spent six months in Rome because he was constantly traveling to get the reform message out. He particularly attacked simony and the marriage of priests. Everybody was clear about the problems that simony created, but the issue of marriage was murky. After all, some of the apostles were married, and priests in the Eastern Church were still allowed to marry. However, being a priest was becoming a kind of hereditary right: Just as the son of a farmer would inherit the farm, the sons of priests were expected to take over for their fathers. This was a real problem because it meant that Church property was being handed down as an inheritance, and it did not say much about the commitment of priests if they were only in their positions because their fathers had done the same thing.

Gregory's Turn

Once Gregory came to the papal throne in 1073, he took the idea of reform to another level. He kept up the fight against simony and clerical marriage, but he honed in on how the Church interacts with society as the center point of his campaign for reform. In fact, he saw the Church as the centerpoint of society and believed that everyone, especially secular rulers, needed to recognize that fact.

Gregory and those he gathered around him wanted to return to a Church centered on the papacy. In actuality, Gregory and his group were calling for more power than the papacy had ever known. Excerpts from a series of propositions he wrote, called the *Dictates,* give a sense of just how far Gregory wanted to go.

1. That the Roman Church was founded by God alone.

2. That the Roman pontiff alone is rightly to be called universal.

3. That he alone can depose or reinstate bishops . . .

7. That for him alone is it lawful to enact new laws according to the needs of the time . . .

9. That the pope is the only one whose feet are to be kissed by all princes . . .

12. That he may depose emperors . . .

Judging the Dead at the Cadaver Synod

One of the most bizarre moments in Church history has come to be known as the Cadaver Synod, so called because a dead man was one of the main players. Pope Formosus died in 896, and eventually Pope Stephen VI was elected. Then Stephen decided to put Formosus on trial. Sound strange? It gets stranger. Stephen had Formosus's body exhumed, dressed in papal robes, and put on the papal throne. Stephen apparently shouted accusations and insults at the dead man, and since Formosus obviously could not answer for himself, a deacon was appointed to speak for him.

The synod found Formosus guilty of perjury and of violating Church law that states bishops cannot transfer from one diocese to another (Formosus had been bishop of Oporto before becoming bishop of Rome, i.e.,

pope). As a result, his election was declared invalid, all his acts as pope were voided, and, in the strangest turn of all, the three fingers of his right hand that he used to give blessings were cut off. His body was buried, then dug up again and thrown into the Tiber River. Eventually the body was retrieved, buried again, exhumed again, and finally given a proper burial in St. Peter's.

The motivation behind this whole thing was actually political, a way of undermining the authority of a ruling house that Formosus had supported. It backfired on Stephen, however, as he was deposed and imprisoned after a public uprising brought on by reports that Formosus's body had begun performing miracles. Stephen was killed in prison and the Cadaver Synod was declared invalid by a later pope.

18. That no sentence of his may be retracted by anyone; and that he, alone of all, can retract it.

19. That he himself may be judged by no one.

20. That no one shall dare to condemn a person who appeals to the Apostolic See . . .

22. That the Roman Church has never erred, nor ever, by the witness of Scripture, shall err to all eternity.

23. That the Roman pontiff, if canonically ordained, is undoubtedly sanctified by the merits of St. Peter . . .

26. That he should not be considered a Catholic who is not in conformity with the Roman Church.

27. That the Pope may absolve subjects of unjust men from their fealty.[1]

Gregory was deeply interested in his own job description, but his reforms went beyond discussions of papal power to affect the entire Church and, in particular, the role of cardinals and the development of canon law.

Cardinals

Under the reforms of Gregory and his successors, the number and power of cardinals expanded considerably. At the time, almost all cardinals lived in Rome, acting as a sort of advisory board for the pope. Gregory and the reformers who came after him, however, sent them everywhere to be the eyes, ears, and mouth of the papacy; they spread word of the reforms, made sure that everyone was obeying, and reported back if there were problems. Essentially, they became the pope's own spy network. Cardinals also took over the leadership of many departments in the papal government, including the curia of papal finances and the chancery, which kept track of all papal appointments, court decisions, political negotiations, and other correspondence.

The single greatest change for cardinals stemming from the reforms, however, was the role they were to play in electing new popes. Prior to this, popes had been appointed by lay rulers, designated by the Roman Church and elected by members of the clergy. However, in 1179, the Third Lateran Council decided that only cardinals could elect a pope.

Canon Law

Reformers looked to laws from the early Church, the works of important early Christian writers, and decrees from councils and other popes as support for their ideas, but up to this point, no one had gathered all these writings together in a systematic way. Gregory and his group began to get them organized, creating the code of canon law along the way. This helped the reformers show the validity of reforms and at the same time centralize administrative power in Rome.

Gathering all those writings clearly proved one point: that they did not all agree. During the next century, the writer Gratian took up the challenge of bringing them into a consistent system. In a work called *A Concordance of Discordant Canons* (usually referred to as the *Decretum*), Gratian worked through almost four thousand writings, deciding what level of authority each had and how they were to be understood in relation to other writings on the same subject—a significant help in making canon law more consistent. Since there were always new decisions from popes, councils, and Church courts to contend with, the body of canon law continued to grow and develop.

All this helped Gregory's reform program. He and later popes were able to use this centralized canon law to help solidify their powers. They were able to show that the decisions they were making were in keeping with earlier rulings, which gave them added clout. Having a clearly organized legal system that explicitly recognized the pope as the ultimate authority in all matters was extremely helpful as well. With all those cardinals moving around Europe, the popes were able to get their decisions recognized and put into practice much more quickly.

One of the consequences Gregory did not anticipate in his reform work was the stirring up of the old Donatist ideas. (Donatists, you recall, believed the benefit of a sacrament depended on the purity of the clergy member performing it.) In his decrees about simony and clerical marriage, Gregory encouraged people to reject priests who were not following the rules. He was not promoting a Donatist idea—he never suggested that the sacraments performed by corrupt priests were any less valid—but he wanted to put pressure on clergy members to reform. Gregory had made an important theological distinction but not one that would necessarily have been recognized by the typical Catholic. Some people began by rejecting priests and ended by rejecting sacraments, leading to problems we will deal with in the next chapter.

Nevertheless, the push for reform continued. Councils in 1179 (Third Lateran Council) and 1215 (Fourth Lateran Council) dealt directly with the roles and lifestyles of bishops and priests. They decreed good morals and a worthwhile education for priests; stated that each cathedral needed to create a way that men could study for the priesthood without paying tuition; ordered bishops to spend more time visiting the churches under their care and less money on lavish living; and demanded that priests be celibate and sober, dress moderately, and not do any work unbefitting one in holy orders. Long after Gregory, the Gregorian reform continued.

Thumbs Up or Thumbs Down?

Cluny's influence spread, and many thought it had the mark of God on it. See for yourself:

Cardinal Peter Damian, after a visit to Cluny in 1063

From the very day of its foundation . . . God's mercy has ordained that, where the burden of earthly subjection has been done away, devotion to his service should be fullest; and that, where there is no liability to earthly service, the full dignity of the monastic profession should be completely revealed. O truly renowned and free-born service of God, which leaves no place for earthly service![2]

Pope Gregory VII, speaking to a council held in Rome in 1080

Although there are many monasteries beyond the mountains which have been nobly and religiously founded to the honour of Almighty God and of the holy apostles St. Peter and St. Paul, there is one in those parts of the world that belongs to St. Peter and to this church by an especial right as its own peculiar possession I mean Cluny . . . By God's mercy, it has come to such a peak of excellence and religion under its holy abbots, that it surpasses all other monasteries that I know, even much older ones, in the service of God and in spiritual warmth. I know of no other in that part of the world to which it can be compared. For it has never had an abbot who was not a saint.[3]

Focus On
Rethinking the Monastery: The Abbey of Cluny

Gregory and the two popes directly after him had a good background for being reformers: they were monks first. In the tenth and eleventh centuries, monasteries were themselves in the midst of change. This did not grow out of the papal reforms and in fact had little to do with them, but both papal and monastic reform point to a strong desire to revitalize the Church and to move away from a focus on worldly things to a deeper connection with the Christian life.

By the tenth century, the nobility had a good grip on monastic life. Most monks and nuns, especially abbots and abbesses, came from the landed classes, and those with money founded new monasteries and donated to old ones, hoping to help along their own salvation. Monasteries were involved in the economics of society, too: many were large landowners, which meant monasteries might actually have vassals or might themselves be vassals owing allegiance to some lord.

Duke William of Aquitaine and Abbot Berno wanted to change all this. As they saw it, monasteries suffered from too much outside interference. In 909, they set up a monastery called Cluny in the Burgundy region of what is now France in such a way that legally it was free to elect its own abbots (no appointments by lay lords or local bishops) and had no feudal obligations (they placed it directly under papal protection). From the start, the monks followed the Benedictine Rule as it had been interpreted by the Second Benedict. Free of

outward restraint and focused on inner holiness, Cluny prospered.

Cluny's abbots set about founding new monasteries and reorganizing older ones along the lines of Cluny with respect to finances, obligations, and the way they lived the Rule. All these other houses actually owed allegiance to Cluny; their monks vowed obedience to the abbot of Cluny rather than to the local leader, who was known as a prior. The Cluny system bore some remarkable similarities to Celtic monasticism. Similar to the places that Columba and his crew founded, Cluniac monasteries would initially be founded by twelve monks sent out from other houses, the main abbot retained control over all the houses, and the main monastery served as a headquarters for the whole group—no wonder there was an altar dedicated to St. Columba at Cluny itself.

The Cluny system was not as highly organized as later religious orders, but still it proved so popular that historians talk about the Cluniac reform of monasticism. Being part of a whole made the Cluny monasteries much more powerful than they could have been on their own. By the beginning of the twelfth century, about three hundred Cluniac monasteries spread across Europe as far as Poland; a century later, the number was fifteen hundred.

Cluny's influence went well beyond the monastery walls. During all the chaos of the fourth and follow-

continued on page 163

continued from page 162

ing centuries, much land that had been used to grow produce had fallen fallow. The Cluny monasteries brought much of this land back into cultivation, and they needed workers to help do this. Villages sprang up around the monasteries to accommodate the people working there, which created a need for artisans and merchants to settle and sell their wares in those villages. All this means that when a new monastery was founded or an older one gathered into the Cluniac system, the surrounding area got an economic boost. Many of the monasteries owned large estates, and Cluny grew so wealthy that its abbots were among the most powerful lords in all of Europe.

Cluniac monks worked with the idea that you could not overdo something if it was for the glory of God. Cost was irrelevant if something was for the liturgy or the church that housed it, and the Great Church built at Cluny at the end of the eleventh century was one of the marvels of Christian architecture until it was destroyed during the French Revolution.

If the church was magnificent, so was the liturgy, which was as serious and splendid as the monks could make it. The first Benedict had wanted his monks to balance their lives between work, prayer, and study, but not so the monks of Cluny. Believing that taking part in certain kinds of spiritual activities like chanting the Psalms could legitimately take the place of manual labor, they left all the physical labor for the servants and spent their time in church. By the eleventh century, some people looking at Cluny began to complain that the liturgy was downright excessive. On feast days,

masses and prayers could go on for twelve hours at a time, and even on normal days, liturgy filled most of the monks' time.

So now we know about the reforms for men; what about the women? Well, you cannot reform what is not already there. We saw in chapter 6 that religious houses for women were beginning to spring up in the sixth century, but there were never anything like the number of men's houses in Western Europe. In fact, until the middle of the tenth century, women's monasteries were rare, and if you were a woman who felt the call to monastic life but did not have money to contribute, you were unlikely to find a place to call home. Sometimes women who desired the religious life simply lived near a monastery and accepted spiritual direction from the monks there, but that did not really equal living the communal monastic life. It was a wondrous thing for many women when houses specifically for them became more common during all the Church and monastic reforms.

Cluny did its bit to help women. It took a century and a half after their own start for them to recognize the need, but in 1061, the first Cluniac women's house was set up in Marcigny in France. As you would expect, the women of this house were completely enclosed, never leaving the monastery for any reason. The nuns took their enclosure so seriously, in fact, that when a fire ripped through their convent, they refused to leave the building. A few other women's houses eventually were set up, but women never had the kind of access to the Cluniac brand of religious life enjoyed by the men. ■

Voices from the Past

▶ Author: Peter Damian, monk, abbot, and cardinal
▶ Written: Mid-eleventh century
▶ Audience: Monks

One of the strongest voices criticizing the idleness and luxury of the traditional monk's life in the eleventh century belonged to Peter Damian. Born in 1007 in the Italian city of Ravenna, Peter was the last child of a large family. His parents died when Peter was young, and his brother Damian stepped up and became the father figure in his life. In fact, Peter later took Damian's name as a sign of the love he felt for this man who gave him so much, including an excellent education. Peter became a teacher, but that did not last long, as he already felt the call to a life of austerity and prayer. He entered a monastery and would happily have stayed there but later was called upon to be a cardinal-bishop and a papal legate, helping out the Gregorian reform by convincing local churchmen of the pope's right to intervene in the affairs of their churches.

It was Peter's brilliance as a preacher, teacher, and writer that got him called away from the life of contemplation that he loved. His surviving writings include 170 letters, 53 sermons, 7 lives of saints, and many other works. He wrote two important treatises about the monk's life, which he saw as a stepping-stone to the more perfect life of the hermit. By nature a man of extremes, Peter envisioned the hermit's life as extreme as well: lots of fasting, few clothes, no socks or shoes even in winter, little sleep, and a good deal of flagellation (beating the body with whips or rods).

A man of his time, Peter saw God as a fearsome king who was angered by the disobedience of his subjects. He wrote approvingly that some of those subjects, "if told of the heavy penalty which is their due, and threatened with the terror of the last judgment"[4] will come to know God; fear, he believed, was a useful motivator and ought to inspire penance and complete rejection of the world. This included rejection of all secular learning: "[W]e are not only forbidden to strive for such worthless learning after we have made our holy profession; we are also commanded to reject all that is unnecessary of what we had previously learned."[5] Peter wrote about these things in a treatise called *On the Perfection of Monks:*

You are well aware, my brothers (I say it with tears), into what lack of zeal our holy order has fallen . . . so that now, having carelessly forgotten almost all its precepts, we seem to be content to wear merely the outward habit of our calling. Under the cloak of religion we live worldly lives, and outrage the spirit of discipline when we abandon ourselves to the flowing stream of pleasures, disgracing the title of our nobility, and vainly bearing the name of monks . . .

[As monks we have not paid all that is necessary to] Christ our king, for whose sake we have abandoned our possessions and spurned marriage; for whom we avoid the eating of meat, hold ourselves apart from the pomp and glory of the world, and exchange the splendour of worldly dress for our humble garb. These, I confess, are great and difficult things, and will be more greatly rewarded with divine gifts; but something is still needed

continued on page 165

continued from page 164

before we can complete the payment of our debt and deserve admittance to the treasure-house of the eternal King ... It is nothing other than this: a fervent love of God and mortification of yourself ...

[When a monk has truly mortified his spirit] he takes no pleasure in frivolous gossip, nor does he waste time in idle conversation; he occupies himself with psalms, hymns and spiritual songs; he desires solitude and seeks a quiet place; the workshops where the brethren speak together and the cloisters of the monastery are to him like the public market-place; he searches for and takes pleasure in remote and lonely places; as far as he can, he avoids all human contact, so that he may more easily stand in the presence of the Creator.[6] ■

However, not everyone agreed. As time went on, the Cluny monks became so involved in liturgy that other duties fell by the wayside. By the twelfth century, a few like Bernard of Clairvaux thought that the monks of Cluny had forgotten what it really meant to live the monastic life.

Bernard's Apology to Abbot William, written in 1125

I am astonished that monks could be so lacking in moderation in matters of food and drink, and with respect to clothing and bedding, carriages and buildings . . . Abstemiousness is accounted miserliness, sobriety strictness, silence gloom . . . Fine clothes and costly caparisons are regarded as mere respectability, and being fussy about bedding is hygiene . . .

Should we laugh or cry at such foolishness? . . . Did the Fathers in Egypt adopt such a manner of life? Finally, did those holy men whom they claim as the founders and teachers of their Order . . . hold with such things or value them? All these men were saints, and because of this they were in accord with what the Apostle said: So long as we have food and clothing, we are content.

To take a single example: what evidence of humility does it give to go about in such pomp and circumstance, attended by so many retainers that an abbot's suite would be enough for two bishops? If I am not mistaken, I have seen an abbot with sixty horses and more in his retinue. If you saw him ride by you would think he were the Lord of the Manor, or a provincial governor, instead of a monastic father and shepherd of souls.[7]

Reforming the Reform: Citeaux

Cluny may have started as a reform in the way monasteries were organized, but by the latter part of the eleventh century, there were rumblings that the reform itself needed to be reformed. Some observers of the monastery were sure that the monks had gotten too far away from the life envisioned by the first Benedict. They did not perform manual labor, fast as much as Benedict required, or do much personal reading or study. The monks were allowed to own private property, candidates for the monastery were not closely screened, and the time they spent as novices was not devoted to spiritual formation. All in all, this was clearly not the simple monk's life anymore. As Cluny relaxed the rules and grew wealthier by the day, it became harder to remember that simplicity was supposed to be one of the monk's goals.

In 1098, a monk named Robert of Molesme founded a monastery in Citeaux (near Dijon, France) that attracted many monks not interested in the cushy life of the Cluny monasteries. At Citeaux, they followed a strict interpretation of the Rule: a simple diet and clothing, the eight traditional worship services each day, and a return to manual labor as part of their lives. They eliminated the practice of accepting children into the monastery, reinstituted the year of the novitiate, and rejected donations, choosing to live only on what they earned. They were not much interested in liturgy, either, focusing instead on the personal conversion of those who came to live at Citeaux. The monks drawn to Citeaux felt that this more austere, demanding lifestyle contributed tremendously to the holiness of their lives.

Just like Cluny before it, the monastery at Citeaux became so popular that more monasteries had to be founded. Soon the one monastery had turned into a full-fledged Order called the Cistercians. By 1115, four monasteries had been founded from Citeaux; by 1200, that number had jumped to 525, spread all across Europe. Their exemption from certain tithes required of all others helped fund their growth, but it also caused some hard feelings with local bishops who felt their authority was being challenged by these monasteries.

The rapid growth of the Cistercian Order owes a large debt to Bernard of Clairvaux. As a young man in 1113, Bernard came to the monastery of Citeaux with thirty friends and relatives whom he had convinced to join along with him. Two years later, the abbot of Citeaux sent Bernard as abbot to a new monastery at Clairvaux. Bernard set to work building up his monastery and helping to start or reform others, but he was much more than an abbot: for more than thirty years, he was one of the most important figures in Western Europe. We will meet up with Bernard again in chapter 10, but for now, let's just note that in his preaching and teaching, he helped spread the word about the new old way of being a monastery.

The Church Then and Now

Faithful Citizenship and Political Action

Most Western nations today tend to be skeptical of religion in the public arena. There is a strong sense that keeping Church and State separate is good for both because it keeps the religious ideas of any one group from overshadowing those of others, while also keeping the State from interfering in the area of religion. Church leaders of the Middle Ages, however, would have laughed at this. Not only did they think the State should support Catholic Christianity to the exclusion of all other religious ideas, but they also wanted the State to recognize itself as a lesser authority than the Church. One look at the statement in Gregory VII's *Dictates* declaring that the pope can depose emperors should prove that point.

Fast forward to the modern world, and the Church must counterbalance both its history of political involvement and the demands in modern Western democracies that Church and State remain separate. The Church communicates its understanding of the role it can play as a religious body in the political realm, and it calls on individual Catholics to get involved in political action. The Church sees this as a direct response to the belief of most Christians, and the majority of people of other faiths as well, that they are called to do good in the world. Helping those who are poor, ill, homeless, imprisoned—Catholics have always believed that God calls them to these tasks, but in the modern world, these responsibilities are inextricably linked to public policy and the political process.

At the Third International Synod of Bishops in Rome in 1971, Church leaders reasoned that because of their baptismal commitment to being the Body of Christ in the world, Catholics have an obligation to work for the common good by bringing their values with them into society, including into politics. This does not mean trying to create a Catholic government such as our medieval popes would have liked; rather, it means being informed and active participants who are guided by their Christian consciences and Catholic beliefs when they vote or are in other ways politically active. The Church calls this faithful citizenship and sees it as a duty to which every Catholic is called.

So just what is it that the Church is stressing when it talks about taking Catholic beliefs into political life? Action in defense of life, in pursuit of peace, and in opposition to poverty, hunger, and injustice. We will talk more about the Church's social teachings in chapter 14, but here we simply need to see that according to the Church, these issues require not just the commitment of the Church as a body but also the involvement of the individual Catholic. In the United States, people like Dorothy Day and her Catholic Worker partner Peter Maurin, peace activists and brothers Daniel and Philip Berrigan, and countless others have devoted their lives to living out their Catholic faith in the political and social arena. In every parish within every diocese, all around the world, you can find people responding to the call to faithful citizenship and making their world better because of it.

Questions and Ideas for Understanding

1. The feudal system is based on the idea that each person has certain rights and responsibilities, although those rights and responsibilities differ greatly from the lord at the top to the peasant at the bottom. In what ways is this system similar to hierarchical structures of work in the modern world, such as in a large corporation?

2. Theologically there is a problem with having local lords appoint bishops, but there is still much to be said for having a local person who knows local issues making this decision. Make a list of the pros and cons of the practice of investiture. Would any of those pros or cons change if

Church leaders made the final decision based on a list put together by the local lord?

3. In Catholic theology, Church reforms come at the prompting of the Holy Spirit, who calls the Church back to its original intent and forward to fuller understanding and service; it is about taking a Church of humans and pulling them closer to the divine, not about taking a sinful Church and making it pure. Still, this Donatist idea plays out over and over again in the Church's history. Why do you think this is?

4. Many modern politicians and workers in the area of social justice have made clear how their Catholic faith leads to their public lives. Research one such person and write a short essay explaining how the person's faith affected his or her decisions and how you think the person's life might have been different if he or she had come from a different set of beliefs.

Notes

[1] *Church and State Through the Centuries: A Collection of Historic Documents with Commentaries,* trans and eds. Sidney Z. Ehler and John B. Morral. London: Burns and Oats, 1954, pp. 43-44.

[2] H. E. J. Cowdrey, *The Cluniacs and the Gregorian Reform.* Oxford, UK: Clarendon Press, 1970, p. xxi.

[3] Cowdrey, *Cluniacs,* p. xx.

[4] Peter Damian, On the Perfection of Monks. In *St. Peter Damian: Selected Writings on the Spiritual Life,* trans. Patricia McNulty. London: Faber and Faber, 1959, p. 89.

[5] Peter Damian, pp. 104–105.

[6] Peter Damian, pp. 84–86.

[7] Bernard of Clairvaux, "Apologia to Abbot William." In *The Works of Bernard of Clairvaux,* Vol I. Spencer, MA: Cistercian Publications, 1970, pp. 52–53, 58–59, 62.

9

New Ideas, New Problems
The Middle of the Middle Ages

Chapter Overview

In this chapter, we will explore:

▶ The growth of towns and new ways of thinking

▶ Heresies that challenged the Church

▶ Some extraordinary saints: Francis of Assisi and Clare

▶ Pope Innocent III

▶ The Crusades and their long-lasting effects

▶ Mary and the saints in medieval times, and how the Church talks about Mary now

Arnulf: Far from Home

Until recently, you had barely wandered beyond the confines of your village, and just look at you now! You have traveled through Germany and Italy and all the way down to the coast of the great sea. Now you are seated in this great ship, feeling it rock and sway, listening to the ship's crew speak some foreign tongue, so many people crowded around you. Next to you is your younger brother Wilhelm. You are glad that he is here. When your lord put out the word that he needed men to go with him on this quest to free the Holy Land, you knew that Christ Jesus himself wanted you to go, despite the hardship of leaving your wife and three little children. You worry about your family, but you know that Anton, your sister Margard's husband, will look after them while you are away.

Many of the others accompanying your lord are younger than you and not yet married, and so more easily spared from the work at home. But there are others even older. How amazing to see these wonderful places your father and grandfather could only dream of: mountains rising toward heaven; lands parched and brown; cities larger than you could have imagined, with merchants selling things you had not even known existed. Who knows what you will find when you finally set foot in the Holy Land.

You and Wilhelm each carry an ax and two knives; these will be your weapons—along with your deep faith that you are fighting for God. The pope himself has commanded Christians to free the Holy Land from the infidels; you heard the bishop preach about it before you left Germany. You know that it is God's will that you help drive them from the land and that if you die fighting, your soul will go straight to heaven. Some of the men hope to be martyred in the fighting, but much as you want to be a good Christian, you hope that you and Wilhelm both make it back home safely.

Many people today reject the idea that God calls people to start a war, but in Arnulf's world, most Christians were convinced that God sometimes commanded exactly that. The idea of fighting for a divine cause was not new, but the way it was being put into practice was.

"New" ought to be the slogan for this point in history. New ideas and attitudes were changing the way people thought about many things, from trade to architecture to what the ideal Christian life should be. And the change come from all over: in this chapter, we will talk about Francis, Clare, and Innocent from Italy; Dominic from Spain; and the Crusades, which carried Europeans to far-off places like Palestine, Egypt, and Constantinople. Violence will be a terrible theme throughout this chapter: in addition to the Crusades, which were one of history's most disturbing examples of Christians using violence against those of other religions, we will discuss the Inquisition, in which Christians used violence against other Christians. Finally, we will look at Mary's place in Catholic thinking, both during the Middle Ages and in the Church today. ■

All about Power: Who Gets It, Who Keeps It

In the twelfth and thirteenth centuries, Europe was head over heels into change, and for once the change was not all about wars and invaders and destruction. Instead, Western Europe was showing distinct signs of stability. Towns and the urban society that go along with them were on the rise everywhere. Life was still largely rural—about 90 percent of the population lived in small villages—but towns were emerging as the new centers of trade and commerce, political power, and even civil liberties. Town dwellers began to recognize themselves as a political group, something villagers had never done, and they wanted their feudal lords to guarantee rights and protections that would give them a measure of independence.

Trade had taken a nosedive during the time of invasions; the constant raiding had made the risks too great. With increased stability, however, commerce picked up. Trade routes opened from the Mediterranean to the Baltic and other points east, and the money began rolling in. The enhanced trade affected cities. Craftspeople could create more merchandise because there were more merchants to sell it and more customers to buy it. Long-distance trade helped create a money economy: You cannot trade your wheat or chickens to merchants in another country in exchange for their silk or spices—the chickens might die, the wheat might get wet and go bad, and so on. Not so with money, and money meant a greater need for banking. All this helped strengthen cities, and some even began to form leagues to make themselves more powerful as trade centers.

Life at the top of the political ladder also was in flux. In 1066, Duke William of Normandy (in France) invaded England, claiming that his cousin Edward, the previous English king, had promised him the throne before he died. King Harold II also claimed the throne, however. The matter was decided at the Battle of Hastings in 1067, with William and his forces killing Harold and making short work of the Anglo-Saxon army.

As Duke of Normandy, William had been a vassal of the French king, but as King of England, he became an equal, and a rival. William also still ruled a big chunk of France—a chunk that got bigger under later kings. With so much of France directly under English control, for centuries to come the kings of England and France would battle to be the most important power in the region.

What might have seemed a thirteenth-century footnote would play large in the evolution of democracy and constitutional law. In 1215, English nobles forced England's King John to sign the Magna Carta, a document guaranteeing them certain rights. This did not do much for the common people—the Magna Carta gave rights only to a privileged elite—but it did establish the principle that the king is bound by the law rather than above it and that at least some citizens have rights even a king cannot take away. This idea proved to have staying power—it is the foundation of the modern democratic society, in which every person has rights and no one is above the law.

Church Fights

William's invasion in 1066 also had a big impact on the Church in England. From the sixth century on, English kings had appointed bishops and abbots to be part of an advisory group called the King's Council, and bishops had acted as judges in the courts. William was having none of this; he was in charge, and he wanted everyone, including the Church, to know it. He said that a Pope could not be recognized or Church decrees implemented in England without the king's permission. He separated the civil courts from those of the Church. Basically, William was claiming control of the Church in his realm just at the time that Pope Gregory VII was fighting other kings and emperors to make them give up that kind of control.

William's successors tried to continue these policies, but the Church regained much of its independence during a period of civil war in the mid-twelfth century that ended with Henry II coming to power.

Henry II had his own problems with the Church, especially in the form of Thomas Becket. Thomas was a friend of the king and his highest-ranking official, so when the Archbishopric of Canterbury came open, Henry figured that getting Thomas elected to the most powerful Church position in the country would make it easy for him to reinstate William's policies.

Henry's plan backfired, however. Thomas, who previously had not been overly religious, as archbishop felt called to a new level of faith and commitment; soon he was fighting his old friend Henry to hold onto the independence the Church had gained during the civil war. Henry was furious and sent Thomas into exile for six years. The two were then reconciled but not for long. When Thomas refused to reinstate some bishops he had excommunicated,

Henry went into a rage and demanded to know why no one would rid him of this annoying priest. Four knights figured Henry was giving them permission to do just that, so on December 29, 1170, they rushed into the cathedral in Canterbury and murdered Thomas. Thomas was canonized three years later, and since then, his tomb in the cathedral of Canterbury has been one of the most important pilgrimage sites in Europe.

The Church's problems ran even deeper than assassinations of future saints, however. While England was dealing with power struggles between Church and State, over in the heart of Catholic Christianity, Rome itself, the power struggles were between pope and pope. In 1130, one group of cardinals elected a pope named Innocent II, but another group elected Anacletus II. Both popes remained in Rome, trying to sway popular opinion to their side. European rulers lined up on both sides of the papal fence, and for a while things were at a standoff. Eventually, Innocent had to move to Pisa, leaving Rome to Anacletus, and so things stayed until Anacletus died in 1138. After that, Innocent returned to Rome and an uncontested papacy. History remembers Innocent as the real pope and Anacletus as an interloper, but it must have been much less clear to Catholics of the time.

Challenging the Church

In the last chapter, we saw that Gregory's reforms had an unintended consequence: some people revived the Donatist thinking that a sacrament was only valid if the priest administering it was worthy. In the eleventh through thirteenth centuries, the longing for a "pure" Church picked up steam. Many started questioning what it meant to be a Christian and wondering whether the Church they knew could truly help them find the answers. Those who ended up deciding "no" found themselves labeled as heretics. Because Church and society were so tightly interwoven, heretics often found themselves on the outer edges of society as well, to the point of imprisonment, exile, and even death for their beliefs.

The Church has never been one great monolithic whole. Throughout its history, the Church has had to contend with political fights and theological disputes. Since the Church had settled in Europe, however, it had never experienced anything like the heresies of these centuries. Typically, a heresy got its start when a group of people rejected some aspect of Church teaching, usually because they had come to different conclusions about what certain things in the Bible meant. Areas of disagreement included whether Christians should marry or eat meat, infant baptism, and the idea of the Mass as a sacrifice. At least one group thought the Hebrew Bible ought to be tossed out entirely.

Many of these things seemed to make sense in light of the Church's ideals, too. Think about it: monks were not supposed to eat meat or marry, and the Church has always taught that the New Testament (NT) is a fuller revelation than the Jewish Scriptures. Sometimes people just took these ideas to a logical extreme and ended up somewhere that the Church regarded as wrong, even heretical.

Other factors were at work, too. Many people were upset that the Church preached simplicity but many of its priests and bishops lived in luxury. The idea of the *vita apostolica,* or living like the apostles—wandering the roads preaching the gospel and the need for repentance, living on what people gave them, and following the path of poverty—inspired many people in the twelfth and thirteenth centuries. These ideas were not heretical in themselves, but they were a short step from thinking that priests and the sacraments they celebrate were unnecessary—beliefs that the Church, and especially the Church of that time, considered seriously heretical ground.

Two groups in particular caused significant problems for the Church in the Middle Ages: the Cathars and the Waldensians.

Cathars

The name the Cathars used for themselves says it all: "Good Christians." They believed that the God of the Hebrew Scriptures, Yahweh, had made the material world solely for the purpose of trapping the souls of humans and keeping them under his command. The good God of the NT sent his son to show people how to break free so that they could return to their true divine home after their deaths.

Cathars believed that breaking free meant separating themselves as much as possible from the world, which meant living an extreme ascetic life: no meat, dairy products, eggs, or wine; no sex; no luxury of any sort. Only the most committed Cathars, the ones known as the perfect, followed this difficult life; others, the hearers, believed in the Cathar message but lived regular lives. The hearers could not return to the good God after their deaths, but they could hope to be reborn with the strength to become one of the perfect in their next life. Souls unaware of their true nature would simply be recycled into new bodies as long as they did not have the key to breaking out of the cycle.

Cathar beliefs were remarkably like those of the Manicheans, the group that Augustine joined and later rejected so vehemently. In fact, medieval theologians often referred to Cathars as Manichees, thinking they were somehow related to that fourth-century religion. Whether a true historical connection exists or not (modern scholars are divided on this), there is no doubt that the Church of the twelfth century was just as horrified—and just as threatened—by Cathar beliefs as the fourth-century Church had been by the Manicheans.

By the time the Church took notice of the Cathars, they were so well established in some parts of Christian Europe that they had already set up their own church hierarchy. Their beliefs spread quickly: within twenty years of their first appearance, Cathars could be found all over Western Europe.

Waldensians

In the 1170s, Peter Valdes, a wealthy French merchant, felt called by God to give away all his money and take to the roads as a wandering preacher. Soon others with the same longing for the *vita apostolica* began gathering around him. The group ran into trouble, however, when their local bishop banned them from preaching. Valdes and his followers felt that the Gospel instructed all Christians to preach, so they went to Rome in 1179 to ask Pope Alexander III for his approval. Valdes and company arrived during the Third Lateran Council, however, so there was a crowd of churchmen hearing their request rather than just the pope. Alexander was deeply moved by their commitment but continued to ban them from preaching unless a bishop specifically gave them permission. The chances of that happening were slim because most churchmen—including those attending the council—thought lay people did not have the training to understand and interpret Scripture in accordance with Church teachings and were likely to lead their hearers into error.

One council attendee, Walter Map, gives us an account of the proceedings. After hearing their request, Map wonders, "Shall the Word be given to the ignorant, whom we know to be incapable of receiving it, much less of giving in their turn what they have received?"[1] Map also shows the deep fear behind this disdain:

They have no fixed habitations. They go about two by two, barefoot, clad in woolen garments, owning nothing, holding all things in common like the apostles, naked, following a naked Christ. They are making their first moves now in the humblest manner because they cannot launch an attack. If we admit them, we shall be driven out.[2]

Map may have been obnoxious, but he did recognize that with their request to take on the priestly function of preaching, Valdes and his followers were ultimately presenting a challenge to the Church's authority. For their part, Valdes and his followers were committed Catholics who wished to stay within the Church, but they simply could not accept that the authority of the Church should take precedence over what they saw as a clear commandment of Scripture. They continued preaching in spite of the pope's ban. Rejecting the pope's authority set them on a path to evaluating and ultimately rejecting more Church teachings. Five years after the trip to Rome, the Waldensians were condemned as heretical by Pope Lucius III.

The Waldensians were certainly not the only group to cross over into heresy during the Middle Ages, but they are the only one that continues to exist to the present day. They became part of the Protestant Reformation in the sixteenth century, and today, Waldensian churches continue to exist in many areas, especially in Italy, the United States, South America, and Germany. They even have a seminary in the heart of Catholic Christianity, in Rome itself.

One of the unusual things about both of these movements was that they allowed women to do things they could not do in the Church: preach and administer sacraments. This attracted many women who wanted to participate in Christian life in these ways and drew plenty of fire from Church leaders who thought the groups' attitude toward women was a sign of their corruption. Clearly, the medieval Church did a poor job of creating ways for women to devote themselves to God, and the Cathars and Waldensians were able to capitalize on this shortcoming.

Fighting the Challenge: The Inquisition

The Church saw heresy as cut and dried: it sprang out of a misunderstanding of Scripture and a refusal to recognize the guiding authority of the Church. Heresy was also considered dangerous: the heretic put his or her own soul in jeopardy and might lead others to do the same. The medieval Church felt compelled to put a stop to this.

The first burning of heretics took place in France in 1022, and by the thirteenth century, the Church was preaching a crusade against the Cathars in Languedoc, a Cathar stronghold in southern France. Called the Albigensian Crusade after a town in Languedoc named Albi with a large population of Cathars, it went on for twenty years. With Church approval and promises of indulgences for the fighters, Cathar areas were decimated and the perfect were massacred en masse. Even this did not kill off the beliefs entirely, though; they went underground, and we still see signs of them a few centuries later.

When large-scale force did not completely get rid of heretical beliefs, Church leaders decided to try something else: the Inquisition, one of the most dreaded organizations in Church history. In 1223, Pope Gregory IX began sending out representatives, usually Franciscans and Dominicans, to investigate and pass judgments in areas with big heresy problems. It is ironic that the Orders founded by one man known for his gentleness and another who wanted to convert heretics by persuasion alone became the backbones of a system that used force and terror to bring people in line with Church thinking.

Before this, bishops had been responsible for finding and fighting the heresy in their dioceses, but the friars assigned to the Inquisition were in a much better position to do the job. They had been educated to spot heresy; they were trained as preachers, which helped them communicate with the common people; and they were directly under the pope's authority, which gave them a lot of freedom to act. When an Inquisitor came into an area, he had authority over everyone except the bishop and his officials and could order anyone to show up in his court.

And it was a court, although the rule of law was not the norm: someone could make an anonymous accusation of heresy against another person; those accused were not allowed legal counsel or witnesses in their favor; and Inquisitors always had the option of using torture to obtain confessions—in fact, a papal document from 1252 specifically allows it.

If you were found guilty of heresy by the Inquisition, the Inquisitor would try to persuade you to return to the Church. If you agreed, things went easily—you were given a penance. However, if you refused or you later fell into heresy again, you would be turned over to secular authorities for punishment. Your possessions would be confiscated by the ruler, anything that could not be taken away (such as your house) would be burnt, and you would be imprisoned or possibly even burnt alive. The Church saw the Inquisition as an effective tool in the fight against heresy, and it continued to use it, most famously in Spain during the fifteenth century and in Rome in the sixteenth century. The Inquisitors believed they were doing what was necessary to protect innocent people from the corrupting influence of heresy. Their legacy of fear, injustice, and a warping of the Christian message of love remains one of the darkest in the history of the Church.

The Man with the Plan: Innocent III

Possibly the pivotal figure of the twelfth and thirteenth centuries is Pope Innocent III. Elected in 1198, Pope Innocent had an extraordinary impact on papal power, was knee deep in the new knowledge that we will talk about in the next chapter, created much of the Church's response to heretical groups, held power during the Fourth Crusade, and approved the new religious Orders started by Francis and Dominic. In many respects, Pope Innocent *was* the Church in the twelfth and thirteenth centuries.

Nowadays popes tend to be older men who have served in the Church for many years, but not Lothar of Segni: He became Pope Innocent III at 37, while still just a deacon. He was pope from 1198 to 1216—eighteen eventful years for the papacy. Innocent followed a different route to the papal throne than did most of the people before him. He soaked up the new philosophy and theology being taught in the Paris schools—probably the first pope to do so—and later studied law at Bologna. Then he put all that book learning and legal knowledge to good use.

Like many Church leaders before him, Innocent was convinced that the pope should be the most important ruler in the Christian world, the one to whom all the other rulers looked for guidance. As he saw it, the most important role of a secular monarch was to aid the Church in its quest to bring more people to Christ and maintain a just society. Where other popes had moved in this direction, none had been able to stake as big a claim to secular power as Innocent. Here are some of the ways he went about it:

Papal States. Like many rulers, Innocent wanted to extend the boundaries of his rule. He built up the Papal States to be a principality of considerable size and strength, and he worked hard to keep other rulers from interfering in his lands.

Arbitrating conflicts. Innocent claimed the right to decide between two men who both claimed the German throne. He also intervened in a fight between the kings of England and France, saying he had the responsibility to rebuke any Christian who is committing a sin, no matter how high his rank. He also got involved in the fight over the Magna Carta, excommunicating the barons who had forced it on King John and even giving the king money to fight those barons.

Information gathering. Innocent had eyes and ears all over Europe in the form of papal legates. These were the pope's ambassadors and representatives to the courts of secular rulers. They gathered information on anything that might be of interest and regularly informed Innocent, making him probably the best-informed man of his time.

Declarations. Innocent also used those legates to spread the word about his own programs and pronouncements, but mainly he did this through mas-

Using the Sacraments as a Weapon

One of the most powerful weapons in Innocent's arsenal was the interdict, and he was not afraid to use it. An interdict is a prohibition that keeps believers from receiving the sacraments or Christian burial or participating in worship services. For a fervent Catholic, sacraments were the ways to mark important events in life, like marriage or death; they also connected the believer to the divine, such as in Mass. Innocent and other popes used it as a political tool to get kinds and emperors to do their bidding. For instance, in 1200, when King Philip of France tried to divorce his wife, Innocent placed an interdict on the whole country. Here's an excerpt from the order:

> Let all the churches be closed; let no one be admitted to them except to baptize infants . . .

Let [the clergy] recite the canonical hours outside the churches, where the people do not hear them; if they recite an epistle or a gospel, let them beware lest the laity hear them; and let them not permit the dead to be interred, nor their bodies to be placed unburied in the cemeteries. Let them, moreover, say to the laity that they sin and transgress grievously by burying bodies in the earth, even in unconsecrated ground.[3]

It worked, too. At first people just went about their business as usual, but after a couple of months the populace got so upset that Philip had to give in and accept Innocent's ruling just to keep peace within his own kingdom.

sive use of the chancery. The chancery handled all the correspondence coming into and going out of the papal government. The records of earlier popes are fragmented, but from Innocent's reign we know that at least six thousand letters were issued. With more than three hundred letters going out every year, Innocent was able to make his decisions known—and keep his power before everyone's eyes—easily and often.

Taking Stock of Popular Religious Movements

One of the thorniest issues with which Innocent had to contend was the growth of popular religious movements. Some of these groups were out and out hostile to the Church, such as the Cathars; others started as movements within the Church but then fell into heresy, like the Waldensians. There were many others. All of them together testify to the huge interest that people of the time had in finding a new kind of spirituality that would fit into their daily lives.

Innocent was sharp, and he recognized that Church leaders sometimes had pushed groups into heresy. For instance, he could see how rejection and humiliation had led Valdes and his followers to turn away from Church authority. Innocent worked hard to prevent similar occurrences and to bring many of these groups back into the Church. As long as they remained orthodox in their teachings, Innocent even went so far as to grant some of them the right to preach. He also made sure others in the Church complied with his rulings. When clergy members in one Italian city excommunicated all those in their parishes associated with movements advocating apostolic poverty, Innocent let them know in no uncertain terms that they had better look again because some of these groups had been approved by the Church. He wanted bishops to always be on the lookout for opportunities to reintegrate those sliding into heresy back into the Church, which is where most of them wanted to be, rather than pushing them out the door entirely.

Not that Innocent was soft on heresy—while he wanted to bring groups back into the fold, he was resolute in dealing with those that refused to recognize the Church's authority. Even with the Cathars, whose beliefs differed so much from those of the Church, Innocent at first wanted to use persuasion to convince them of the error of their ways. That way of thinking fell apart when a papal legate to the region of Languedoc was murdered in 1208, at which point Innocent authorized the Albigensian Crusade. It was a horrific use of force on the Church's part but not a step that Innocent took lightly.

Francis and Innocent

In 1210, Innocent had an audience with a group of laymen asking approval to live lives of apostolic poverty and wandering preaching. The leader of this contingent was none other than Francis of Assisi. When Innocent welcomed Francis with open arms, he gave a place within the Church to the lay desire for a new way to live the Christian life.

Innocent was moved by the purity of Francis's ideas, but he was also wily and wise. Francis was not off by himself at the fringes of society; he was right in the middle of that big push for holiness known as the *vita apostolica* that pervaded the twelfth and thirteenth centuries. Innocent knew that if he kept Francis and his followers in the fold, he had a much better chance of keeping them from developing the anticlerical tendencies that marked many of the other heretical groups of the time. This man, Innocent was convinced, could actually help combat the spread of heresy rather than helping to complete it.

Brother to All: Francis of Assisi

Francis was born in 1181, the son of the wealthy and successful merchant Peter Benardone. No one could have predicted that he would eventually give up his easy life to live in absolute poverty, but that is exactly what happened.

When he was in his early 20s, Francis began to feel that something was missing from his life, and as he thought about it over the next few years, he came to realize that the "something" was "nothing"—owning nothing, wanting nothing, and living just for God. Disturbed by his son's thinking, Peter hauled him before the bishop, hoping he could talk some sense into Francis. However, the boy had ideas of his own: he wanted no more of his father's money or the comfort it brought, so he stripped to the skin, handed the clothes to his father, and began his life of begging. Within a few years, he was out in the streets preaching repentance to the same people who had watched his transformation.

The popular image of Francis is of a man so gentle that even the birds would listen to him, but Francis attracted more than birds. Charismatic and forceful, he could set people on fire to give up all they had to wander the world as impoverished, homeless preachers. So many young men began flocking to his side that within a year, Francis realized he needed to give them instructions on how they were to live. He wrote a short Rule in 1209, but it was clear to him that with all the heretics preaching poverty and repentance, he needed some official approval, so he headed off to Rome to see Pope Innocent.

Today we talk about the Order that Francis started as the Franciscans, but he called them the Friars Minor, the lesser brothers. They did not live all in one place like most monks or focus on book learning. Francis wanted them to concentrate on being humble, preaching, praying constantly, and above all, following the ideal of poverty. Just as knights in the popular stories of the time devoted themselves to their ladies, so Francis devoted himself and his Order to what he called Lady Poverty. He ended up creating a new form of religious life: the mendicants—monks who renounced all possessions, were granted the right to beg for their bread in Church law, and were not bound to particular monasteries but to the Order as a whole. Making a choice for poverty often has more meaning for those not born poor, so it is no surprise that the early Franciscans came mainly from the merchant and aristocratic classes; the real news is that they came by the thousands.

Francis was more interested in being an example to his fellow monks than in making decisions about what they should do, and he showed this with his life. Twice he set out to preach to nonbelievers in foreign lands, and though he was turned back by circumstances beyond his control, his desire to reach out to others became central to the Order. In 1220, he resigned as the Order's leader and became a simple brother.

Four years later, Francis claimed that he had received the stigmata, miraculous markings on the hands, feet, side, or head—the same places that the Gospels report Jesus being wounded during his Passion. The stigmata was very painful for Francis, but he and those around him also understood it as a great blessing. Francis's pains lasted until he died in 1226. It only took two years for him to be canonized, but even that short time was not needed by most people, who began venerating him as a saint almost immediately after his death.

A Woman of Strength: Clare of Assisi

Clare was just 18 when she ran away from home to follow Francis in 1212. Like Francis, she left behind a life of privilege—an aristocratic family in Assisi. They disagreed heartily with her decision—her father even tried to drag her home by force—but she was determined, on fire to serve God by living in poverty. However, there was a catch: she was a woman, which at that time meant she should be enclosed, not wandering around preaching. As soon as Clare professed her vows as a nun, Francis sent her to live in a Benedictine monastery, where the sisters lived in luxury.

Clare was miserable. She did not want the comfortable Benedictine life; she wanted the hardship that Francis and his companions endured. She could not do much about being enclosed, but she decided that she could at least live in complete poverty within the monastery walls. So when Francis finished refurbishing a simple dwelling near the chapel of San Damiano in Assisi, Clare moved there as abbess of a new Order of nuns, the Poor Clares.

Determined that her Order would follow Lady Poverty just as the Friars Minor were doing out in the world, Clare decreed that her nuns would beg for charity and work with their hands in order to live. She rejected a Rule that seemed too easy and refused to accept gifts of property and income for her monastery, even when they came from the pope. The only thing she wanted was to be granted what she called "the privilege of poverty."

Despite her strength of will, Clare could not keep other houses of Poor Clares—and many sprang up even in her lifetime—from being forced to accept property, but she won the day for the women of San Damiano. In 1228, Pope Gregory issued an order granting the privilege of poverty to Clare and her companions, the first such order ever granted. The next pope, Innocent IV, wanted to soften the Poor Clares' approach to poverty, but again Clare held out, and two days before her death in 1253, she received Innocent's official confirmation of the Rule for her Order that included absolute poverty.

Preaching by Example: Dominic

Francis was not alone in thinking that people devoted to the Christian ideal needed to get out and live simple lives among the laity. When a thirteenth-century Spanish bishop and his assistant were traveling through southern

Women's Ways: Beguines and Anchorites

Clare committed her entire life to her quest for God, but not all women yearning for holiness wanted or were able to take the nuns' vows. A group called the Beguines, developed during the thirteenth century, offered women a life focused on God but not bound to monastery life. In fact, the Beguines fell somewhere between nuns and everyday lay people. They led lives of celibacy, worked to support themselves, engaged in acts of charity, and spent much time in prayer. However, they did not live under a Rule or take any permanent vows, and they could leave the community whenever they wished. For most of their history, they were not an organized group like the monastic Orders but simply a collection of individual communities. The Beguines produced quite a few mystics, people who claim to experience a deep level of communion with God. The sort of freedom that Beguines enjoyed was not common for women in those times, and it made many people in the Church uncomfortable. These women were not directly under any male control, and while some Church writers praised them for their lives of simplicity and devotion, others could not get past the idea that the women needed to be regulated more closely.

In fact, the whole Beguine movement came under suspicion as time went on. They were formally condemned by the Council of Vienne in 1312, and Pope Clement V decreed that women could no longer live this sort of common life without taking vows or working within an approved Rule—in effect, he told them to become nuns or get out. The prohibition against them was later relaxed, but most communities of Beguines eventually either converted into convents of approved Orders or made their way out of the Church altogether by joining forces with various heretical groups of their time. Still, a few have continued to exist to the present day, especially in Belgium.

While Beguines wanted lives of devotion but with more freedom than a monastery offered, some women in England sought God by giving up their freedom altogether. These women, called anchorites, gave a new twist to the old hermit idea: They lived alone but in small rooms attached to their parish churches. Many of them were actually sealed within those structures—they walked into the little room and then watched as the door was sealed up behind them so that they could never leave. Anchorites talked about their way of life as a "living death." In fact, prayers for the dying were usually said as the woman entered what would be her last home on earth.

So what did the anchorite do with her time? Pray, mainly. She was supposed to pray over every activity: getting up, washing, putting on her shoes, and so on. She ate little, probably only one meal a day, and practiced other forms of asceticism. Although she kept silent most of the time, the anchorite was not completely cut off from the world. She had a small window through which she could receive food and the other necessities of life, and she could talk with people there; in fact, since they were thought of as holy people, many anchorites spent time counseling people who came to them for advice. But the anchorite was not supposed to spend too much of her time talking or even looking out the window; that would be showing too much interest in the outside world that the anchorite had vowed to leave behind.

France, they saw how deeply Cathar ideas had affected the area, and they realized that the laity thought of the Cathar perfect as living much holier lives than the Catholic clergy. They decided to fight the Cathars on their own turf: they would go barefoot, sleep on the floor, eat only the simplest foods, preach the good news, and beg for their bread. When the bishop died, the assistant, Dominic de Guzman, continued the work they had started together.

Others began joining Dominic, and soon the Dominican Order had been approved by Innocent III. The Dominicans took a different tack than the Franciscans: they focused on preaching rather than on the spirituality of poverty, and to preach effectively, they needed to study theology and learn about the ideas that were affecting the Church. Dominic believed heresy had gripped the laity because they did not have enough instruction in the Christian faith to recognize heresy when they saw it, and he was sure that a firm understanding of theology was the best foundation for building a truly Christian life.

Dominic soon realized that his Order needed to do more than just combat the Cathars; they also needed to preach the gospel in a way that would reach all people, so he began sending out his friars two by two to do just that. The Order grew tremendously; within a generation they had spread across Europe and soon after could be found in non-Christian lands to the north, east, and south.

The reason the Dominicans, as well as the Franciscans, were so successful is that they met a need that traditional monasteries could not fill: they fit in with the urban culture taking off in the new towns. The Dominicans and Franciscans could live simply in the middle of a town and work with the people there, rather than being dependent on gifts of land and endowments as were traditional monasteries. In addition, unlike those traditional monks, they did not retreat from the world but rather lived in it and tried to change it.

Belief and Violence: The Crusades

Mendicant monks were not the only ones trying to change the world. Church leaders, secular rulers, and common folk alike came together in an attempt to change things in a far-off land they believed should rightfully be ruled by Christians—specifically, European Christians. The impetus behind the Crusades was the desire to free from the hands of infidels the land in which Jesus had lived and carried out his ministry. The Crusaders could not know that the

Living the Spirit: Popular Devotions

The desire for the *vita apostolica* and a more dynamic faith carried right on through the fourteenth and fifteenth centuries. Over and over, we see regular laypeople looking for more than Sunday Mass and access to the sacraments; they were looking for ways to reshape their thoughts and actions to be closer to God, ways to change their lives.

For some, the desire for a new spiritual practice stemmed from a feeling that their sins were overwhelming and that they needed to do penance to pay a penalty for them. But what if someone else could help them pay? Here is where indulgences came in. Think of it like a divine bank account of merit: When you sin, you take merit out of the account, and when you do something good, you add merit to it. Most of us try at least to keep things even, but the saints put in a lot more than they took out. This means that there is merit available for others to use. With an indulgence, the Church draws on this treasury of merit to cancel some or all of the penalty that a person would normally have to pay for sinning.

We first start hearing about indulgences being granted to Crusaders in the eleventh century in return for their military service. As time went on, indulgences were given both for service to the Church and for performing certain devotions. Soon gathering indulgences became itself a kind of devotion. By the fifteenth century, indulgences were actually being sold by the Church. As we shall see, this source of income led to a lot of corruption and the most serious protest the Church has ever known.

Living and Dying with Christ and the Saints

Some wanted to focus on identifying with the suffering of Christ, and this became a major emphasis in the popular devotions of the fourteenth and fifteenth centuries. Many turned to devotions like those that follow to help them in their meditations.

Pilgrimages. Going to pray at holy places was nothing new, but pilgrimages became much more popular around this time. You could travel as far as the Holy Land, the homeland of Jesus, or as close as the next town to a church that contained a saint's relic. In either case, you could get a sense of being in the presence of the divine in a way that you did not experience in your everyday life.

Stations of the cross. Tablets on the wall of the church showed pictures of events in the passion and death of Jesus, and by walking from station to station and meditating on each one, you could feel like a pilgrim following in the footsteps of Jesus.

Passion plays. Plays depicting the life and passion of Jesus had been around for centuries, but now their popularity hit a new high. The plays offered people a way to experience the story of Jesus rather than just reading about it.

The rosary. The meditation of the rosary developed over a couple of centuries until assuming its present form in the fifteenth century. Using prayer beads such as the rosary is not a practice restricted to Catholics; Muslims, Hindus, and Buddhists also use prayer beads to count repetitions of prayers. In all these traditions, the prayers are used as a kind of mental background noise that helps the person praying meditate on some aspect of the divine. In the Catholic tradition, the person praying will usually meditate on one of three sets of mysteries associated with the rosary: the joyous mysteries of Jesus' birth, the sorrowful mysteries of his death, and the glorious mysteries of his resurrection.

tensions and hatreds sparked by the conflict they were starting would erupt into tragedy so many times over the centuries to follow.

In the second half of the eleventh century, many Westerners headed out on pilgrimage to the Holy Land. The area was controlled by a Saracen group known as the Seljuks, and they were unhappy at this influx of European Christians. They began to make life difficult for the pilgrims.

In 1095, Pope Urban II decided he had heard enough of these stories, so he called on the French to liberate the land from Seljuk control. In doing so, he was also asserting his power over the French ruler, declaring the authority of a pope to get kings and princes to put their resources at the service of the Church. In fact, political power played a large role in all of the Crusades, but the slogan adopted for the First Crusade, *Deus volt!* or "God wills it!" gives us insight into what was in the hearts of the pope, the French king, and all the Crusaders.

The First Crusade was a military success; the Crusaders captured Jerusalem and other lands. They set up four kingdoms ruled by Western knights, congratulated themselves on a job well done, and then most of them returned home. However, the lands under Western rule were mainly along the coastline, and the Seljuks still controlled the inland, which inevitably meant more fighting. Six more Crusades aimed at taking control of the Holy Land were preached and fought over the next two centuries. Some had a little success and some were terrible failures, but in the end, the Westerners had to give up and the Saracens remained in charge.

In this history of tragedies, one of the greatest belongs to the Fourth Crusade. Innocent III wanted the Crusaders to conquer a port in Egypt that would serve as a base for another campaign against Jerusalem. Instead, the Crusaders got diverted and turned their destructive attention to the great city of Constantinople, where they had been asked to help a deposed emperor regain his throne.

The resulting devastation was far ranging: After setting fires, massacring Muslim citizens, and pillaging, the Crusaders completed their destruction during Easter week of 1204, leaving much of the city in ruins. Entire libraries and priceless works of art were destroyed, churches were plundered, and the beautiful Hagia Sophia suffered more damage from these Christian invaders than it would experience when the city was taken by the Turks in 1453. Even the great altar was torn apart so that the Crusaders could get to the gold and silver within it. Finally, one of the crusading nobles was appointed the new emperor, a situation that lasted until 1261.

Although Pope Innocent had protested at first, he decided after the fact that this was as good a way as any to get the Eastern and Western parts of the Church back together. He could not have been more wrong. History sees this as the final break, the moment when the divide between the two branches of Christianity became insurmountable. What trust could there be after this? What ties of Christian love could overcome this act of Christian violence?

The following table provides a snapshot of the Crusades: when, why, and how each went.

Crusade	When	Why Called	How It Went
First	1096-1099	Pilgrims' problems	French knights set up kingdom in Jerusalem and three other areas.
Second	1146-1149	Loss of one of the Crusader kingdoms to Saracens	Called by Pope Eugenius II and preached by Bernard of Clairvaux. Fought by French and Germans. Ended in total defeat.
Third	1187-1190	Saracen leader Saladin's conquest of Jerusalem	Fell apart when the French king took his knights and went home. English king Richard the Lionhearted negotiated treaty that permitted Christian pilgrims to visit the holy places.
Fourth	1201-1204	Failure to recapture Jerusalem during Third Crusade	Crusaders turned aside to Constantinople and ended up conquering a Christian city. Complete break of communion between East and West.
Fifth & Sixth	1228-1229	Wanted to capture Egypt, which would pave the way to recapture Jerusalem	After some initial success, ended in defeat, although an unstable kingdom was established in Jerusalem.
Seventh	1248-1254	Loss of Jerusalem in 1244 and vow of Louis IX of France to go on Crusade if he recovered from an illness	Terrible loss of life and money, with little to show for it. In 1270, Louis returned, wanting to finish what he had started, but both he and a son died on this Crusade.

Most of the time we hear about rulers and their knights in the history of the Crusades, but in two famous instances, it was everyday people, peasants on the one hand and children on the other, who took up the call to free the Holy Land.

When the First Crusade was being preached in 1095 and 1096, about fifty thousand people in Germany, including entire families with small children, were inspired by a wandering preacher called Peter the Hermit to march on Jerusalem. Along the way, the members of this People's Crusade, as it came to be called, directed their crusading zeal to the task of massacring thousands of Jews in German towns and ravaging the lands of Christians in Bulgaria. The group had become quite a bit smaller by the time they reached Constantinople, and when they landed on Saracen territory, most were killed. In 1212, tens of thousands of children from France and Germany felt inspired to make their own Crusade. They headed toward Italy, expecting that their innocence would be the decisive factor in God granting them victory when well-prepared armies had failed. What they got instead was a one-way ticket to slavery; unscrupulous traders boarded them on ships and then sold them for profit. Thus ended the Children's Crusade.

And All This Leads To . . .

The impact of the Crusades goes well beyond their military failure. We will see in the next chapter how contact with Arab civilizations profoundly affected the West's access to philosophical and scientific knowledge. In spite of the disaster of the Fourth Crusade and the final break between the Eastern and Western churches, the East and West actually got to know each other again. This helped prompt trade between the two former parts of the empire, which was a big help to Italian port cities. Since all those people traveling far from home needed a way to be able pay for things, the Crusades also were key in getting a money economy going in Europe. With so much aggression being turned toward the Saracens, the West experienced a significant drop in social tension. A European peasant now had to worry less about his lands being destroyed in a fight between warring lords.

The Crusades also got people thinking about what it means to fight a holy war and when violence may be used in the service of religious goals. Sadly, most decided in favor of force. This led to Christians feeling justified in using brutality to evangelize areas that were not traditionally Christian. Hatred of the Jews also became more prominent, leading to the expulsion of all Jews from England in 1290, from France in 1306, from Spain in 1492, and from Portugal in 1497.

Finally, the idea of the religious crusade became important in Western thought. Spanish Christians fighting the Saracens in Spain from the eleventh through the fifteenth centuries talked about it as a crusade; so did German Christians fighting the pagan Wends in the twelfth century and northern French nobles fighting the Cathars in the early part of the thirteenth century. It did not take long for popes to begin declaring crusades against any European leaders who challenged them. In the modern world, the word *crusade* remains a flashpoint between Christians and their Muslim and Jewish neighbors. When Christians hear "crusade," they usually think of fighting for a noble cause, but when Jews and Muslims hear it, they often think of outsiders' trampling on their religious beliefs.

The Holiest of Christians: Medieval Thinking about Mary and the Saints

Along with new ideas, the Crusaders brought back many relics from their sojourns in the Holy Land. A relic is a fragment of the body or clothing of a saint, believed to carry with it some of the saint's holiness. The practice of venerating saints skyrocketed during the Middle Ages. In fact, modern scholars have collected hagiographies (stories about saints) for more than twenty-five thousand saints who were venerated in one place or another during the Middle Ages. The upsurge of interest in saints even had an effect on the medieval economy. Pilgrimages to the sites of saints' tombs became extremely popular, and all those people traveling needed food and shelter, and therefore vendors to provide them. Those relics flooding in during the Crusades, and the even larger number of fakes, were an economic boon, too, because charging people to see or touch the relics brought in a tidy sum.

The Church has always made a clear distinction between the worship that is owed to God and the veneration that is appropriate for saints, but that does not mean the average peasant in twelfth-century Germany understood the difference. In times of need, people prayed to saints for help, believing they had the power to perform all kinds of miracles, from big things like curing disease to small things like helping someone find a lost object. When prayers were answered, people regularly missed the Church's theological point that the power to answer the prayer was given to the saint by God. Many people turned to saints because they thought of God the Father and Christ as being unapproachable, while the saints, however holy, remained people like us who understood everyday life.

No saint was more highly venerated than Mary. People felt they could turn to Mary for miracles and that she could appease the wrath of God. As a woman and a mother, Mary understood the pain of loss and would comfort and care for her children no matter what their sins. Theologians saw Mary as having a central role in redemption because she was the channel through which Christ came to the world. In the great cathedrals built during this time, there is much evidence of Mary and her power: she is shown as queen of heaven and earth, the one who presents her Son for the people's adoration, and the most important advocate on the Day of Judgment. Mary was seen as the ultimate combination of incredible power and incomparable love, which is why the line between venerating a holy human and worshipping a divine being was often crossed with Mary.

The Church Then and Now

Mary in the Modern Church

Modern Catholics and their medieval counterparts have much in common in terms of their devotion to Mary, but the way the Church talks about Mary has changed over the centuries. When medieval thinkers organized their understanding of God and the world into theologies, they described Mary's roles in the section that talked about Christ, but in modern theologies, Mary has her own unique place. Two things found in the modern works and not in the medieval ones are discussions of Mary's Immaculate Conception and her Assumption.

Calling Mary "the Immaculate Conception" means affirming that she was free from original sin from the moment she was conceived. Some medieval thinkers accepted this idea and others did not, but belief in this doctrine grew over time, and it was officially defined in 1854. The Assumption is the Catholic belief that Mary was taken bodily into heaven at the end of her life. Whether this occurred while she was still alive or after her death is a question the doctrine leaves unanswered. There is no mention of this in the Bible, and the idea seems not to have been known in the early Church, but it became widely accepted by the eighth century. The doctrine was officially defined under Pope Pius XII in 1950.

If you hear a modern Catholic theologian talking about Mary's role, he or she is less likely to be talking about these doctrines than about Mary as mother of the Church and mediatrix of grace. Catholics see Mary as the mother of all Christians because she is the mother of Christ, who brings about a new life in Christians. The bishops at Vatican II said that Mary cooperated by her obedience, faith, hope, and burning charity in the Savior's work of restoring supernatural life to souls. For this reason she is a mother to us in the order of grace. While the Church always affirms that Christ is the one Mediator between God and humans, it recognizes that others can be mediators when they bring people to God through knowledge and acceptance of Christ. Mary is understood as a mediatrix (the female version of mediator) because she gave her consent to the Incarnation, cared for Jesus during his years on Earth, shared in his suffering at his death, and continues this work after her Assumption.

Pope John Paul II, whose pontificate defined the Church at the end of the twentieth century and formed the Church that moved into the twenty-first century, was particularly devoted to Mary, speaking and writing much about her. He dedicated himself to Mary during his speech accepting the papacy and even took the phrase, "I am wholly yours, O Mary!" as his motto. He designated 1987–1988 as a Marian year, delivered a series of seventy short speeches on Mary between 1995 and 1997, and wrote an encyclical on Mary's role in the Church called *Redemptoris Mater* (*Mother of the Redeemer*). All of this has led to John Paul being known as the Marian Pope.

The "Hail Mary" is one of the basic prayers that all Catholics learn, and the rosary, which is dedicated to her, continues to be one of the most popular devotions in the Church. In different times and places, people have pictured Mary in ways that would speak to them. Some have thought of her as a great and powerful queen, others as a poor and humble young girl. The veneration given to Mary by Catholics is sometimes a stumbling block for those from other Christian traditions, but Mary's place at the heart of Catholic Christianity is solid.

Questions and Ideas for Understanding

1. What sorts of theological problems do you think the presence of two men claiming to be pope made for the Church?

2. If Valdes and his followers had been given approval to preach by Pope Alexander, do you think they would have ended up in the heretic category? If Francis had not been given approval by Pope Innocent, would he have been a heretic rather than a saint?

3. Read Francis of Assisi's "The Canticle of Brother Sun." Write an essay reflecting on why Francis is a hero to many in the modern environmental movement.

4. Research the ideal of the *vita apostolica* in the twelfth and thirteenth centuries as it was practiced both within and outside the Church, and write an essay explaining how political and social factors contributed to this movement.

5. Think about the persecution of Christians in the early Church and the persecution of heretics under the Inquisition. In what ways were they similar? The fears out of which they grew? The methods they used?

6. Look more deeply into the theology behind the Crusades. What in medieval Christianity supported this use of violence? What could have counteracted it?

Notes

[1] *Chronicon Universale Anonymi Laudunensis*, ed. Georg Waitz, in *Monumenta Germaniae Historica, Scriptores*, XXVI, 447. In *Heresies of the High Middle Ages*, trans. Walter Wakefield and Austin P. Evans. New York: Columbia University Press, 1991, p. 203.

[2] *Chronicon*, p. 204.

[3] Quoted in *A Source Book of Mediaeval History*, ed. Frederic Austin Ogg. New York: Cooper Square Publishers, Inc., 1972, p. 382.

10

Bringing It All Together
Thomas Aquinas and New Ways of Thinking

Chapter Overview

In this chapter, we will explore:

▶ Political breakdowns and cultural buildups

▶ Anselm, Abelard, and explaining God's existence

▶ Thomas Aquinas, the greatest medieval theologian

▶ The beginnings of universities

▶ The Church's teaching role

Alina: A Boy's Dreams in a Girl's Life

You are lucky and you know it. Most girls never learn to read and write, except maybe the ones who become nuns. Okay, boys from servant and peasant families do not usually learn either, but well-born boys like your brothers and their friends do. They go off to monastery or cathedral schools, while girls like you stay home learning how to sew or make candles. At least your mom taught you how to read using her book of Psalms. Your dad was not sure what use it was to teach girls these things, but he does not mind you reading his two books over and over again. Your friend Camille's mom lets both of you read wonderful romantic stories of brave knights and beautiful ladies from a book she has, but still you want more.

Why couldn't you go to the university, like your brother François? He has only been home once in the three years since he left for Paris, but on that visit you loved hearing him talk about the lectures and the books he had read on math, philosophy, logic. You long to be there yourself, but even François laughed at the idea of a girl sitting beside him in the lecture hall. "God gave you your place in life, little sister, and you just need to accept it." He said something like that every time you let slip how much you yearn to study and learn and open your mind and *think*.

Mom is always telling you that you have your head in the clouds, that you should pay attention to the things that really matter to a woman: running the household and raising children. You will need those skills once Armaund comes home next year. Your future husband has been away fighting the Crusades. You are not looking forward to the marriage—after all, you barely know Armaund—but that is how life goes for a girl. Until he comes home, though, you will spend your time imagining the world of François, the world of learning to which you will never belong.

The last chapter was all about what people were doing; this time around, we will be looking at what people were thinking. The twelfth and thirteenth centuries were an incredible time for big ideas. You had Dante creating a masterpiece of literature; Hildegard writing medical texts, morality plays, musical compositions, and much more; Thomas Aquinas teaching and writing a theology that would become foundational for the Roman Catholic Church; scholars working out new ways of doing philosophy, theology, and science; and universities springing up all over the place. A lot of this was made possible by the new learning of the time; okay, maybe it was not so new, because a good bit of it was more than a thousand years old, but to the Europeans rediscovering it as they came into contact with Arab civilizations in the twelfth and thirteenth centuries, it sure seemed new. We will look at all this, plus at how the Church understands its role as teacher. ■

Falling States and Rising Cathedrals

Kings and emperors kept wanting more power, but in the latter part of the thirteenth century, the end was in sight for the empires they had tried to build. German kings wanted to control the entire Germanic region, but the small principalities that made up the area refused to play along. The result? A weak king, independent principalities, and a messy situation that continued until late in the nineteenth century.

Italy was not faring much better. Although Innocent III had regained control of the Papal States, things were chaotic and later popes could not hold onto them. Moreover, it seemed like every European monarch wanted to rule Sicily. During the twelfth century, the island had been one of the wealthiest states in Europe, with a cultural richness garnered from its time as an Arab holding. However, in all the fighting over who should control it, the monarchs managed to destroy the prosperity that had made them all lust after the island in the first place.

Over in Spain, things were slightly more ambivalent. A Christian living in a Christian-controlled area probably caught the crusading spirit and wanted to help push the Moors out—exactly what the Christian rulers began doing in the thirteenth century, and with much success. But those living in one of the "recovered" areas, whether Christian or not, probably thought the whole thing was a disaster. The Muslim society being kicked out was more culturally advanced and more tolerant than the Christian society coming in, and the whole situation depressed the economy. Between the invasions and the Christian rulers' practice of letting all the land come under the control of a few powerful families, the new rulers managed to mangle the urbanization and great economy that had been the norm under the Muslims.

Farther east, people were dealing with yet more invasions, this time from the Mongols. When Genghis Khan came to power in the early part of the thirteenth century, he managed to gain control over what had been a bunch of disorganized tribes and started expanding his empire. The Mongols took over all of China and most of the Middle East before heading into Europe. There, they took over Russia as well as parts of Poland and Hungary and up to the borders of Germany before they turned back to the East.

While empires toppled, art was on the rise. Have you ever seen a Gothic cathedral? Gorgeous, with soaring spires and stained-glass windows, this cathedral style started in France, but before long it had spread throughout Western Europe. In the thirteenth century alone, a number of incredible Gothic cathedrals were built in Paris, Chartres, Reims, Amiens, Gloucester, Canterbury, Brussels, Bamberg, and Siena.

There were innovations in literature, too. A Crusader named Geoffroy de Villehardouin wrote an eyewitness account of the Fourth Crusade; what makes this interesting is that he did it in French instead of in Latin. People

Dante

When I had journeyed half of our life's way,
I found myself within a shadowed forest,
for I had lost the path that does not stray.

Inferno, Canto I[1]

That is how Dante's *Divine Comedy* begins. Parts of it are quite funny, but to Dante, "comedy" meant something that had a happy ending, not something that makes you laugh. For the good Catholic Dante, his poem had the happiest ending of all: a vision of "the Light that moves the sun and the other stars,"[2] otherwise known as God.

In the poem, Dante travels through Hell, Purgatory, and Paradise, talking to the people in each realm and finding out what got them there. He builds an entire structure showing what happens in the afterlife and how people's vices and virtues in this life affect their ultimate destination. The source of this structure? The Catholic theology of Thomas Aquinas's *Summa Theologica.*

Dante received his education at a Dominican church, where he learned about the teachings of Thomas, who began writing the *Summa* the year Dante was born. He uses Thomas's ideas constantly, picking up on ideas about what is good and what is sinful, how grace transforms and perfects human nature, and how the

entire cosmos is put together. Readers follow along as Dante goes down to Hell in the center of the earth (which is not just a place of fire: at the core is Lucifer, frozen by his lack of love), then back to the surface to the mountain of Purgatory. Dante climbs the mountain and then ascends through the planets and stars, all in their proper order, to the highest Heaven called the Empyrean. Following Thomas, Dante sees all of these realms as concentric circles, with Earth at the center and the Empyrean on the outside; this may sound like putting Earth at the place of honor, but it shows that Earth is the farthest point from the source of all truth and reality.

Dante may have been a faithful Catholic, but he was also critical of the Church. He put no fewer than seven popes in Hell, and even the great saints we see in Heaven often speak disapprovingly of what is going on in various parts of the Church back on Earth. Thomas, for instance, is happily hanging out in the sphere of the Sun, but Dante has him painting a scathing portrait of the greed of his fellow Dominicans. However, even in his criticism, Dante's ultimate concern is to show the truth of Catholic Christianity and how it contains and continues what God has revealed to the world.

were beginning to write in their native tongue. Others picked up the style, and before long, Dante was writing *The Divine Comedy* in Italian, as well as his defense of writing in the vernacular.

The New (Old) Knowledge

The best-known Renaissance is the tremendous revival of learning that occurred in the sixteenth century, but that is not the only time Western society has experienced a rebirth, which is what *renaissance* means. It also happened in the twelfth and thirteenth centuries, and this rebirth was big as well. New ideas were springing up and old ones being renovated—in education, society, law, politics, architecture, religion, philosophy, science, and literature.

The biggest catalyst for this was the rediscovery of works by Euclid on mathematics, Ptolemy on astronomy, Archimedes on engineering, Hippocrates and Galen on medicine, and Aristotle on just about everything. For centuries, most scholars in the West had not been able to read Greek, so many works by ancient Greeks simply went unnoticed. Starting in the tenth century, though, Westerners began to have increased contact with Saracens, who controlled Sicily and Spain. While the contact was often violent as Westerners tried to regain control of these regions from the Muslims, even violent contact is contact, and some European scholars began to learn Arabic. A happy side effect of this was bringing all those Greek works back into the European worldview. The Saracens, it turned out, had translated many Greek works into Arabic, and Western scholars jumped at the chance to translate them into Latin—which means they came to the Western world courtesy of double translations: once from Greek into Arabic, once from Arabic into Latin. That may not bode well for the accuracy of the texts, but it was still enough to prompt a revival of learning that got European scholars thinking in new ways about everything around them.

One of the astounding things about the rediscovery of so many of Aristotle's works was that they appeared in the West ready for use. The Saracens had not just been sitting on these works for all those centuries; some of their most exciting philosophers and scientists had pondered Aristotle's works and written commentaries on them, and these entered the West's cultural universe at the same time as the Aristotelian works themselves. It was like being handed a gallon of gas rather than a barrel of crude oil for your car: the commentaries made Aristotle's ideas immediately accessible.

Accepting the works of Aristotle and Euclid did not come without tension. Western Christianity had to deal with the fact that rediscovery of their own cultural past was coming via their biggest rival, the Islamic world. In other words, the Islamic world they were trying so hard to defeat was more culturally advanced than they were.

In addition, Aristotle and the other ancients were pagans. These treasures of philosophical and scientific thought were coming from persons who did not believe in Christ or accept the Bible as foundational. What were Christians supposed to do with Aristotle's optimism about the material world and avoidance of mystical explanations? How could they reconcile these with the Christian conviction of the time that the world is a vale of tears in which God works directly? Some simply could not. In 1210, certain of Aristotle's scientific writings were banned at the trendsetting University of Paris because they contradicted biblical explanations. This did not last long, though; by 1255, that same university not only allowed the teaching of Aristotle but actually required that all his works be taught. Aristotle became known to Western scholars as "the Philosopher," as though there was only one; his ideas, once deeply controversial, became so entrenched in Western thought that within a few centuries, those who contradicted his thinking were considered heretical. In the twelfth century, though, all this was just beginning.

Signs of Contradiction: Bernard of Clairvaux and Hildegard of Bingen

Two of the brightest stars in the twelfth-century European intellectual community were not part of this new learning. The rediscovered works of Aristotle had not yet permeated their world, and they played little or no part in the thinking of Bernard of Clairvaux and Hildegard of Bingen. No matter; these two had plenty of other things to think, speak, and write about, and neither was ever known to keep an opinion quietly to him- or herself. Bernard and Hildegard were signs of contradiction for their times: an abbot and an abbess whose vocation led them away from the world but whose lives led them right back into it.

Crusading Mystic: Bernard of Clairvaux

> [I] saw
> an elder dressed like those who are in glory.
> His gracious gladness filled his eyes, suffused
> his cheeks; his manner had that kindliness
> which suits a tender father
>
> *Paradiso*, Canto XXXI[3]

This is how Dante introduces Bernard of Clairvaux, whom he places among the highest souls in Paradise. Bernard was a remarkable man: an inspiring preacher, a mystic of love, an adviser to popes and kings, and perhaps the most powerful man of his time. Not everyone would have agreed with Dante's presentation of Bernard as a "tender father"; the man made enemies, in no small part because he was implacable against those whom he thought strayed from the narrow path.

We ran into Bernard a couple of chapters ago, heading up a monastery of the Cistercian Order. This was a role he cherished, but the monastery was simply too small for Bernard's big personality. Bernard was mentor to four popes and counselor to secular rulers as well. In other words, he had influence. For example, when one of the kingdoms set up during the First Crusade fell to the Saracens, Pope Eugenius III decided a new Crusade was in order. He made an official declaration to this effect in 1145 but had little luck generating any enthusiasm. Enter Bernard, a charismatic preacher and by this time a powerful abbot, as well as a friend and former teacher of the pope. Bernard went on a preaching tour, building support for the Crusade among both the nobility and the regular folk. It worked, and the Crusaders set off in 1147. While the Crusade was a disaster, it says a lot about Bernard's influence that he could gather support where the pope could not.

Bernard also preached against the various heresies of his day, especially against the Cathars, and when Anacletus and Innocent II both claimed the papacy at the same time, Bernard tried to convince people that Innocent was the proper pope. Bernard also found time for quiet and contemplation. He wrote hundreds of sermons, many works on the monastic life, and quite a few masterpieces of mysticism and theology. He wrote a Rule for the Knights Templar as well as a number of hymns.

Look at Bernard's writings and his life, and you will see that he was something of a contradiction. He was a big proponent of retiring from the world, but it would be hard to find anyone in the twelfth century who was more involved in it. He attacked his opponents in and out of the Church ferociously, but he was also a mystic and completely dedicated to the Virgin Mary. He could preach killing infidels one minute and write a beautiful reflection on love the next.

Writer, Preacher, and Twelfth-Century "Dear Abby": Hildegard of Bingen

Hildegard of Bingen had nothing like Bernard's power; she was simply a force of nature. That came later in life, however. Born in 1098, Hildegard was the last of ten children and, in her parents' view, a perfect tithe. So off she went to the convent at age 8. That may seem young to take on the nun's life, but little Hildegard had her first vision when she was only 3. She was still having them thirty-five years later when she became abbess of her convent.

Hildegard's life was filled with visions, but they did not come to her in pictures and words. She said she would see a brightness so great that her soul trembled, which led her to think of God as the "Living Light." At age 40, she felt called to start writing down her visions, and after one vision a couple of years later, Hildegard tells us that she suddenly "grasped the underlying meaning of the books—of the Psalter, the Gospels and other Catholic books of the Old and New Testaments."[4] Knowledge of Scripture was not the only thing that came to her this way. After another vision, she says, she began to compose music without having previously known anything about musical structure or notation.

Hildegard's visions attracted lots of attention. In 1147, she sent her major work, the *Scivias* (short for *Scito vias Domini,* which means "Know the Ways of the Lord"), to Pope Eugenius. The *Scivias* is both a record of Hildegard's visions and a work of theology in which she presents her teachings on the sacraments, monastic vows, salvation history, and the moral life. Eugenius was hugely impressed and declared the work to be inspired. This was a big deal; not many mystical or theological texts by women were accepted by the pope himself.

If this was all that Hildegard had written, she would be seen as an important theologian of the twelfth century. Hildegard, however, was prolific. Her writings include works of theology; books of medicine, natural history, and saints' lives; the first known morality play; musical compositions; and a huge number of letters. All kinds of people wrote asking her for advice—she exchanged letters with three popes and five monarchs, as well as other members of the nobility, Church leaders, and regular folk. She did not just sit around waiting to be asked for advice, either. If Hildegard thought someone was headed off the path of righteousness, she would write and tell him or her so in no uncertain terms, whether a nun in her convent or the German Emperor Frederick Barbarossa, whom she raked over the coals for supporting a schismatic pope.

Those not familiar with the long and rich Christian tradition of talking about God in female terms—and most modern people are not—may be surprised by Hildegard's writings. When she talks about God working in history, her imagery is masculine, but she presents God as feminine when speaking of the continuing divine presence in the world. Hildegard accepted the understanding of the time that women were weaker than men but saw no reason why that should mean that women were less important than men. On the contrary, she presented women as full participants in doing God's work in the world. As she writes in *The Book of Divine Works,* "Man is the work of God perfected, because God is known through him . . . But Man needed a helper in his own likeness. So God gave him a helper that was his mirror-image, Woman, in whom the whole human race lay hidden. And the man and the woman were thus complementary, so that the one works through the other . . . And man signifies the divinity of the Son of God, woman His humanity."[5]

Hildegard was just as much of a contradiction as Bernard was. She may have called herself "a foolish and uneducated woman,"[6] but she also claimed divine approval for her work. At a time when nuns were supposed to be enclosed, Hildegard went out on preaching tours, giving sermons in monasteries and churches. She was wildly unusual: an unordained person and a woman whose sermons were warmly received by abbots and bishops as well as the laity. Hildegard was certainly not a feminist before her time, though. Even given her activities, she believed wholeheartedly that women should not preach or be priests. She said of her own ministries that God had to work through the weakness of women only when the Church leaders who should be strong had fallen from their calling.

New Thoughts from New Thinkers: Anselm and Abelard

Bernard and Hildegard were not part of the new learning; Anselm of Canterbury and Peter Abelard were. Theologically speaking, Anselm and Abelard were in opposite corners on most issues, but both took traditional problems and came at them from fresh angles. They are part of a movement that historians call *scholasticism,* from the Latin word *scholasticus,* the title used for the head teacher who most often taught theology in a school.

What defines the scholastics as a group is not a common theology but a common method: the use of reason and logic in the service of theology. Scholastics took as their starting point that faith and reason are gifts from God, so any seeming contradiction just means there is a flaw in the logic somewhere. Where earlier theologians had been content to look at Scripture or the works of early Christian writers like Augustine for answers to questions about things like the purpose of life or God's existence, the scholastics tried to reason their way through these things. Not that reason was the be-all and end-all of truth in the scholastic worldview—reason, they believed, is not in error, but the way humans use it can be, so one must always check things discovered by reason against the yardstick of God's revealed truths.

"I Believe in Order to Understand": Anselm[7]

This statement from, Anselm's *Proslogion,* is probably his most famous even if it is really an echo of something Augustine had said almost eight centuries earlier. It is a great phrase for the man called the "father of scholasticism," and it describes Anselm's thought process perfectly: start with faith in what God has revealed, and then use reason as an aid to understanding those revelations.

What is the first and most important thing that God has revealed? That he exists. Anselm tried a number of approaches to proving God's existence, but there is one proof based solely on reason that has kept Anselm's name at the top of the charts for centuries. It is called the ontological argument (ontology is the philosophical study of being or existence), and Anselm starts it by looking at Psalm 14:1: "Fools say in their hearts, 'There is no God.'" Anselm uses this to move by logical steps to the conclusion that God must exist:

Now we believe that thou art a being than which none greater can be thought. Or can it be there is no such being, since the fool hath said in his heart, "There is no God"? But when this same fool hears what I am saying—"A being than which none greater can be thought"—he understands what he hears, and what he understands is in his understanding, even if he does not understand that it exists. For it is one thing for an object to be in the understanding, and another thing to understand that it exists . . . Even the fool, then, must be convinced that a being than which none greater can be thought exists at least in his understanding, since when he hears this he understands it, and whatever is understood is in the understanding. But clearly that than which a greater cannot be thought cannot exist in the understanding alone. For if it is actually in the understanding alone, it can be thought of as existing also in reality, and this is greater. Therefore, if that than which a greater cannot be thought is in the understanding alone, this same thing than which a greater cannot be thought is that than which a greater can be thought. But obviously this is impossible. Without doubt, therefore, there exists, both in the understanding and in reality, something than which a greater cannot be thought.[8]

Many people think there is something sneaky going on in this argument, but it is hard to figure out where it goes wrong. Bertrand Russell, a famous philosopher and atheist, said that one day while he was still a student, it came to him in a flash that the proof worked and God must exist—but later he recovered. Even where philosophers thinking through the existence of God have rejected the argument, most have felt the need to deal with it, and many—perhaps most famously Rene Descartes, whose "I think, therefore I am" was followed quickly by "I think, therefore God exists"—have used this argument in some form.

Anselm (1034–1109) was born in Italy, but he seemed always to be heading west: first to France as abbot of a monastery, then to England as Archbishop of Canterbury. However, the reason people still talk about Anselm has more to do with what he wrote than what he did. Anselm reasoned his way through a number of thorny theological issues, like the atonement, the Incarnation, predestination, and free will. One historian says that Anselm's most original trait is the "strong and serene confidence with which he explores the great mysteries of the faith,"[9] a confidence we see in his ontological argument. Anselm was not struggling with revealed truths or the corpus of Catholic tradition; instead, he started with a straightforward acceptance of these things and used that as grounding from which to work through them. Anselm was not trying to prove these things but to see where reason took him in understanding them.

"The First Academic"[10]

That is what a modern scholar has called Peter Abelard (1079–1142), who was probably the most brilliant philosopher and theologian of the twelfth century. Abelard's father wanted him to have a military career, but Abelard was not interested. He took to the road in search of an education and ended up in Paris, where he soon decided that he knew more than any of his teachers—as brilliant as he was, he probably did. So he set up his own school, and students flocked to his classes.

Abelard agreed with Anselm that reason was important, but he inverted the scholastic understanding that everything must be checked against revealed truth. Abelard believed reason took precedence over faith, or at least over what anybody said about faith. Many scholars wanted to quote some authority figure like a pope or an early Christian writer in response to any theological issue, believing that this solved the problem, so Abelard put together a work called *Sic et Non* (*Yes and No*) that brought together statements from many different Church authorities on 157 different issues of doctrine. The statements often contradicted one another, and that was Abelard's whole point: how could you just quote an authority to make your case if someone else could quote another authority and prove the opposite? He did not want to throw out the authorities, because he truly believed that what they had to say was valid, but he did think that a person had to go below the surface and look more carefully to find the underlying agreement between what the various authorities said on an issue.

Abelard made enemies. Some people thought he was just trying to cast doubt on the Church's authority altogether. *Sic et Non* was not itself the cause of these difficulties, but the basic methodology that Abelard used in it was: his questioning of what had been handed down. Anselm wanted to understand what had been revealed; Abelard wanted to look at it from different angles and see what happened. Bernard of Clairvaux disliked Abelard immensely and in 1141 hauled him before an ecclesiastical council on charges of heresy. With characteristic arrogance, Abelard refused to answer the charges and ap-

Coming to Terms with the Atonement

Medieval Christians agreed that Jesus' death made it possible for humans to be saved, but they were not sure how. Many believed people had put themselves in bondage to the devil by sinning; humans had to die so the devil could collect his due. But Jesus was different. Having never sinned, he was not bound; and as the Christ, he was a great prize for the devil. Christ did not have to die, but he offered himself as a ransom, agreeing to die and descend into Hell if the devil would set humanity free. The joke was on the devil, of course: Jesus died but then rose again, freeing himself from the bondage he had voluntarily embraced and leaving the devil with no absolute rights to any human soul.

Questions remained, however. Why did sin make death inevitable? Why couldn't God simply free humanity without Jesus having to die? Anselm of Canterbury thought that this theory gave too much power to the devil and wrongly made atonement an issue between humans and the devil. The problem was between humans and God, he argued. Humans owed God total obedience, but instead sinned. God could simply forgive humans, but then he would be letting his mercy take precedence over his justice. Humans owed God a perfect life, but even if someone managed never to sin, he

or she was already stained with original sin even before birth. On their own, humans were helpless. But God could do something by becoming human. Jesus was born without sin and lived a perfect life, so as a human he owed God nothing more. But he gave more – his life – and with that extra gift he paid the debt humans owed to God, redeeming them.

Peter Abelard, however, had little use for Anselm's idea: "How cruel and wicked it seems that anyone should demand the blood of an innocent person as the price for anything...still less that God should consider the death of his Son so agreeable that by it he should be reconciled to the whole world!" (*Exposition of the Epistle to the Romans*).[11] Atonement was not about satisfying some sense of justice on the part of God, argued Abelard, but about God's perfect love for humanity that inspired it to love him in return. God's love, he said, frees humanity from bondage to sin. Critics like Bernard of Clairvaux decided Abelard was a heretic who tried to turn Christ into nothing more than an example, leaving humanity to earn salvation on its own. But Abelard believed we can only love God because he first loved us – in other words, God's grace makes our love, and therefore our salvation, possible.

pealed to Rome; with characteristic self-righteousness, Bernard wrote to the pope that Abelard was a persecutor of the faith, an enemy of the cross, a man who perverted doctrine and of questionable morals to boot. Bernard won the day and Abelard was excommunicated, but later reconciled with both the Church and Bernard. Abelard rightly felt misunderstood: Those who battled him disliked his belief that reason is necessary as a starting point in theology, but they also missed his belief that faith is the necessary starting point for life and salvation: "I do not want to be a philosopher if it means resisting St. Paul; I do not wish to be Aristotle if it must separate me from Christ."[12]

Angel and Ox: Thomas Aquinas

Those are just two of the names that Thomas Aquinas was called. He is the Angelic Doctor (as in "Doctor of the Church," a title given to some of the most important theologians in the Church's development) whose writings go right to the heart of how Catholicism understands God and the world, and he is the dumb ox who kept so quiet as a student that people thought he was physically unable to speak. No one ever accused Thomas of having charisma, but his work laid the foundation for the way Catholic theology has developed ever since.

Born in the Italian town of Aquino in 1225, Thomas did not stay little for long: At least part of that "ox" comment had to do with his size, and there is a story that in his later years he was so round that a semicircle had to be cut out of the table so he could get close enough to eat. At age 6, his parents sent him to live in a monastery, where he stayed for nine years—until a political situation forced all the monks to leave. By then, his family had begun to recognize his intellect, so they sent him to the University of Naples, where he got a glimpse of the philosophical and scientific works starting to spread around Europe.

While in Naples, Thomas also became acquainted with the Dominicans. Their passion for God and for learning hooked him early. Although his parents had wanted him to be a monk, this was not what they had in mind. As an aristocratic family, they had hoped their son would become a Benedictine monk, maybe abbot someday, in a prestigious monastery—not some impoverished wandering scholar. Thomas's family hoped he would outgrow this phase, so his brothers kidnapped him and took him to a fortress, where he stayed for more than a year. However, Thomas proved to be just as stubborn as an ox, too, and he would not change his mind. Eventually the family had to give in.

Thomas's Dominican superiors sent him to Paris to continue his studies, and it was in Paris that everything began to come together for him. He studied under a professor named Albertus Magnus, one of the greatest teachers of his time and the first important scholar of Aristotle in the West. Thomas had come across Aristotle before, but now he began to see how he could use Aristotle's philosophy in bringing reason and faith together.

Thomas finished his studies and started teaching in Paris, where he died in 1274 when he was only 48. About a year before that, though, he had a mystical experience, a vision of something so sublime that he stopped writing altogether—this from the man who wrote so very much. When a friend asked him to get back to his work, he replied, "I can write no more. I have seen things which make all my writings seem like straw."[13] But before that, Thomas had written an extraordinary amount: commentaries on Scripture; philosophical treatises and expositions of Aristotle's writings; sermons, prayers, and hymns; works on politics; and three theological syntheses. In these works, he developed theories of logic, metaphysics, theology, psychology, ethics, and politics that still have an impact on thinkers to this day. Moreover, he spent years working on maybe the greatest enterprise in Christian theology ever: the *Summa Theologica*.

Work, Work, Work

If you squeezed all of Thomas's thought into a bottle, the label would say *Summa Theologica*. The *Summa Theologica*—usually just called the *Summa*—was Thomas's attempt to deal with every major aspect of Christian theology. It tries to answer 630 theological questions in depth, which means it is massive: one modern edition runs to more than 3,200 pages.[14] But as big as it is, it is not complete—Thomas was not able to get through everything he had planned before his death.

The method Thomas used to answer all these questions was unique. In *Sic et Non,* Abelard had shown how various authorities did not always seem to agree on a subject and then left it to the reader to figure out what to do with all those different opinions. Thomas modified this approach: first he laid out the issue, then he presented all the different authorities whose words seem contrary to what he was finally going to conclude. This is not so different from Abelard up to here, but where (in his writing, at least) Abelard had left the final resolution of the issue up to the reader, Thomas laid it all out. He used reason to come up with an answer and then refuted each of the objections he had laid out earlier. In the course of the *Summa,* Thomas dealt with ten thousand objections this way.

Thomas's reach was massive; the only other thinker in the Church's history that we can compare to him is Augustine, whose work Thomas turned to more frequently than that of any other Christian writer. However, the two had fundamentally different ways of going about their work. Augustine was all about practicality, trying to deal with issues that arose in the course of his work as a bishop. Thomas was all about logic, attempting to create a logical intellectual system of Christianity. Where Augustine reaches back to the works of the Neoplatonists for many of his most basic understandings, Thomas goes right to Aristotle, whom he usually just calls "the Philosopher." Aristotle created precise definitions and moved from point A to point B in clearly laid out logical steps, a system that Aquinas picks up and applies to theology.

This is not to say that Thomas in any way wanted to put reason above faith. Rather, his life's work was to bring the two together, a synthesis he pulled off brilliantly. Even within the synthesis, though, Thomas always believed reason cannot take one to salvation; for that, faith and revealed truth are necessary.

In all of his writings, Thomas worked with the belief that faith and reason are completely compatible. Anselm had put reason in the service of theology, but Thomas did not think you needed to make one subservient to the other because they fit together perfectly. Knowledge and revelation, theology and philosophy, traditional understandings and new ideas—all of these things could be reconciled if you just looked at them properly. We saw back in chapter 3 that Origen and Tertullian clashed over what sorts of knowledge could be useful to Christians, but Thomas had no doubts on the subject: use it all, he says, because all knowledge comes from a divine source.

Not everyone was thrilled with Thomas's work. He made big use of Aristotle, but some Church leaders thought the pagan philosopher's ideas were contrary to Christian faith. Thomas, however, was sure the problem lay in the ways some scholars were using Aristotle's ideas. He did not accept everything Aristotle said at face value; he worked hard to figure out how those rational and scientific ideas fit in with faith. Still, three years after Thomas died, thirteen of his teachings were condemned as heretical by the masters of the Parisian school. However, the orthodoxy and downright usefulness of Thomas's writings soon became clear, and by 1309, his work was the standard for all Dominican thought and eventually became a major grounding for the development of Catholic doctrine.

Making the Grade: Medieval Universities

Thomas Aquinas and Abelard were brilliant examples of the heights to which a medieval education could take you, but they were certainly not the norm. In fact, just getting an education in the Middle Ages could be rough going. You did not simply traipse down to your local public school at age 7 and then

Voices from the Past

Thinking about the First Mover

▶ Author: Thomas Aquinas

▶ Written: Late-thirteenth century

▶ Audience: Beginners in Catholic Christian Faith

Here is one of the most famous passages in the *Summa,* where Thomas Aquinas goes down Anselm's road of trying to prove the existence of God. Thomas comes up with five different ways of doing this; here is the first:

Objection 1. It seems that God does not exist; because if . . . God existed there would be no evil discoverable; but there is evil in the world. There-fore God does not exist.

Objection 2. Further, it is superfluous to suppose that what can be accounted for by a few principles has been produced by many. But it seems that everything we see in the world can be accounted for by other principles, supposing God did not exist . . . Therefore there is no need to suppose God's existence.

On the contrary, It is said in the person of God: "I am Who I am" (Exod.iii.14)

I answer that, The existence of God can be proved in five ways.

The first . . . is the argument from motion . . . [It is] impossible that . . . a thing should be both mover and moved, i.e., that it should move itself. Therefore, whatever is in motion must be put in motion by another. If that by which it is put in motion be itself put in motion, then this also must needs be put in motion by another, and that by

another again. But this cannot go on to infinity . . . Therefore, it is necessary to arrive at a first mover, put in motion by no other; and this everyone understands to be God.[15]

Here is a snapshot of Thomas's other four arguments:

- The First Cause: Every effect has a cause, which is in turn the effect of another cause. This cannot go on forever, so there must be a First Cause.

- The Necessary Being: Everything that exists was at some point just a possibility that later came into being. There was a time in the past when none of these possibilities had yet come into existence. But things exist now, so something which was necessary, not just a possibility, must have made them come into existence.

- The Standard of Perfection: We talk about things having more or less truth or goodness, but for us to understand these distinctions there must be something that is the maximum of truth and goodness.

- The Intelligent Designer: Things in the world act in certain orderly ways, like the laws of nature. But something must have laid out what those laws would be. ■

around age 18 decide where you wanted to head for college. People often had to leave their hometowns to receive any kind of education, and the in-depth learning of a university might lie days or even weeks away from your family home.

If you were a typical person of the thirteenth century, you would probably be a peasant in a small village who spent little or no time thinking about any kind of book learning. However, if you were just a little less typical—if your parents were merchants, say, or artisans—and you happened to live in town, then you at least had a chance that your parents would send you to the school at the local cathedral to learn Latin and a little math. (That is, if you were a boy. There were far fewer schools, and far fewer parents, willing to spend the money for girls' education.) A few centuries back, you might have been sent to a monastery school, but by the twelfth century, many monasteries had decided to limit their monks' contact with the outside world, getting rid of their schools for nonmonks in the process. Cathedral schools, on the other hand, were set up mainly for secular students. They taught the basic reading and math skills that a merchant or craftsman might need, and by the late twelfth century, some were teaching higher-level subjects—the first inklings of universities. Teachers at these schools were usually independent, which means that if they got the urge (like Abelard did) to set up their own schools, they could just go rent some rooms and do it—and if you the student liked that teacher, you probably went with him. Why was it so easy to move? Because the schools did not have libraries, laboratories, museums, or buildings of their own—just a teacher whom you hoped actually knew something you wanted to learn.

Originally, a university was just a group of students and teachers who banded together to form a guild, which is like a labor union. The first *university* (short for the Latin phrase *universitas magistrorum et scholarium,* meaning "the whole community of masters and scholars") was set up in Bologna, Italy, when a group of students figured out that the townspeople were doing a little price-fixing at their expense. They decided that if they all worked together and threatened to leave, they could get some more reasonable prices set and it worked. In fact, animosity with the locals was a fact of life for medieval students. In some areas, battles between townspeople and students happened more or less regularly, with people on both sides ending up hurt or dead, but most of the time the tensions stayed under control.

From the twelfth century on, universities popped up all over the place. Peter Abelard and his students were laying the foundations for the University of Paris. Oxford had started to turn into a university town by the end of the century, with Cambridge going the same way just a few decades later. By the end of the Middle Ages, there were at least eighty universities spread around Europe.

Education was entirely lectures, with the teacher seated in a chair while students sat on the floor at his feet. The teacher would explain a text word by word and then discuss opposing views about the subject. Students would rent the pages of the lectures from a local bookstore and copy them by hand. There were no written assignments, but students were expected to take part in debates, which were all in Latin. In fact, everything was done in Latin, so

A Sign of Transformation

By the third century, the welcoming ceremony in most Christian communities included both baptism by water and a laying on of hands that bestowed the Holy Spirit on the person. As Christian communities grew bigger and priests took over more and more of the work that bishops used to do, the two parts of the ritual were separated in many places. A priest could perform the baptism, but only a bishop, as successor to the apostles, had the authority to confer the Holy Spirit, which is what the sacrament of confirmation is understood to do.

It took awhile for the confirmation ritual to be performed in the same way throughout the Church. In ninth-century France, bishops fighting local nobles in order to protect the Church's rights wanted to change the way some things were done, but they had to be able to show that the change was already Church practice in Rome. Around 850, some clerics decided to "discover" the needed proof. They put together a collection of letters and decrees—some real, some falsely attributed to early councils and popes, some flat out forged—that

gave them the rights they needed. A couple of the documents said that people needed the laying on of hands by a bishop in order to be full participants in the life of Christ. The statements actually came from the preaching of a fifth-century bishop, but they got passed off as being in letters from two popes, one from the third century and one who never even existed. But the "discovery" was so successful that it was soon accepted as law all over Europe.

Medieval theologians were clear that confirmation was needed, but they had a hard time explaining exactly what it did. It could not give a person anything necessary for salvation—that all came through baptism. Some thought it gave Christians extra strength to fight off temptation; others, like Aquinas, said it gave Christians the grace needed to achieve spiritual perfection. Nowadays, Catholic theologians talk about confirmation as a sign of interior transformation: The person experiencing the ritual recognizes the Holy Spirit's presence in his or her life and is publicly proclaiming that he or she has decided to live out what it means to be a Christian.

regardless where you attended, you would still be able to understand the readings and lectures and talk to the other students. It is no coincidence that *university* and *universal* have the same Latin root, *universus,* meaning "whole" or "entire": being part of a university meant being part of something more encompassing than any local school could ever be.

The Church Then and Now

Teaching God's Truth

Some Christian groups say they only teach what the Bible says (although we have seen repeatedly that different interpretations lead to different teachings), but Catholics also believe that God's interaction with and revelation to humanity continues. From this perspective, somebody has to be in charge of figuring out and passing along what God continues to reveal, and that is where the *magisterium* comes into play.

Today we use the term *magisterium* from the Latin word *magister,* meaning "one who teaches and has authority," to refer to the right and responsibility of bishops to teach what God has revealed, a role that Catholic theology says bishops derive from their place as successors to the apostles. *Magisterium* also refers to the bishops collectively as the bearers of this responsibility. In Catholic understanding, it is always God who reveals the truths of the deposit of faith (the things that God has revealed for human salvation); the role of the magisterium is to help humans understand it. The Vatican II document *Constitution on Divine Revelation (Dei Verbum)* puts it this way:

> The task of authentically interpreting the word of God, whether written or handed on, has been entrusted exclusively to the living magisterium of the Church, whose authority is exercised in the name of Jesus Christ. This magisterium is not above the word of God, but serves it, teaching only what has been handed on, listening to it devoutly, guarding it scrupulously, and explaining it faithfully by divine commission and with the help of the Holy Spirit; it draws from this one deposit of faith everything which it presents for belief as divinely revealed. (*Constitution on Divine Revelation,* no. 10)

All of this is based in the understanding that while God's revelations are made *for* all people, they are not immediately evident *to* all people. If it were evident, everyone would agree and that would be that. But one quick look at a book on world religions, or even a glance at the Churches section in any phone directory, shows that people most emphatically do not agree, nor is everyone interested in trying to work it all out for themselves; most people take much on faith when it comes to their beliefs. Christians take the Bible on faith; they did not experience the events described or even know the authors, nor do they know the people who wrote the Nicene Creed or worked out other Christian doctrines. The same is true of peoples of other religions when they look at their own sacred writings and the doctrines that have developed over the centuries. The teaching authority of the magisterium is the Catholic answer to the question of who to trust in matters of faith.

The bishops collectively make up the magisterium; does this mean that individually they have all this teaching authority? What about when they disagree? There are different levels of magisterial authority.

ordinary magisterium	Exercised by individual bishops, including the pope; bishops have this teaching authority but not the promise that what they teach is infallible.
ordinary universal magisterium	The authority bishops have when they collectively maintain a bond of unity with each other and the pope and teach in accordance with Church doctrines. Teachings at this level are guaranteed to be infallible; the teaching authority of ecumenical councils like Vatican II is in this category.
extraordinary magisterium	When an ecumenical council solemnly defines a doctrine or when the pope speaks in a way that fits the requirements for infallibility, they exercise this level of authority.

Catholics are expected to accept teachings of ordinary magisterium, but they are required to accept those of the ordinary universal and extraordinary magisterium. Not to do so is to step totally outside of Catholic teaching and to reject the Church's authority.

Questions and Ideas for Understanding

1. Do you think a medieval Christian would find Bernard of Clairvaux to be something of a contradiction because he preached love, mysticism, and violence? Why or why not?

2. What does it mean to believe something first and then seek to understand it afterward? What sorts of things do most people today believe without understanding? What about things in areas outside of theology, like science?

3. Research one circle (one level of sin) in Dante's *Inferno*. In a short essay, explain how the sin goes against Catholic teaching as expressed in Thomas's *Summa* and how the punishment of the sinner fits the sin.

4. Write your own version of a *Summa* question-and-answer strategy: Start with a proposition; next, lay out every item you can think of refuting that proposition, then each one supporting it; finally, show the conclusion to which you come and how you have overcome every opposition to it.

Notes

[1] Dante, *Inferno,* trans. Allen Mandelbaum. New York: Bantam Books, 1980, Canto I, pp. 1–3.

[2] Dante, *Paradiso,* trans. Allen Mandelbaum. New York: Bantam Books, 1983, Canto XXXIII, p. 145.

[3] Dante, *Paradiso,* trans. Allen Mandelbaum. New York: Bantam Books, 1984, p. 281.

[4] Hildegard of Bingen, *Secrets of God: Writings of Hildegard of Bingen,* trans. Sabina Flanagan. Boston: Shambhala, 1996, p. 9.

[5] Hildegard of Bingen, *Secrets of God,* p. 70 (1.4.100).

[6] Quoted in Barbara Newman, *Sister of Wisdom.* Berkeley: University of California Press, 1987, p. 34.

[7] Anselm, *Proslogion,* trans. Eugene Fairweather. In *A Scholastic Miscellany.* Philadelphia: Westminster Press, 1956, p. 73.

[8] Anselm, *Proslogion,* pp. 73–74.

[9] David Knowles, *The Evolution of Medieval Thought.* Baltimore, MD: Helicon Press, 1962, p. 100.

[10] Anders Piltz, *The World of Medieval Learning,* trans. David Jones. Totowa, NJ: Barnes & Noble Books, 1981, p. 53.

[11] Peter Abelard, *Exposition of the Epistle to the Romans.* trans. Eugene Fairweather. In *A Scholastic Miscellany.* Philadelphia: Westminster Press, 1956, p. 283.

[12] "Confession of Faith." In *The Letters of Abelard and Heloise,* trans. Betty Radice. New York: Penguin Books, 1974, p. 270.

[13] G. K. Chesterton, *Saint Thomas Aquinas.* New York: Image Books Doubleday, 1956, p. 141.

[14] Thomas Aquinas, *Summa Theologiae,* Vols I–IV. Taurini: Marietti, 1948.

[15] Thomas Aquinas, *Summa Theologica* I:2.3, English Dominican trans. New York: Benziger Brothers, 1947. In *Readings in Christian Thought,* ed. Hugh T. Kerr. Nashville, TN: Abingdon Press, 1990, pp. 112–113.

11
Changing the Rules
Re-Forming Christianity

Chapter Overview

In this chapter, we will explore:

▶ New feelings of nationalism and the birth of the Renaissance

▶ Luther and the call for change in the Church

▶ The Protestants and their Reformations

▶ The Catholic Reformation

Michael: Being Catholic in a Protestant Land

You shut the door of the shop behind you with a sigh of relief—it is finally your half-day off! You like working with the printer, and you know that in a few years you will be able to open your own print shop. Your father has been setting aside money to help you begin the business; combined with the wages you have saved as an assistant, you almost have enough to buy your own press. A few more years and you will be able to afford a set of printing blocks, too. Then maybe you will think about taking a wife.

All this runs through your head as you walk down the street to the pub to meet your friends. You already know what they are talking about—Lord Wilhelm's declaration that all churches in his lands are to be reformed like the churches in Saxony. Priests are no longer required to be celibate; bishops may not hold public office; people do not need to confess their sins to a priest; and instead of receiving only the bread at the Eucharist, they have begun drinking the wine as well. These are big changes, and no doubt more will follow. Your friend Gunther believes strongly in these changes—he calls them reforms. He says that Christians are getting back to the Church of the New Testament. He has read many of Dr. Luther's pamphlets and thinks they tell God's truth. Hans, on the other hand, is just as sure that Dr. Luther is wrong to stand against the Church. "Lord Wilhelm is bringing the downfall of true Christianity in the principality," Hans says.

Your own views fall somewhere in the middle. You know the Church needs to change—your local bishop has lived like a rich man while the poor are taxed to pay for it, your parish priest has a mistress and two children, and both the bishop and your pastor urge people to pay for indulgences rather than to repent and turn to God. On the other hand, people's mistakes cannot change the fact that God is present in the world through the Church and its sacraments. You do not think it right that Lord Wilhelm should make people break communion with the Church—you and everyone else are being forced to fall in line with the Protestants, even if you do not agree with them. How can believers hope to live a Christian life if they cannot even love one another?

In the sixteenth century, many people faced the same dilemma that Michael faced. As the Protestant Reformations rolled across Europe, rulers often took it upon themselves to decide how Christianity should be practiced in their lands. Some places became solidly Protestant, others remained firmly Catholic, and still others wavered, leaning toward Protestantism early on but returning to communion with the Church once the Catholic Reformation revitalized it. We will take a look at all these changes and at one of the many results of these Reformations: the different ways that Protestants and Catholics understand what it means to be Church. ■

Plagues, Problems, and a Rebirth

Everything was changing in the fourteenth century—the economy, the importance of city vs. rural life, the expectations of workers, political alliances. The biggest reason for all this change was the appearance of the bubonic plague, an illness so horrible that it has become known as the Black Death. The plague first hit Europe in 1347, carried there by Italian ships returning from trade runs along the Black Sea. It was spread by fleas that had feasted on the infected blood of rats. People had no immunity to the illness and no idea how to treat it, which meant they died in droves: more than a quarter of the population of Europe was wiped out in just three years. The epidemic tapered off but resumed less than ten years later, and then again a decade after that. By the last part of the century, outbreaks were less frequent and less severe, but they still had enough power to keep populations low for more than a century. People were terrified and hysterical. Some decided life was too short to worry about anything, so they lived just for pleasure; others thought God was punishing society for its sins and felt the need to do extraordinary penance. The latter included the flagellants, bands of men and women who wandered from town to town beating themselves with sharp-tipped whips as a way to call people to repentance.

Around this time, we also see the beginning of a climate shift so severe that it has come to be called the Little Ice Age. This shift led to record crop failures, meaning food was sometimes scarce. Even so, the plague had wiped out so many people that there were still not enough agricultural workers to keep everything running.

There were other impacts as well, good for some, not for others. With more jobs available than people, workers could be choosy and demand higher wages. Landowners were squeezed and started asking for money from their tenants, instead of the services they had always accepted before. Some peasants revolted against the landowners' demands, while others got tired of the situation and moved to the cities, but life was not necessarily better there. The new urbanites found high unemployment and much tension between rich and poor.

Even with people streaming in from the countryside, overall lower population meant that cities were becoming smaller and poorer in the fourteenth and fifteenth centuries. Combine this with entire villages disappearing due to plague, famine, and general unrest, and we have a situation rulers do not like: decreasing revenue. Many rulers began demanding taxes, a decidedly unpopular move. However, the money had to come from somewhere, and trade was stagnant.

If you lived in England or France during this time, the economy looked worse because those countries were caught up in the Hundred Years' War. The war started in 1337 when the French decided they had had enough of England controlling the French region of Aquitaine. The French king, Philip VI, attacked Aquitaine, and the English king, Edward III, responded by claiming he was the true heir to the French crown through inheritance from his mother. Things deteriorated from there, and the war dragged on for more than a hundred years. It ended in 1453 with the English having lost almost all their properties in France. Still, the war was harder on the French than on the English as it was fought almost entirely on French soil.

In Spain, things did not look so bad—if you happened to be Christian. If you were a Jew or a Moor, however, life was downright grim. In 1492, the Spanish rulers Ferdinand and Isabella retook southern Spain from the Moors who had controlled it for centuries and expelled all the Jews from Spanish territory. That same year they sent Columbus on his voyage to the New World, where many native peoples would soon have reason to curse the coming of the Christians.

By the beginning of the sixteenth century, things were looking better. The population was increasing, with most of that increase taking place in small villages. Even with the migration of peasants into cities, 85 percent of the people still lived and worked in rural communities. In addition, throughout Europe people were beginning to identify themselves as citizens of nations, rather than just of their local communities—something made easier by the fact that the nations themselves were taking shape. A whirlwind tour of Europe at the beginning of the sixteenth century would find France and England more or less set, Switzerland coming along nicely, and Spain and Portugal now colonial powerhouses. However, Eastern Europe remained disorganized, and in Italy, rather than national unity, there were separate political units bickering among themselves.

The situation in Germany was ugly, with the area divided into more than a hundred principalities. There was still a Holy Roman Emperor, but he was not in Rome and did not have much of an empire. He was elected by the leaders of the seven most powerful principalities, but they still ruled their own roosts; the other ninety-three or so principalities did their own thing as well. The whole business was unstable because the emperor, principalities, and free German cities formed constantly shifting alliances as they fought each other.

As we will see, it was in the midst of these little divisions that the big division in the Church came about.

Old Ideals Made New Again: The Renaissance

After the horrors of the Black Death and the scandals in the Church, people were facing a crisis of values. They were trying to figure out what should be the central force in society and what ideas should guide a person's life. The questions were not new, but they took on new life as people began thinking more about human capabilities in this world than about what happens in the next. This emphasis on human ability and potential is called humanism, and it kicked off an intellectual movement called the Renaissance. As they explored the role of the individual in society, writers and thinkers looked to the ancient Greeks and Romans, whose learning had been held up as the highest point of human achievement. They decided the ideals expressed in classical literature and ancient civilization were better than what they saw around them, so they tried to reinvent those ideals for their own time. This is what gave us our concept of the "Middle Ages": scholars and intellectuals wanting to reconnect with ancient learning began thinking about the centuries between the fall of Rome and their own time as a low point in history. What drove the Renaissance was the desire to bring civilization to a new peak.

This was a time of enormous creativity, and literature, music, art, and architecture soared. This was the time of Michelangelo, Leonardo da Vinci, and many others whose genius is still recognized. After centuries devoted to the works of Aristotle, other Greek philosophies like Platonism and Neoplatonism were once again on the must-read list. While known, these works had not received much attention in recent centuries. Now all that was changing as scholars put together better editions of classical Greek and Latin texts and broadcast them widely, thanks to the printing press.

Looking with new eyes through all these ancient texts, scholars began to notice many disagreements over scientific facts and theories. This led to a scientific push as scholars began trying to work out the theories for themselves. The sense of renewal did not stop at the doors of the university, either.

Nations were developing more sophisticated ideas about diplomacy, and political theory was a hot topic. The Middle Ages were gone and with them the time when European society was more concerned with the prospect of heaven than with the realities of life on earth.

Papal Brawls: The Babylonian Captivity, the Great Schism, and Beyond

The fourteenth and fifteenth centuries were the great age of papal scandals. First came a series of popes who were under the thumb of the French king, a situation known as the Babylonian Captivity of the papacy. Then came the Great Schism, a ridiculous situation in which no less than three people claimed to be pope at the same time.

At the beginning of the fourteenth century, most of the power and influence Innocent III had gathered a century before was gone, but Boniface VIII (1294–1303) was determined to turn that around. A lawyer and diplomat, Boniface managed to restore order to the Papal States and the Church's finances and tried to help resolve both the Hundred Years' War and Italian wars being fought at the time. However, Boniface met his match in King Philip IV of France (1285–1314). Philip annoyed Boniface: against tradition, he taxed clergy members, kept churches in France from sending money to the Vatican, and—ignoring canon law's claim that only a Church court can try clergy members—put a bishop in prison. When the pope protested, Philip made the French clergy send Boniface a letter stating they would no longer recognize him as pope. Boniface responded by issuing *Unum Sanctum*, a papal bull that declared the pope's authority is greater than that of kings. Philip responded by sending a small army to Rome to imprison and harass Boniface, who died just a month later. (Boniface had many enemies but few whose words about him have had the staying power of Dante. After Boniface exiled the Italian writer, Dante gave him a place of honor in the Eighth Circle of Hell in *Inferno*.)

Popes after Boniface did not have the means to keep fighting the French king, so they went with the "if you can't beat 'em, join 'em" idea: they moved to France. Clement V (1305–1314), the pope after Boniface and a Frenchman, decided to move the papacy's headquarters from Rome to Avignon, and there it stayed for the next seven popes and seventy years. Every one of those popes was French, as were most of the cardinals during this time.

French pope, French cardinals, all making their home on French land—the French king was delighted and had a huge say in Church affairs. Not everyone shared his enthusiasm, however, and as time went on, many in the Church began protesting this move away from the papacy's historical home of Rome. The great Italian poet Petrarch saw parallels between the Old Testament (OT) description of how sixth-century Israelites were held captive in Babylon and the current situation between the French monarchy and the papacy; he called the situation the "Babylonian Captivity of the papacy."

Eventually those protesting the "captivity" won. It was not Church officials or secular rulers who got the papacy moved back to Rome, however; it was two women, Bridget of Sweden and Catherine of Siena, who protested so loudly and so well that two popes decided the women must be right.

Bridget, the patron saint of Sweden, was an exceptionally strong-willed woman. After raising eight children and being widowed, she took the veil as a nun. A woman of action, Bridget started a new religious order for women and spent her time advising bishops and royalty in Sweden on how to act in a Christian manner. In 1349, she headed to Rome, where she called for Church reform and the papacy's return. For eighteen years, she prayed and worked up public opinion on the matter, and it was mainly due to her that Urban VI decided in 1367 to return to Rome. However, much of the Church's administration was still run from Avignon, and three years later, Urban returned there. Bridget, who had received revelations for many years, warned him that he would die if he returned to Avignon—which was exactly what happened within a few months.

A few years later, Catherine came on the scene. The twenty-third of twenty-four children born to a wool trader and his wife, Catherine had visions from the time she was 5 and vowed herself to Christ at age 7. She did not let the fact that she was not wealthy or noble—or that she was illiterate—stop her from sending dictated letters to the powerful people in her world, giving them advice (often unsolicited) on how they should perform their duties. She wrote for years to Pope Gregory IX, telling him that God commanded three things of him: reform the Church, return to Rome, and assemble a new crusade to the Holy Land. The third part did not go far, but Gregory did work on reform, and although he really did not want to, Catherine's revelations on the matter shook him enough that he made the move back to Rome in 1376, just four years before Catherine's early death at age 33.

There were more and bigger conflicts to come. Gregory died within two years of the move, and when it came time to elect a new pope, a mob gathered in Rome demanding that an Italian fill the office. Every pope for the last seventy-five years had been French. The cardinals felt pressured and elected an Italian who took the name Urban VI, but the French cardinals hit back by gathering a few months later and deposing Urban, saying his election was not valid because they had felt threatened. They elected a new—French—pope, Clement VII, who promptly moved back to Avignon.

However, Urban was not going to give up. Now there were two popes, who set up two colleges of cardinals, two sets of papal administration, and two centers of power. The problem went all the way down to the local level; in some places, there were two different bishops chosen by the two different popes. The situation has become known in history as the Great Schism.

Secular rulers supported one pope or the other based on their own political needs, but everyday Catholics were horrified at the mess. Something had to be done. Some cardinals from both sides decided the situation had gone on long enough, and in 1409, they met in Pisa to discuss the situation. Their solution was to depose both popes and elect a new one. Of course, neither pope accepted this, so there were three popes claiming control of the universal Church. Another council, held in the German city of Constance, was called in 1414 to find a solution. This council deposed all three popes and elected Martin V. This time it worked, and the Church was once again united behind one pope based in Rome.

It was good for the papacy to get beyond the Great Schism, but issues remained. A series of problematic popes began with Alexander VI (1492–1503), who bribed his way into the papacy. He was a master of simony (selling church offices) and nepotism (giving important favors to relatives), had at least eight children with his mistresses, and was even rumored to have been involved in assassination plots. The next pope, Julius II (1503–1513), was more interested in art and architecture than in theology. A big supporter of artists like Michelangelo, he was so enthusiastic to rebuild St. Peter's Basilica that he authorized the sale of indulgences, which eventually sparked the Protestant Reformations. Leo X (1513–1521) would be the first to face the protesters, but with his

Focus On
Rumbles and Roars: Calling for Change in the Church

So how do you start a revolution in the Church? Not necessarily by trying to. Martin Luther wanted to lead the Church to reform and renewal, not splinter Western Christianity into a thousand pieces. However, even before Luther arrived on the scene, others were calling for much-needed changes; the idea that the Church needed a tune-up had been growing for more than a century. In 1412, a Czech priest and university teacher named Jan Hus got involved in a controversy about the sale of indulgences. At first, Hus called for reform, but he came to believe that simony and corruption had become too ingrained in the Church for it ever to be removed. He also thought the Church had gotten off track with its insistence that Tradition is just as important as Scripture. He gained a lot of support in his native land, but in 1415, he was condemned as a heretic and burned at the stake.

Hus developed his beliefs partly as a response to reading what the Englishman John Wycliffe, a professor at Oxford, had written a generation earlier about the need for reform. Wycliffe believed the gospel required the Church to embrace poverty. This did not win him many friends among the Church's leaders, but it was a hit with the regular people in England. Like Hus,

Wycliffe was convinced that the Bible was the only true guide for human behavior and belief. He made the first translation of the Bible into English so that people would be able to interpret Scripture for themselves. Wycliffe ended up being declared a heretic in 1380, and his followers were persecuted.

There are many similarities between these men and Martin Luther, and one big difference: while Hus and Wycliffe's actions lit candles, Luther's sparked a bonfire.

Timing is everything. Part of the reason people were ready to listen to Luther was that others like Hus and Wycliffe had already been saying similar things. Moreover, Luther had political support for his religious ideas, which gave him some leeway in spreading them. In addition, the printing press allowed Luther's ideas to spread rapidly. Luther saw the press as a gift from God, and it certainly was a boon to the movement he was starting. More than 2,500 editions of his various writings in German were made between 1518 and 1544, and that is not counting his most popular work, the German translation of the New Testament. All told, Luther printed more than five times as many works as all his opponents combined. ■

first words as pope he proved how ill-equipped he was to face a serious challenge to the Church: "Now that God has given us the papacy, let us enjoy it."

Given all this, the idea that popes should not have so much political authority was spreading. As people found their trust in Church leadership challenged, they began to look to their secular rulers for guidance on political and social matters. This trend played a big role in how people dealt with the issues raised by the Protestant Reformations.

In the Eye of the Storm

You would never know from Martin Luther's background that he was destined to have a profound effect on the entire Christian West. He was a middle-class child who did well in school and was training to be a lawyer when he got caught in a terrible storm. Terrified, he vowed to become a monk if he survived—and survive he did. Eventually, Luther became a priest, and in 1513, he started teaching Scripture at the university in Wittenberg.

Luther was moody, with a tendency toward depression. He felt deeply guilty for his sins, and even the aid of the sacraments and the advice of his superiors could not dispel this guilt. In the letters of Paul in the New Testament (NT), Luther saw someone who shared his sense of unworthiness. Luther studied Paul's letters and came to believe they showed a way out of the guilt: the recognition that even though humans are sinners and cannot do anything to merit salvation, God will treat those who have faith as though they were righteous. The principle is called justification by faith, and it is at the center of Luther's theology.

Luther felt the Church had gotten away from this truth. He saw people saying prayers and going on pilgrimages in the hopes of making themselves worthy of salvation, rather than simply depending on God's mercy. He was particularly upset at the way indulgences were used: people tried to buy their way out of sins rather than repenting, and the Church used this to make money. When a Dominican named Johann Tetzel came to the Wittenberg area to sell indulgences, Luther decided to start a discussion with his colleagues at the university about the practice. He did what any Wittenberg professor who wanted to start a debate did: he posted a series of theses (statements) on the door of the local church as a way of inviting others to agree or disagree with him. The theses sparked a controversy, however, as Church leaders lined up either to defend the practice of selling indulgences or to condemn it, and Luther unexpectedly found himself at the center of a different kind of storm.

"Here I Stand"

The money from the indulgences Tetzel was selling was supposed to go partly to a local Church leader named Albrecht and partly to fund Pope Leo X's pet project of St. Peter's. When Luther began protesting this sale, he inter-rupted Albrecht's revenue stream and got much more attention than he had anticipated. In danger of being arrested for his public statements, Luther only remained free due to the protection of his local ruler, Frederick, whom the pope did not wish to alienate.

Luther was constantly put on the spot to defend his condemnation of Church practice, and this led him to cast a wider net and start speaking out against more of what he saw as corruption in the Church. In 1520, he published a series of works detailing his new understandings. In *To the Christian Nobility of the German Nation,* he called on Germans to begin reforming the Church in their midst by stopping the payments they made to Rome, acknowledging that the pope should not have political power in the secular sphere, and allow-ing priests to marry, among other things. He turned his attention to doctrinal matters in *On the Babylonian Captivity of the Church,* in which he took on the Church's sacramental system, contending that only baptism and the Eucharist are sacraments, the others being human rather than divine institutions. In his third work, *On the Freedom of a Christian,* Luther set out the heart of his belief in justification, which comes through belief in Christ rather than through any works one may do. Basically, he took on the Catholic Church and its peniten-tial system—and the fight was on.

In the midst of all this, Pope Leo X declared Luther to be a heretic and demanded, in effect, that he take it all back. Luther publicly burned Leo's let-ter. The pope proceeded to excommunicate him.

Luther's fate might have been sealed except that his ruler, Frederick, re-mained on his side. Frederick appealed to the German Emperor Charles V, who decided Germans should only be tried in German courts, meaning Lu-ther was not sent off to Rome. In April 1521, he was called to stand before the Diet of Worms, which was something like a parliament led by the emperor. Asked to renounce his views, Luther replied, "I am bound by the Scriptures I have quoted and my conscience is captive to the Word of God. I cannot and I will not recant anything . . . I cannot do otherwise, here I stand, may God help me."[1] So there he stood, and there he was convicted. The emperor had him declared a heretic, but by then Luther had disappeared from Worms. He headed back toward Wittenberg, but along the way was "kidnapped"—Luther himself was in on the planning—on Frederick's orders and taken to Wartburg

Castle. This kept him safe and out of Rome's and the emperor's control and gave Luther the freedom to translate the entire NT into German.

Luther may have been out of the public eye, but his ideas had gained such popularity that nothing could stop the coming changes. Back in Wittenberg, people devoted to his ideas had taken the lead in reforming their local church, making changes to the way people received communion and dropping the requirement that priests be celibate. The call for reform in the Church was growing louder and clearer, and by 1525, it was clear that Western Christianity was splitting down the middle.

"In the Beginning" in Their Own Languages

Martin Luther and the other Protestant Reformers thought people should read and interpret the Bible for themselves. This sounds easy enough, but there were two problems: up until now, Bibles were only available in Latin, which most people could not read; and they cost a lot of money, which most people did not have. The answer was to make the Bible available in translation and at an affordable price.

Translating the Scriptures was not a new idea; after all, the Church's official edition, the Vulgate, was a Latin translation from Hebrew and Greek. When Jerome created the Vulgate in the fourth century, many people spoke Latin. However, as fewer people used Latin as a spoken language, only an educated minority could read the Bible or even understand what it said if it was read to them. This was not a bad thing, according to Church leaders who were worried people would misinterpret the Scriptures and fall into heresy. In fact, it was heresy that got them thinking this way; when the Cathars and Waldensians started making translations in the twelfth century and encouraging people to interpret Scripture

in ways that went against Catholic teaching, Church leaders decided to ban the reading of the Bible in the vernacular, the languages people spoke. When Wycliffe translated the Bible into English early in the fifteenth century, Church authorities were sure his followers would not have leapt into heresy if they had not been reading the Scriptures in their own language, so the Church established a new round of prohibitions on reading vernacular translations.

Translations are all well and good but only if people can afford to buy them. Paper had been in use in China for more than a millennium by the time it was introduced into Europe in the thirteenth century, and it helped lower the cost of books. The printing press is what really made books affordable, however. Luther's translation of the NT into German was a best seller, and other vernacular translations began to appear. Fast forward to the present and your local bookstore, and you will likely find a dozen different translations of the Bible in English for sale. It would make the Reformers proud.

Scripture and Faith

Luther's rallying cry for his theology was *"Sola scriptura"*—Scripture alone. By this, he meant that popes and councils, bishops and writings do not even collectively have the authority of the Bible. It alone is the direct revelation of God, and everything else must flow from it. This idea wreaks havoc not just with papal power and with Catholic belief in the equal value of Scripture and Tradition but with the Church's understanding of itself as the mediator of grace for humanity. If the Bible is the central way that God speaks to people, then why would people need anything else? If the sacraments the Church dispenses are not needed for salvation, then in what way is the Church necessary? Luther and others who followed him finally came to believe it simply was not. God works directly in each human being, they said; the community of Christians is a help and support for the person but is not a necessary element in receiving God's grace.

Nor is the Church necessary for understanding Scripture, Luther declared. *Sola scriptura* does not mean "Scripture alone as interpreted by Holy Mother Church." Luther and his followers denied the authority of popes and Church councils to be the ultimate arbiters of what Scripture means, a move that carried with it a denial of the theological value of the apostolic succession that was supposed to give them this authority. Every believer, Luther held, can interpret Scripture because every believer has the same value before God: the priesthood of all believers, as he called it.

So Scripture alone is God's revelation to humans, and faith alone is what is necessary for salvation. As Luther saw it, knowing that works cannot contribute to salvation gives you complete freedom, not to sin but to live fully and without fear. Sinning will not condemn you anymore than not sinning will save you; all that is required—and therefore all that is useful—is faith. Luther believed Catholic teaching had perverted this, and he placed his contempt on the teachers of this tradition: "[A]lthough we should boldly resist the teachers of traditions and sharply censure the laws of the popes by means of which they plunder the people of God . . . we must spare the timid multitude whom those impious tyrants hold captive by means of these laws."[2]

Introducing the Protestants

Martin Luther got the Reformation ball rolling, but many others picked it up and ran with it. These other Protestant reformers agreed that their consciences would not let them continue in communion with the Catholic Church, but they often disagreed about what beliefs to hold and how Christians should organize themselves. Soon there was a patchwork of Protestant groups and a number of Protestant Reformations. Here is a rundown of some of the most important:

Group	Main Issues	Modern Christian Denominations That Developed from This Group
John Calvin and followers	Calvin preached the Reformation in Geneva and ended up as leader of the city, which became a showplace of Protestantism. His writings influenced people all over Europe. He taught double predestination, which is the idea that God has already chosen who will be saved and who will be damned, and there is nothing you can do about it.	Presbyterians, the Church of Scotland
Anabaptists	Their name comes from the belief that only adult baptism is valid. They focused on the individual's ability to interpret Scripture and on living according to what they saw in the New Testament. They shared all their property, did not perform military service or take oaths, and tended to live in communities separated from the rest of society.	Mennonites, Amish, Quakers, Baptists
Church of England	It split from Rome over whether or not the English King Henry VIII could divorce his first wife and take another. The pope said no, so Henry declared himself the head of the Church in England. Under Henry's daughter, Elizabeth, a national church developed that walked a middle ground: it rejected what was seen as too great an emphasis on the hierarchy in Catholicism but continued to focus on the sacraments.	Anglicans, Episcopalians, Methodists
Puritans	These people picked up on Calvin's understanding of the Church and split off from the new Church of England. They wanted a theocracy, where secular society is ruled by religious leaders, so some Puritans decided to start over and crossed the ocean to the New World—America.	Congregationalists, Disciples of Christ, United Church of Christ

These groups represent many differing points of view, but what they had in common was a desire literally to re-form the Christian community. In the fourteenth and fifteenth centuries, people were turning inward, wanting to serve God in the midst of their daily lives. Here we see how this inward desire turned outward: from wanting to change just themselves, people developed a desire to change the world around them.

And change it they did. In 1500, Europe was basically Catholic; by the end of the century, it was deeply divided. Some areas were firmly in favor of the Church, others were solidly on the side of Protestantism, and still others were an uneasy mixture. Germany was particularly divided, with some princes lining up to support the Church and others to leave it, but either way they expected their people to line up with them. Some kings and princes were surely led to support Luther and the other reformers because of their own deep beliefs, but for others it did not hurt that disbanding the Roman Catholic Church in their territories gave them an opportunity to take over all the Church's lands.

With everyone taking sides, it was just a matter of time until violence erupted. We will talk a bit more about the devastating Thirty Years' War (1618–1648) in the next chapter, but it is enough to say here that it pitted Protestant against Catholic all across Europe. Western Christianity had come apart at the seams, and the splintering would only get worse as the years went by. There are more than 33,000 Christian denominations in the world today, and most of them can trace their roots back to the Protestant Reformations.

The Reformations affected much more than just religion. What started as protests over faith and beliefs turned out to be a catalyst for change in many areas of Western life.

Political ideas. People decided that if they had the right to follow their conscience when it went against Church teachings, then they certainly had a right to follow it when it went against State laws. This led to the conscientious objector, and more broadly, it influenced the development of democracy and the idea of fundamental human rights.

A new regard for women. Where the Church of the Middle Ages had held up the monastic life as the highest ideal, Protestants emphasized marriage and family, which helped create a new view of women as companions and near equals. This does not mean the patriarchal ideas about women disappeared, but society did begin the long, slow move toward greater equality.

A higher view of work. Another aspect of rejecting monasticism as the ideal was that Protestants tended to see the true Christian vocation as serving God in the world through one's work. This is the origin of what is called the Protestant work ethic, a belief that hard work is a sign of good character. The Church had traditionally seen the accumulation of wealth as a threat to salvation, but the Protestants saw it as a sign of God's favor.

The use of the vernacular. Reformers did most of their writing in the languages of the people. Luther published an enormous amount of literature in German, Calvin published works in French, and other reformers wrote in their own native languages. In fact, these reformers helped shape the modern versions of many western European languages, most especially through their vernacular translations of the Bible.

Responding to the Call: The Catholic Reformation

Those who became Protestants were not the only ones doing reform at this time; the Catholic Reformation was up and running within a few years of Luther's stand at Worms. It does not get as much press, but in a way it is truest to Luther's original intent: he started by wanting to reform the Church from within, which is exactly what the Catholic Reformation accomplished.

It would be easy to think the Catholic move for reform was just a reaction to the success of Luther and the others, but such is not the case. While the Catholic Reformation responded to the issues raised by Protestantism and the criticisms it leveled at the Church, the seeds of the movement were already in place before Luther's theses hit the door of the Wittenberg church. We already saw that Jan Hus in the Czech lands and John Wycliffe in England had not only called for reform but had gotten others interested in their ideas. Many other Catholics were just as deeply concerned about the need to change the direction in which the Church was headed, so it was only a matter of time before this need exploded into change.

One of the strongest voices calling for change in the Church belonged to a Dutch priest named Desiderius Erasmus (ca. 1467–1536). While greatly respected among the Renaissance humanists and brilliant as well, Erasmus was in an uneasy position as a reformer. He fought against a slew of problems in the Church, including monks breaking their vows, the pitiful level of education among the clergy, the misuse of indulgences and other devotions, and theol-

"From This Day Forward"

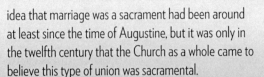

You have picked out the cake, ordered the flowers, and decided on a menu for the reception. You and your spouse-to-be have spent hours thinking about the wedding, but how much time have you given to thinking about the marriage itself? If the answer is "none," then theologically speaking, you are missing the whole point. From the Catholic viewpoint, it is the marriage, not the wedding, which is a sacrament, a point of grace in the lives of the partners. You do not have to read far in the Bible to find the grounding for the Catholic belief that marriage is a gift from God: Genesis 2:24 says that "a man leaves his father and mother and clings to his wife, and the two of them become one body." Jump to the NT, and in the Gospel of John you will see Jesus attending a wedding and blessing it by performing his first public miracle. The author of Ephesians describes marriage as a symbol of the relationship between Christ and the Church (5:21-33), a continuation of the Jewish understanding that God's covenant with Israel is similar to a marriage.

It may be a great symbol, but marriage is also a practical issue. It involves families, children, and property, and it raises questions about who can marry and if marriages can end. In the Roman Empire, marriage was a secular matter, and there were laws governing these issues. Christians of the time believed they should make marriage sacred by living it "in the Lord," but they did not really see it as a sacrament. In fact, it took awhile to get from "marriage as gift and symbol" to "marriage as sacrament"—about eleven centuries, in fact. The idea that marriage was a sacrament had been around at least since the time of Augustine, but it was only in the twelfth century that the Church as a whole came to believe this type of union was sacramental.

Unfortunately, when you talk about marriage, you also have to talk about divorce. It was permitted by Jewish law, but Jesus said divorce should only be granted in cases involving immorality. Over time, it became clear that the Church could not grant divorces—how could it agree to the breaking of a union that symbolized Christ's love for his people? However, in some circumstances, a marriage had not been properly made—maybe one of the partners had been deceived in some way, or the marriage partners had been too young to make such an important decision. In these cases, ecclesiastical courts could annul a marriage, declaring that the sacrament was never truly administered. Sure, there may have been a wedding and a priest presiding, but a priest simply witnesses to a marriage; the actual sacrament is administered by the bride and groom to each other. If they did not or could not do it properly, there was no real marriage.

For centuries, the Church taught that the main purpose of marriage was to bring children into the world. Starting in the middle of the twentieth century, Church theologians began talking about marriage more in terms of what great good it brings to the spouses. Catholics still see having children as a central aspect of marriage, but they talk about the mutual love and support of the marriage partners as being just as central.

ogy that was concerned more with its own beauty than with bringing people to God. He did not hesitate to criticize greed, ambition, and abuses of power wherever he saw them in the Church, including among the popes. Some people in the Church thought that Erasmus's criticisms were helping Luther in his fight, and Luther himself thought of Erasmus as an ally—that is, until Erasmus made it clear that he had no intention of leaving the Church.

Erasmus was in a difficult position. He drew fire from the powerful over his writings against the greed, corruption, and lack of spiritual depth he saw in the Church around him; he also drew the wrath of the reformers for his writings against Luther's take on Christianity. Erasmus could not agree with the extremists on either side. He attacked many of the same issues that provoked Luther's ire, but he seemed always to be starting from a different position: Where Luther rejected indulgences because human works are worthless in receiving justification from God, Erasmus thought people were substituting these pieces of paper for actually changing the ethical standards that had led them to sin in the first place. Where Luther came to believe the human's sole hope was to humbly have faith in God's mercy while accepting that humans are sinful to the core, Erasmus believed humans could grow in Christian wisdom and come closer to God by imitating Christ ever more closely. Luther and other Protestants thought that Erasmus simply caved in when the going got tough, but Erasmus thought that even if the aim of the reformers was good, their methods were not: they were raging and condemning the Church, when what the Church truly needed was education and change brought about from the inside.

Church leaders recognized the need for reform, too. Pope Adrian VI (1522–1523), for example, realized the protests pointed to issues that not only needed serious attention but also presented a real challenge to Church unity. He moved quickly to begin reforming the curia and bring German princes back into communion with the Church but died before he could accomplish much. A decade later, Pope Paul III (1534–1549) appointed a committee to report on problems in the Church. The committee came back with a long list: nepotism, simony, pluralism (bishops heading up more than one diocese), absenteeism (bishops not living in their home dioceses), immorality among the clergy, and corruption among Church leaders. Paul took decisive action: he called for a council to meet and deal with these issues head on. That council, held at Trent in Italy, marked a turning point in the Church's history.

The Council of Trent

Decades earlier, Luther and other reformers had called for a council to deal with the serious issues facing the Church. By the time the Council of Trent was convened in 1545, Luther had long gone his own way, and the council that resulted was not going to bring about the sweeping changes in doctrine that he wanted. Nonetheless, this council was a huge event. The bishops gathered there may not have made the changes Luther and other reformers wanted, but they did give the clearest and most precise statements to date about many Catholic doctrines. This was work enough in itself, but the biggest success of the council lay in its complete overhaul of the way the Church was organized and run.

The council met in three stages over the period 1545–1563. Why did it take almost twenty years for the council to do its work? On the one hand, the bishops had too many things to deal with; on the other, wars were being fought over the very issues they were discussing, which meant the council had to disband at times to avoid danger. We can break down the council's work into three main categories: the authority of Scripture and Tradition, issues related to doctrines and sacraments, and organizational reforms.

The Authority of Scripture and Tradition

This was really at the heart of the disagreements between Protestants and Catholics. The Protestant Reformers held that Scripture was the only true guide for Christian belief. Catholics then and now accept the authority of Scripture but also believe that early Christian writings, the statements of popes, and documents from Church councils—collectively known as Tradition—are also part of the divine revelation to humanity. In the face of the Protestant declarations to the contrary, Trent affirmed that the Holy Spirit continues to lead the Church—that revelation did not end with the final book of the Bible.

This belief in the ongoing process of revelation had implications for the Catholic position on who should interpret Scripture. Protestants generally said that every believer could interpret Scripture, although they quickly realized that this led to many different interpretations and much fragmenting among Christians. The Council said that bishops are the ones given authority over interpretation because they are in the line of apostolic succession, which guarantees that they maintain the wisdom and knowledge of the early Church and of succeeding generations.

Doctrines and Sacraments

The Protestant reformers hit hard at the sacraments, with Luther and others holding that only baptism and the Eucharist can be shown from the NT to be valid. The bishops at Trent reaffirmed that each of the seven sacraments was instituted by Jesus during his ministry on earth and explained the theology behind each one in detail. In addition, many Protestant reformers had thrown the tricky issue of transubstantiation out the window, explaining that the purpose of the Eucharist was to serve as a remembrance of Christ's sacrifice, not a reenactment of it. Trent, however, continued the Catholic understanding that the bread and wine are truly changed into the body and blood of Christ, meaning that the Mass is a continuation of the work of Christ.

The council also explained how Catholics think about grace. Luther had become convinced that even though humans remain sinful, God justifies them because of their faith. Trent rejected this, saying that the believer plays a role in cooperating with God's grace. God justifies people not only based on what they believe but also on what they do with that belief—their works. This in no way implies that belief is unimportant; rather, it is a statement that belief must result in action in order for it to be effective.

Reforms

Here we find the most innovative part of the council. The bishops decided that reform needed to begin where most people's point of contact with the Church begins: with the local parish priest. Too many priests were poorly educated and did not understand the theology they were supposed to teach. The bishops came up with a novel solution to this problem: the creation of seminaries. The word *seminary* comes from the Latin for "seed"—in seminaries, the seeds of good priests are planted and grown. Before Trent, the education of priests had been haphazard; in some places, the ability to speak enough Latin to say the Mass was all that was required. Now priest candidates would be well trained and thoroughly examined, both on their theological knowledge and on their worthiness to perform such an important role in the life of the Church.

There were top-down reforms of the Church as well. Church leaders were made to stop the disturbing practices of simony and nepotism. Bishops were required to hold regular synods as a way of dealing with clerical abuses and theological questions and to spend time in their home parishes with the souls under their care. The teaching authority of the bishops was reaffirmed, because they connect the Church's head (the hierarchy) with its body (the believers), but bishops were reminded that their role as teachers meant they had to make sure the laity knew the faith and stayed in line with it.

The council also laid out guidelines to ensure that people viewed relics and images with the proper reverence but not in a magical or superstitious way. As for indulgences, which sparked Luther's protests in the first place, Trent said they really were valid, but the way they had been used at times was disgraceful. They were for devotional purposes, and the Church should not make money on them.

The council dealt with many other issues, but you can see from these main points how it worked to answer the questions Protestants had raised in the minds of believers. It was a big success in explaining exactly what the Church taught about Christian faith and Catholic practice, and it helped bring new life into the Church. On the academic side, Catholics made big leaps in biblical and theological scholarship in the decades following the council. On the personal side, we see a renewed interest in moral reform and spiritual growth among people throughout the Church. In the last half of the sixteenth century, more than half of the popes were men who had been involved in the council, and they helped keep its spirit alive and growing in the Church—a big change from the "Now that God has given us the papacy, let us enjoy it" mentality earlier in the century.

What the council could not do is heal the divisions among Christians and bring them into unity once again. This was due partly to a fundamental divide between Protestants and Catholics over what exactly needed to be reformed. Protestants thought the problems in the Church ultimately stemmed from incorrect theology, while Catholics believed their theology to be grounded in God's truth and thought reform was needed in the areas of ethics and morality. The Council of Trent is where it became completely clear that Western Christianity was not going to reunite.

Oppression, Intimidation, and Reformation

The Council of Trent and the rest of the Catholic Reformation were serious attempts to right wrongs and correct abuses within the Church, but many of those involved in the fight to make these changes also had a circle-the-wagons mentality. The Church was under attack in a way it had not experienced before, and they knew it. Many were willing to fight back with all the tools at hand, including intimidation and violence.

Two of the most important tools used by popes to suppress ideas they considered heretical were the Index of Prohibited Books and the Inquisition. The Index was first published in 1559, under Pope Paul IV. As we have seen, the Protestant reformers had realized the printing press was a boon to their movement, and Paul caught on to this as well. He realized that if dangerous books were not printed, it would be much more difficult for dangerous ideas to be spread, so he ordered the creation of the Index, which listed all works that were not to be printed or read by Catholics. This included not only the works of Protestants but also others that were considered dangerous in the wrong hands; even the Bible and works by Church Fathers were either prohibited outright or allowed only with written permission from a bishop. After all, it was Luther reading Augustine and the NT that led to this whole mess in the first place. At least, that is how Paul and the Inquisition saw it.

The Index was actually part of the Inquisition. We last saw Inquisitors out battling heretics, especially the Cathars in France. In 1542, Pope Paul III set up the Congregation for the Holy Office, otherwise known as the Roman Inquisition, to deal with Protestants in Italy. Over time, it began spreading a wider net, bringing charges against an array of people who were judged to say or do something that took them outside the boundaries that the Church considered acceptable. We will run into the Holy Office again when we talk about the most famous case it ever brought, the one against Galileo Galilei.

The Roman Inquisition was in some ways less offensive than earlier Inquisitions; the one in Spain in the fifteenth century had destroyed the lives of countless *conversos*—Jews and Muslims who had been forcibly converted to Christianity and were then accused of practicing their native religions in secret. In fact, the terrible excesses of the Spanish Inquisition made a number of popes uneasy enough that they established more stringent limits on the

Roman Inquisition. Still, *less offensive* is a relative term; there is no question that the use of the Inquisition in support of the Church's stand against Protestantism is one of the dark moments in Church history.

The Church Then and Now

What Makes People into a Church?

In the first chapter we discussed "church" as an assembly of God's people called forth by God. But what does it mean to be called forth? Given that people do not see eye to eye on many other things, it probably does not come as a shock to know that different Christian groups have a variety of opinions on this matter as well. Let's take a look at what Catholics and a few different Protestant groups mean when they talk about being Church.

The Priesthood of All Believers: The Lutheran View

Lutherans see the Church as the gathering of believers who respond to the Holy Spirit's call. It is not about hierarchy and it is not a place you go for blessings; it is an earthly institution meant for the help and support of believers. The Spirit works through the Church in its preaching and the sacraments it administers, but the Church is not itself a source of grace for believers; grace can only come from God directly to the believer. That is why all believers are understood to be priests – nothing stands between them and God.

A Place for Moral Action: The Calvinist View

Calvinists work mainly from a "what you see is what you get" understanding of the Church – it is more about the visible institution than about the group of those called by God; after all, only God knows whom he has called. For Calvinists, encouraging people to act in a moral manner is one of the main functions of being Church; salvation comes from God without any action on our part, so the best we can do is to try to follow God's laws.

Submitting to Christ: The Anabaptist View

People in these traditions think of the Church as the group of those who have submitted their lives to Christ. The Bible is important to them, but the Holy Spirit working directly in their lives is even more important. The believer has a personal relationship with Christ; the community is not necessary, but it is useful in helping people understand how to have that personal relationship.

The People of God: The Catholic View

For Catholics, being Church means being part of the community through which the Holy Spirit moves and works in the world. It is recognizing that the individual does not stand alone before God but is part of the community of those whom God has called together. The connection between the individual and Christ is made through the Church, particularly through the sacraments.

Overall we can say that the difference between Catholic and Protestant understandings of what it means to be Church centers around the roles of the individual and the community. Protestants see being Church as being brought together with others who have a personal relationship with Christ, while for Catholics being Church is what creates that relationship in the first place.

Questions and Ideas for Understanding

1. Imagine that you are living through a period of plague. People all around you are dying, but you remain healthy. Would you feel guilty, blessed, or just lucky? Would you try to run away to a place without plague, or would you stay to help those who were ill?

2. Luther said that every believer has the ability to interpret Scripture. This sounds good in theory and may be true in actuality, but history has shown that differing interpretations lead to conflict and disunity. Hold a debate in which the one side argues for the necessity of having a unifying central authority for Scriptural interpretation and the other argues for recognition of the direct connection between God and humans that makes such an authority unnecessary.

3. Look more deeply into the theological issue of justification by faith and the way it was expressed in various Protestant movements. Explain the difference between various Protestant understandings of this issue and the Catholic position.

4. Sometimes it is said that conservative Catholics think the Council of Trent marks the highest point in Christian history after the time of

Jesus. Research what this statement means, why it is said, and from what viewpoints it could be true.

Notes

[1] *Luther's Works*, Vol. 32, ed. George W. Forell. Philadelphia: Muhlenberg Press, 1958, pp. 112–113.

[2] Martin Luther, *On Christian Liberty*, ed. Harold J. Grimm. Minneapolis, MN: Augsburg Fortress Press, 2003, p. 68.

12

Discoveries Near and Far
New Lands, New Science, and New Ways of Serving

Chapter Overview

In this chapter, we will explore:

▶ European wars and voyages of discovery in the seventeenth century

▶ Ignatius of Loyola and the Jesuits

▶ The story of Church missions around the world

▶ The Church's interaction with science

Leilani: Living the Mission Life

When you were a little girl, the man in the black robe first came to your people. At first, you thought he was some kind of devil, with his pale skin and strange speech. Your parents were afraid at first, but as the Black Robe learned to speak as your people, they began to listen to him. They came to understand that he was a holy man from the tribe of the Sky Spirit. The Black Robe wanted you and your family to learn a new way of living. He and others who came after him helped the men of your tribe make a clearing and build houses, so your people would not have to roam the forest. Then they built a bigger house with a cross on it for the Sky Spirit, whom they taught you to call God. Every seven days, the pale skins called your people together and spoke to this God using strange words.

The Black Robes did wonderful things for your tribe. They showed your father and brothers how to farm, and now there was food all the time. They showed you strange symbols on what you learned was paper and told you that each symbol represented a sound from your language. You had never heard of language being put down this way, but now you could do it yourself. Best of all, they brought music! You and your younger brother were both learning to play a pipe that they called a flute. You had come to love these men from the tribe of the Sky Spirit, because they were gentle and kind and taught you how to live like God wanted.

Lately, though, there have been other men with pale skin, only they do not wear black robes and they do not seem so gentle. They carry fire sticks, and when they find young people from your tribe in the forest, they carry them off as prisoners. The Black Robes say these are bad men who are forcing your friends into slavery, but this does not make sense to you. After all, they are pale like the Black Robes, so are they not from the tribe of the Sky Spirit as well? You are confused, and you miss your friends who have been taken. Two things can make you feel better, at least for a time—playing your flute and going to the house of God for the seventh-day meeting. You still do not know what exactly the Black Robe is saying when he speaks to God, but it soothes you to be there with all the members of your tribe. It makes you realize that all of you are now part of the tribe of God, too.

In the sixteenth and seventeenth centuries, all over the world people like Leilani were learning about Christianity from missionaries, who were often the first Europeans these people had ever seen. The Europeans were discovering a lot, too: they explored lands and cultures that were new to them, found new trade routes to get them to these places, researched new scientific fields, and created new ways of working in existing ones. We will look at the Church's role in all these discoveries, and we will talk about the Jesuits, who were involved in many of them. After we explore the Church's struggles with some of the scientific developments of the time, we will take a quick look at how the Church views faith and science in the modern world. ■

Destruction and Discovery

European history in the seventeenth century is a mixed bag of seemingly non-stop warfare on the continent and incredible discovery.

The constant warring caused great destruction. By 1618, the religious and political situation in Germany had gotten out of hand, with Protestant and Catholic rulers of the various principalities ready for a fight. They set the Thirty Years' War in motion, and it did not take long for most of Europe to get involved. Both Protestant and Catholic nations were fighting to make their religious preference the standard for Europe, but political and territorial struggles played a big role as well, and many countries shifted alliances as the war dragged on. Religious differences also set the stage for a civil war over in Britain: Scotland's Presbyterians chafed under the rule of the Anglican King Charles I of England, and they started an uprising in 1642. King Charles was unpopular at home as well, resulting finally in his imprisonment and ultimate beheading. The monarchy was restored to power in 1660, but by that time, Ireland and Scotland had both come directly under the authority of the English government, and the British Isles were born. In northern Europe, Sweden became a powerhouse during the Thirty Years' War, but it lost a great deal of ground to Peter the Great's Russia during the Great Northern War in the first part of the eighteenth century. And Austria was on a roll: it defeated the Turks in 1683 and conquered Hungary over the course of the following fifteen years.

With all this fighting going on, it is a wonder anybody had time to engage in trade—but they did. Changes in trading patterns helped shift the power centers in Europe from Germany and the area around the Mediterranean to the countries in the northwest of the continent, especially England. Even Spain and Portugal, which had gotten rich by engaging in trade and conquest, lost ground to the Netherlands—it seemed like the Dutch traders were everywhere for awhile—and then to England, which got a huge boost by trading with its various colonies. With foods and other products pouring into Europe from the Americas, India, and the Far East, we can see the first inklings of a worldwide economy.

Making a New Map

The Age of Exploration—that is what historians call the fifteenth through seventeenth centuries. Around the beginning of the fifteenth century, Europeans started looking for new ways to get places because the old ways were no longer working. With the Mongol Empire falling apart in the East and the Ottoman Empire getting strong to the south, the overland trade routes Europeans had been using were blocked. They took to the waters, and literally a whole new world opened up to them. Bartholomew Diaz found a new trade route to the East when he went around the Cape of Good Hope at the bottom of Africa in 1486; Vasco da Gama made it to India in 1497; and Christopher Columbus sailed the ocean in 1492. Ferdinand Magellan set out to sail around the globe and nearly made it; he died in the Philippines in 1521, but his second in command, a Basque named Juan Sebastian del Cano, finished the trip for him. In the sixteenth century, the Spanish explored (and conquered) in the Americas. The French showed up in North America in the next century, and not too long after, a Dutch ship headed for the East Indies accidentally blew onto the coast of Australia.

These contacts with foreign lands were a boon to Europeans, bringing them new kinds of foods and other goods, new sources of revenue, and new ideas about the world. However, for the peoples "discovered," it was often another story. Countless thousands of Native Americans in North and South America and the islands of the Caribbean were enslaved to work for Spanish and Portuguese traders, and when the native peoples started dying off, the traders took to kidnapping and transporting Africans as slaves. The slave trade was big business during the sixteenth and seventeenth centuries.

From the perspective of the twenty-first century, it is clear that the destruction of a way of life and the enslaving of humans are terrible things, but it was not so clear to the Europeans at the time. Most of them had never traveled outside Europe and knew nothing about the cultures of the peoples they encountered on these explorations. In fact, they could not even recognize what they saw in Africa or the Americas as "culture" at all because they were not centered on what the Europeans considered to be the most important elements of civilization, namely Christianity and the classical traditions of Rome and Greece. By and large, the Europeans saw the native peoples as, at best, innocent children and, at worst, barbarous animals. Either way, they had no basis for understanding or even respecting the peoples they encountered, and they found themselves far too often on both the giving and receiving ends of complete misunderstandings and dangerous judgments. While the Europeans might have been guilty of cultural arrogance, it was the deeper issue of their cultural blindness that led to terrible actions and hostilities that have passed down through the generations into the present day.

Fighting the Good Fight: The Jesuits

By the sixteenth century in the Church's history, Jesuits seemed to be every-where. Members of this religious Order were on the front lines of renewing Catholicism in Europe, preaching the gospel in new ways and to new peoples around the world, educating everyone from natives of the Americas to the wealthy sons of nobles in Europe, and inventing new ways to do science. They developed a great deal of influence but found a world of trouble to go along with it, much more than their founder Ignatius of Loyola could ever have imagined.

Ignatius was born in 1491 into a large Basque family. The youngest of twelve children, he grew up around the royal court and spent the better part of his first twenty-six years thinking mainly about wine, women, and song. In 1517, he entered the military and four years later suffered a terrible leg wound in battle. During his recovery, he began reading stories about the lives of Christ and the saints, and he found his outlook changing. He said good-bye to his frivolous past and decided to devote his life to serving Christ.

At first, Ignatius was unclear what his path should be. He tried living as a hermit and then traveled to Jerusalem before he decided to study for the priesthood. Even in this setting, Ignatius stood out for the intensity of his faith, and before long, he had gathered a group of followers from among his fellow students. He led them in a series of meditations he called the Spiritual Exercises, which he designed as a way to help people learn to follow God's will. The men formed a new religious Order and traveled to Rome to ask for Pope Paul III's blessing.

They received the pope's blessing and more. When Paul ordained them priests, Ignatius and the others took the usual monk's vows—poverty, chastity, and obedience—and then one more: they swore absolute obedience to the pope.

The fledgling priests got a chance to put their vows into practice immediately. Although they had wanted to travel to the Holy Land to convert non-Christians, Paul told them to look closer to home. In a Europe so divided by religious conflict—this was just two decades after Luther's theses touched off the Protestant Reformations—there was plenty to do for Catholics dedicated to protecting the faith. As Ignatius saw it, people were drawn to Protestantism not because the Church's teachings were flawed but because they were not putting those teachings into practice in their daily lives. He and his men decided to devote themselves to preaching and promoting the ideas of the Catholic Reformation, and in 1540, Paul approved their new Order as the Society of Jesus—or the Jesuits, as they came to be called.

The Jesuits were not your typical religious Order, neither living the enclosed life of the traditional monasteries nor the mendicant life of the Franciscans and Dominicans. Instead, the Jesuits' big focus was on being active in the world: praying with and ministering to people in the streets, hospitals, prisons, and foreign lands. Their great work lay especially in two fields: missions and education. We will see more about their missionary activity later in the chapter, but first let's look at their work in education.

The Jesuits fell into being teachers simply because they were so popular. When Ignatius died in 1556, there were already more than a thousand members in the Order; seventy years later, there were fifteen thousand. Somehow or other, the Jesuits had to get all those young men educated, so they founded colleges to train them. More than thirty-five Jesuit colleges were up and running by 1556; a hundred years later, there were more than four hundred colleges, plus a hundred or so seminaries and schools. By that time, you did not have to be planning a career as a Jesuit to go to one of their schools; any boy who wanted to could attend.

Being teachers may not have been the Jesuits' original intention, but Ignatius and company came to realize they had a wonderful opportunity to serve the Church in this way; after all, they were training young minds in Catholic moral values, helping to instill a commitment to service, and creating better-educated Catholic members of society. Between running these schools and writing thousands of textbooks to be used in them, it is no wonder that people called the Jesuits the schoolmasters of Europe.

Jesuit education became popular because it was excellent. The Jesuits emphasized Latin and Greek, Catholic theology, philosophy, and ethics. At-

Voices from the Past
"Rule for Thinking with the Church"

▶ Author: Ignatius of Loyola

▶ Written: Mid-sixteenth century

▶ Audience: Catholics seeking spiritual direction

Ignatius definitely saw himself as a soldier of Christ, and even the spiritual direction he gave reflected this. His *Spiritual Exercises* were intended to help people enter more deeply into their connection with God as mediated through the Church. In a time when Europe was falling into chaos and warfare over what Christianity should look like, Ignatius never wavered. His Church was under attack, it had become the Church Militant, and he would use all the weapons in his arsenal to fight for it. In an appendix to the *Spiritual Exercises,* he wrote this list of rules; glancing through even a few of these, you will be able to see how much of it is directed against fighting the Protestant Reformations.

In order to have the proper attitude of mind in the Church Militant we should observe the following rules:

1. Putting aside all private judgment, we should keep our minds prepared and ready to obey promptly and in all things the true spouse of Christ our Lord, our Holy Mother, the hierarchical Church.

2. To praise sacramental confession and the reception of the Most Holy Sacrament . . .

3. To praise the frequent hearing of Mass, singing of hymns and psalms, and the recitation of long prayers . . .

4. To praise highly religious life, virginity, and continence; and also matrimony, but not as highly as any of the foregoing . . .

6. To praise the relics of saints by venerating them and by praying to these saints . . .

9. Finally, to praise all the precepts of the Church, holding ourselves ready at all times to find reason for their defense, and never offending against them . . .

11. To praise both positive and scholastic theology . . .

13. If we wish to be sure that we are right in all things, we should be ready always to accept this principle: I will believe that the white that I see is black, if the hierarchical Church so defines it.[1] ■

tending their schools was free, although many of their graduates later supported Jesuit education—and the schools were turning out kings and emperors, cardinals and philosophers, and scientists by the dozen. Today, the Jesuits have 28 colleges and universities in the United States alone and 90 worldwide, plus 430 high schools in more than 50 countries.

Big Trouble for the Jesuits

Soon the Jesuits were a bona fide political power, and not just inside the Church. Since the Jesuits answered directly to the papacy, popes began to use them for diplomatic matters, for example, sending them as ambassadors to various countries. In many cases, the people with power in those countries chose Jesuits as confessors, which gave them access and insight into the workings of many governments. Catholics educated by the Jesuits also continued to turn to them for help and support as they got older and became powerful.

In the seventeenth century, the Jesuits were riding high in influence and prestige, but they also faced challenges. They had traveled as missionaries with the Portuguese as the latter built their empire, and when that empire began to decline, so did the fate of those Jesuit missions. Moreover, the Jesuit emphasis on a classical education in Greek and Latin put them out of touch with the new trend toward reading and writing in the vernacular, which meant Jesuit schools were not as popular as they had been.

In the eighteenth century, Jesuit fortunes grew dimmer yet. Their missions were in trouble, their political power and wealth made them targets of attack, and their work as the pope's personal brigade put them in the crosshairs of rulers who wanted to undercut papal power. They were seen as threats to national power, both because they were such a strong international force and because of their direct allegiance to the pope. As the century wore on, anti-Jesuit feeling reached a fever pitch among European governments. A number of Catholic rulers got together and asked the pope to disband the Jesuits, and even those rulers that did not actively ask did not protest, either. Finally, in 1773, Pope Clement XIV decided he had no choice but to dissolve the Order, and the 23,000 Jesuits worldwide were either dismissed or allowed to do other service in the Church. Everywhere, national governments pounced on the Jesuit holdings in their countries.

That was not the last word on the Jesuits, however. In 1814, as Pope Pius VII was trying to help reconstruct Europe after the Napoleonic Wars, he decided to call the Jesuits into service to do it. The Order was restored, but it never again reached the level of influence that it once had. Jesuits could no longer afford to offer free education, and they did not have the same kinds of access to people in power, but they did have the will to serve the Church, and there are nearly 25,000 members of the Order working in more than a hundred different countries today.

Around the World in More than Eighty Days

Let's take a glance around the globe to see some of the missionary efforts that began during the fifteenth through seventeenth centuries.

China

The Franciscan John of Monte Corvino arrived in China in 1294 and worked alone for eleven years before any other missionaries reached him. He baptized thousands, but not long after his death in 1330, the missionaries were expelled from the country and Christianity died out. In 1583, a Jesuit missionary, Matteo Ricci (1552–1610), arrived on the scene. Dressing as a Confucian scholar and speaking Mandarin, he interested the local intellectuals in Christianity by talking about mathematics, physics, and astronomy and by filling his home with all sorts of mathematical and astronomical instruments, clocks, musical instruments, and printed books and maps. He figured these things would lead people to ask him about his life and work—just the opening he needed to tell them about his beliefs. Eventually, the emperor summoned Ricci to Peking, where for nine years he spent his time lecturing on scientific topics and writing Chinese texts about the Catholic faith. By the time he died in 1610, he had made more than two thousand converts. He had also opened the door for others to come, and his Jesuit brethren carried on his work.

The number of Christians in China had grown to more than 800,000 by 1724, but trouble was brewing. The Jesuits had made the gospel accessible to the Chinese by adopting many of their customs and using Confucian words to talk about Christian concepts. The problem was that the Confusion understanding of these terms differed significantly from what Christians usually meant by them. Later missionaries from other Orders, especially the Franciscans and Dominicans, thought the Jesuits had gone halfway to being pagans, and the two groups started fighting. In 1700, the Chinese emperor declared that all missionaries had to follow the Jesuit model or leave the country. Many were expelled, and by the 1720s, the Church in China was being persecuted.

Speaking from Silence: Prophetic Nuns ◀ ◀ ◀ ◀ ◀

To live the cloistered life is no easy thing, and most women who choose this path walk it unknown to the outside world. A few, however, do make their voices heard. In the sixteenth and seventeenth centuries, two of the strongest voices belonged to Spanish-speaking Carmelite nuns: Teresa of Avila and Juana Ines de la Cruz.

Teresa of Avila (1515–1582) When just out of her teens, Teresa entered a Carmelite monastery in her hometown of Avila, Spain. For the next twenty years, she did all that was required but somehow always felt that something was missing. She began to have visions, and in 1562, those visions led her to found a new Carmelite house, one that followed stricter rules. She and the thirteen nuns who went with her lived in serious poverty: They wore habits of coarse brown wool and leather sandals even in winter, slept on beds of straw, did manual work, ate no meat, and spent much time praying alone. Despite these self-imposed deprivations, Teresa's monastery was no gloomy place. In everything, she focused on love and on joy in living for God. She ran her monastery with humor and wisdom, and it became the model for sixteen others she founded in her lifetime. Eventually, she was able to make these houses into a separate Order known as the Discalced Carmelites.

Teresa wanted to get her message out beyond the monastery walls. She wrote a number of works, including an autobiography, a history of her Order, works on meditation and prayer, and many letters, but it is her descriptions of her mystical experiences that have captivated people for more than four centuries. In *The Interior Castle,* Teresa urges the nuns for whom she is writing to think of the soul as "a castle made entirely out of diamond or of very clear crystal, in which there are many rooms." People give far too much attention to the castle's outer wall, the body, and far too little to its center, "where the very secret exchanges between God and the soul take place."[2] Her writings were hugely popular and are now the most-widely read works in Spanish behind *Don Quixote.* In 1970, Teresa's work as a reformer and writer led to her being named a Doctor of the Church.

Juana Ines de la Cruz (1651–1695) Half a world away and almost a century later, Juana was born outside of Mexico City to a woman of Spanish descent who had an affair with a Spanish military officer. Juana never knew her father, but she had a loving mother and a grandfather who let her roam his enormous library. Juana taught herself to read at age 3, and from then on, she read everything she could find: history, science, the classics, early Christian writers, the Bible—if it was in a book, she wanted to know about it. She entered a Carmelite monastery at age 18, but it was not especially strict and the women could own possessions. What did Juana own? Books—thousands of them. A few even listed Juana as author; she wrote poetry, plays, and even theology.

One day, Juana heard what she considered a poor sermon, so she wrote an analysis of it and sent it to some friends. The local bishop got hold of the letter and had it published. He congratulated her on making such a clear argument—and then wrote a letter himself stating that women should remain silent, which he also circulated. Juana wrote a response that talked about the rights of women. She said that ability, not gender, should determine who does the talking and writing, and argued that it was wrong to keep women away from education as many people wanted to do. Juana pointed to a list of learned women from history and the Bible, and commented on the Church's tradition of respecting the works of great female saints like Teresa of Avila. All this started a firestorm that left Juana exhausted. She gave away her books, entered a stricter monastery, and devoted herself to silence. She died at age 44 while tending sick nuns in her convent.

Japan

Jesuits made it to Japan almost as soon as they came into being as an Order. Francis Xavier, one of Ignatius's closest companions, headed to Japan in 1549 with two other Jesuits and a translator. By 1581, the Jesuits had set up 200 churches in the country and baptized 150,000 Christians. That number reached half a million by the turn of the century, but Japanese leaders became suspicious that the missionaries were really there to act as spies for Spain and Portugal and started persecuting Christians. Eventually, all the missionaries were either killed or banished, and the Christian communities were destroyed. Japan closed its borders and would not allow missionaries back into the country for almost two centuries. However, in 1865, when the French were allowed to build a church in Nagasaki, they discovered that a small number of Japanese Christians had kept the faith alive through all that time.

India

Franciscan priests were on the ship with the Portuguese explorer Vasco da Gama as he made his way to India in 1500, but hanging out with the Portuguese turned out to be a problem: the Portuguese merchants and traders acted so badly that it seemed ridiculous to Indians when the missionaries spoke of Christians as people of love and integrity. Francis Xavier stopped in India in 1542 before heading to Japan, but it was another man from his Order, Robert de Nobili, who had the most success. De Nobili went the Ricci route: From the time he arrived in 1605, he ate, dressed, and lived like an Indian and studied the Hindu scriptures. De Nobili presented Christianity in a way that made sense to Indians, and he and the Jesuits who followed him made thousands of converts. However, the Indian Catholic Church ran into hard times in the seventeenth and eighteenth centuries. Priests were in short supply, conflicts between Portugal and Rome made life hard for the missionaries in Portuguese colonies, Dutch and English Protestants worked to keep Catholicism out of the colonies they had set up, and many colleges and mission houses were destroyed when the Jesuits were disbanded.

These Age of Exploration missionaries were not the first to bring Christianity to India, though. Legend tells us that the apostle Thomas traveled to India in 52 BCE and founded Christian communities there. When the Catholic missionaries arrived fourteen centuries later, they discovered that these communities of "Thomas Christians" were still around. The Thomas Christians had their own church structures and worship services, which did not sit well with the Portuguese explorers who first encountered them. There was lots of tension and outright hostility at times, but the Thomas Christians considered themselves then, and remain today, in full communion with the Roman Catholic Church.

Africa

Eight years after missionaries arrived in the Congo in 1483, they had the spectacular success of converting the king and his family. The king returned to his old beliefs after a while, but his son remained Christian and helped the missionaries when he came to the throne. The Congo was not the only region where missionaries worked, but by the mid-eighteenth century, you could barely find a trace of the Catholic missions anywhere in Africa. Many missionaries died due to the difficult climate and lack of medical care, and the Church did a poor job of training priests from among the locals. Sometimes missionaries used the promise of food or other forms of help as a way to get people to agree to baptism, which is not a recipe for lasting conversion. The unstable political situation in many areas of the continent did not help, but the greatest disadvantage for the missionaries was simply that they were all Portuguese—just like the slave traders whom they accompanied. The combined efforts of slave traders and missionaries gave the native peoples good reason to associate Christianity with slavery.

The Americas

Conquest and mission went hand in hand as Spanish and Portuguese explorers and missionaries fanned out all over the Americas. By 1555, you could find missionaries in the West Indies, Mexico, Central America, Colombia, Venezuela, Ecuador, Peru, Chile, and Brazil. They founded mission settlements, churches and cathedrals, hospitals, and schools. Religious Orders set up universities in Mexico City and Lima, Peru, almost a century before Harvard opened its doors. While the missionaries usually did bring their own culture to the indigenous peoples, they did not stop there: Books in twelve Indian languages were being printed in Mexico by 1575. It took longer for missionaries to make their way through North America, but by the end of the sixteenth century, you could find missions in many areas of the continent.

There is no denying the dark side to the mission work in the Americas. Missionaries often urged on the early conquistadors as they destroyed native temples and massacred their priests. They worked with civil authorities to resettle the natives and force them to accept Christianity, but many missionaries were horrified at the treatment of the natives. They thundered from the pulpits and tried to get the soldiers and settlers to treat the natives more humanely but with mixed success at best; the European settlement of Central and South America was so devastating for the peoples who were already there that the natives were killed or died off by the millions.

One of the most beautiful and most tragic stories from the South American missions comes from the region of Paraguay and Argentina. Jesuit missionaries converted whole tribes of the Guaraní natives there and helped protect them from European slave hunters. The Jesuits set up *reducciones,* communal settings where the Guaraní practiced agriculture, architecture, metallurgy, farming, ranching, and even music and printing. The *reducciones* lasted for a hundred years but were destroyed in the 1750s when a land treaty between Spain and Portugal changed everything. The Portuguese demanded that the *reducciones* be evacuated, leaving the Guaraní once again open to the slave hunters. The Guaraní rebelled, and many Jesuits joined them in fighting, but the rebellion was crushed in 1767 by a joint Spanish–Portuguese army. This act of defiance was one of the strongest reasons given for the disbanding of the Jesuits in 1773.

Bringing Faith and Science Together

While some Catholics were off discovering new lands, others were discovering more about their world through science. Read certain kinds of modern Christian literature, and you will get the impression that Christian faith and scientific knowledge are sworn enemies, but this is not true of Catholic Christianity. Many people think the Church has a long history of conflict with science, but actually the opposite is true: Despite some spectacular fights, the Church has nearly always supported scientific research, and for centuries, most of the great scientists in the West had their day job in the Church. They include Albert the Great, who began the study of geology; Georges Lemaitre, originator of the big bang theory; Gregor Mendel, the first to research genetics;

and many others. Many Church missionaries were also conducting scientific studies, making huge contributions in the areas of geography, natural history, botany, and medicine.

The list of Jesuit scientists is amazing. Angelo Secchi initiated the study of astrophysics; Francesco Grimaldi came up with the wave theory of light and drew the map that remains the basis of all modern moon maps; Jose de Acosta pioneered the geophysical sciences; Francesco Lana-Terzi is known as the father of aeronautics; Girolamo Saccheri invented non-Euclidean geometry; and Gregory Saint Vincent discovered the polar coordinates. Thirty-five moon craters have been named for Jesuits. A Jesuit determined how to put together the Gregorian calendar, another made a final determination of the border between Russia and China, and five of the world's eight largest rivers were first charted by Jesuit explorers. Seismology is called "the Jesuit science" because members of the Order contributed so much to its development.

This is not to say that science has always been a top Church priority. During the Middle Ages, scholars tended to think more about the glories of the next world than about the details of this one. For centuries, science advanced little, not because the Church was trying to put the brakes on research but because it was not a deep part of the mind-set of the times. Things began to change in the thirteenth century when Aristotle's scientific texts were rediscovered, which got people thinking about how the world works. Just who did that thinking? Mainly people in universities—which, of course, were almost always Church institutions. Students studied the natural sciences as part of their university education, and many professors looked at science as a complement to theology, seeing both as ways that God communicates with humanity. Two scientists in particular stand out: Robert Grosseteste and his student Roger Bacon.

Robert Grosseteste (1175–1253) was a thirteenth-century bishop and reformer; he also happened to be a brilliant professor who helped turn Oxford into the leading center of scientific research. Having studied the works of Aristotle and his Arab commentators, he realized that to know how something works, one could not just think through the problem as scholars were used to doing—you needed to observe, create a hypothesis, and test it. Grosseteste's approach laid the groundwork for the scientific method, which is the basis of modern science. He also wrote works about physics, mathematics, astronomy, optics, light, motion, color, and psychology.

Like his teacher Grosseteste, the Franciscan monk Roger Bacon (1214–1294) taught at Oxford and worked with the scientific method. In fact, he came to believe that scientific observation was the true foundation for all knowledge because it gave us a way to know the world, which meant learning more about the world's Creator. Bacon wrote many works of both science and theology. He dabbled in alchemy, which at times got him into trouble with his Franciscan superiors. Alchemy is more than just a superstitious attempt to change base metals into gold; it is based on the idea that all elements come from the same Being, so if understood properly, one could be converted into another. To Bacon, it seemed like a science that could help cure sick bodies and even sick souls—the perfect way to bring science and theology together.

The work of Grosseteste, Bacon, and others like them helped revitalize interest in science. In the fourteenth and fifteenth centuries, scholars—mostly men who belonged to Church Orders—created astronomical calendars, built new measuring instruments, started working out trigonometry, figured out how to use graphs for scientific knowledge, and formulated many new laws of science. For its part, the Church was not in the business of trying to impose one point of view on all scientists. Church leaders did sometimes let scientists know where they were bucking up against the boundaries of Christian doctrine—boundaries they were not allowed to cross—but the Church was never interested in determining the content of the science that was being discovered.

Moving the Earth

In the sixteenth century, all kinds of new scientific ideas were swirling around. Book printing made it easier to get the word out about theories and discoveries, and illustrated books could show drawings of plants or animals rather than just describing them.

However, illustrations could be confusing, too. For example, a drawing of the universe as most people of the time understood it would have Earth at the center, with circles around it showing the orbit of the sun, stars, and planets, with heaven surrounding all. The theology behind the picture was that the celestial bodies were higher up and closer to heaven; Earth was in the center because it was the farthest from God and the lowest part of creation. The idea that the entire universe swirled around Earth was so much a part of people's thinking that it affected how they interpreted the Bible. When they read in verses like Ecclesiastes 1:5 that "The sun rises and the sun goes down," they thought it proved the matter—the sun was moving around Earth. Not that there weren't other views—Nicolas of Cusa wrote about his belief that there were thousands and thousands of worlds, and having such an opinion did not keep Nicolas from being made a cardinal in 1446. However, the majority of people, including those learned in science, accepted without question that the world was at the center of everything God had made.

It took awhile, but in the sixteenth century, scientists began to appreciate Grosseteste's and Bacon's idea that scientific truth could only be uncovered by observation. When the idea was applied to astronomy, it quickly became clear that the model with Earth in the middle and everything moving around it did not work. Nicholas Copernicus published a book in 1543 claiming that the planets move around the sun. He had not figured out exactly how they do this, but he got people looking at the universe differently. Copernicus's work was welcomed by the Church—in fact, it took the urging of a cardinal to get him to publish his theories in the first place. His work got good press for half a century and was even used in reforming the calendar ordered by Pope Gregory XIII. Combine the works of Copernicus and two other sixteenth-century astronomers, Tycho Brahe and Johannes Kepler, and we have the picture of a universe with the sun at the center and the planets rotating around it in elliptical orbits—which is much closer to what modern science tells us. We cannot say that the Church immediately accepted all this, but it certainly did not condemn it.

During the seventeenth century, scientists used the scientific method to make discoveries in many fields. Many of those scientists were Catholics, but they sometimes had to be careful how they performed their research. The Church did not accept all these new theories at once, even when they had good science behind them; for that matter, neither did any of the other Christian religious bodies. What made the Church different was that it had ways to keep ideas it deemed heretical or dangerous from being printed; other religious groups simply did not have this kind of control, much as they often wanted it. It is true that some Catholic scientists felt the heat of censorship and surely there were others who felt constricted in what they could say, but the majority of Catholic scientists went about their work just like everyone else.

Setting the Record Straight: Galileo

When people think of conflict between the Church and science, they almost always think first of Galileo, but the condemnation of Galileo's work is one of the most misunderstood points in the Church's history.

By age 25, Galileo Galilei (1564–1642) was a professor of mathematics at the University of Pisa. Brilliant and arrogant, he got along so badly with his coworkers that a few years later he moved to the University of Padua, where he became interested in astronomy. Galileo heard about a new invention, the telescope, and decided he could build a better one—and he was right. By his third try, his telescope could show objects a thousand times larger and thirty times closer than could be seen with the eye. That may be puny compared to modern telescopes, but at the time it was astounding; suddenly things far off could be seen more accurately, and things close up could be studied in a way that had not been possible before. Galileo used his invention to make some important discoveries about space: He saw mountains and valleys on the moon, which everyone had thought was smooth; he determined that Jupiter had moons, which showed that not all heavenly objects moved around Earth; he discovered sunspots, proving that stars could change; and he saw that Venus went through phases, which indicated that it moved around the sun. Obviously what people were used to thinking about the heavenly spheres and what the spheres actually did were two separate things: Earth was not at the center of the universe, and planets moved around the sun.

So how did the Church respond to all of this? Quite well. Galileo had support among the Jesuit astronomers and from Cardinal Maffeo Barberini, who later became pope. However, some people thought that Galileo's ideas went against Scripture, and they started to protest. Galileo really hoped the Church would come out in support of his statements, but the leadership was not ready to take this step. After all, Galileo's ideas were still in the theoretical stage; he had some observations but did not yet have solid scientific proof that his interpretations of them were true. His many friends in the hierarchy encouraged him to keep writing about his ideas as theories rather than facts, but Galileo refused, and the Church finally condemned his ideas as heretical.

When Cardinal Barberini came to the papacy as Urban VIII in 1623, Galileo hoped the decision against him might be reversed. Urban went so far as to say that Galileo could teach his theories as hypotheses, but Galileo got this inch and took a mile: he wrote a dialogue about his ideas, which he had agreed not to do, and then went and took some scientific ideas the pope had expressed and put them in the mouth of the dumb guy in his dialogue! Urban was deeply offended and angry. He ordered Galileo brought to trial, and that is when Galileo was actually condemned and ordered to say that his theories were wrong.

This was not the Church's total rejection of a truth it simply did not like, which is the popular view of the Galileo incident. The real issue was not whether science and religion are incompatible or whether the Church should have a say in what science gets done. It was about who had the right to interpret Scripture: could Galileo do so in such a way as to support his scientific theories, or was the Church the only true source of interpretation? That was a much more loaded question in 1623 than it had been in 1423. The Protestant Reformations had torn apart Western Christianity based partly on the belief that people should be able to interpret Scripture for themselves, and the Thirty Years' War was still going on. The Church felt like it had its back to the wall, and it came out with guns blazing in defense of the faith and of its own position.

So who was right? Maybe nobody. The Church was wrong because obviously Earth is not at the center of the universe; Galileo was wrong because a good scientist should not expect support for his theories until he has the proof to back them up; and people who claim the Galileo case shows that the Church is against science are wrong because it was a particular situation in a particular time in history.

Still, there is no denying that Galileo got a bum deal, and in 1992, Pope John Paul II admitted this. Four hundred years after Galileo's views were condemned, John Paul acknowledged that the Church had been in the wrong. He said that Galileo had been good for the Church, helping its leaders realize that Scripture is about faith and should not be used to explain the physical world.

The Church Then and Now

The Church and Science in the Modern World

After the time of Galileo, the most controversial scientific theory was evolution. Charles Darwin was the first to recognize that his theory had deep implications for Christian belief. Traditionally, Christians had thought of humanity as totally different from other species, made in the image of God in ways that other species were not. Darwin's theory undercut this fundamental distinction and saw humans as simply farther down the evolutionary path. For Darwin, though, this did not negate Christian belief; he held that an infinitely powerful God certainly had the ability to create in an evolutionary manner, producing a few life forms that were then capable of evolving into any number of species. The Church's response to all this has been cautious but never hostile. Even when popes have noted that the theory calls certain Catholic doctrines into question, they have also stressed that the Church does not want to inhibit discussion and research on the theory: "[T]he Teaching Authority of the Church does not forbid that, in conformity with the present state of human sciences and sacred theology, research and discussions . . . take place with regard to the doctrine of evolution."[3] So the greatest modern scientific controversy in the public mind, including in the mind of some Catholics, has been no big deal for Catholic theology.

Modern advances in science have presented new challenges to certain Christian understandings, and sometimes the Church feels it necessary to wade into the fray. Issues such as stem cell research and human cloning have moral and religious implications, the Church says, that require it to respond. The Catholic Church does not reject science, but it does sometimes object to the way science gets done, specifically when Church leaders believe that those doing or applying the research do not show respect for the human being as God's creation. Still, the modern Church supports science, even to the extent of having its own scientific community—the Pontifical Academy of Science. Founded in 1936 under Pope Pius XI, the academy includes members working in many of the major areas of science and mathematics. People enter the academy by invitation only; the current members vote on new members, who are then appointed by the pope. This is a prestigious group: more than forty members have been Nobel Prize winners. The academy's role is to provide a framework for interdisciplinary cooperation among scientists through meetings, conferences, and publications.

The members of the academy are not usually members of the Church, but the days of the church member/scientist are not gone. In fact, the Vatican even has its own observatory at Castel Gandolfo, the pope's summer palace outside Rome. It is run by—who else?—Jesuits, who also run the Vatican Observatory Research Group's telescope in Arizona. Some peculiar ideas have been put out there about these Jesuit astronomers: they have been accused of being the pope's astrologers or of training to be missionaries on Mars. Ask the astronomers themselves, however, and you get a picture of good Catholics who try to be good scientists as well.

One of them, Brother Guy Consolmagno, has written about his life as a Church astronomer. He believes that when people see a conflict between science and religion, it is usually because they think science has all the answers—a mistake a scientist would never make—and he sees himself as a "living witness to the Church's commitment to truth and the scientist's commitment to God."[4] Other scientists, including Galileo, might have reasons to question the Church's commitment, but there can be no doubt that the scientific world would look very different today were it not for the long history of Catholics creating new fields of study and discovering new ideas.

Questions and Ideas for Understanding

1. The Jesuits were formed to fight for the Catholic faith; in what ways were they doing this as educators?

2. Do you think the Christian missionaries of the fifteenth through seventeenth centuries went about their work in ways that fully respected the peoples and cultures they encountered? If not, what sort of change do you think would have made this possible?

3. Do you think the Church has the right or the responsibility to speak out about scientific matters? Why or why not?

4. Select some writings from the work of either Teresa of Avila or Juana Ines de la Cruz; write an essay explaining the work and placing it in the context of its time.

Notes

[1] Ignatius Loyola, from *The Spiritual Exercises of St. Ignatius,* trans. Anthony Mottola. New York: Doubleday & Company, 1964, pp. 139–142.

[2] *Teresa of Avila: Selections from* The Interior Castle, trans. Kieran Kavanaugh and Otilio Rodriguez. New York: Harper San Francisco, 2004, pp. 6–7.

[3] Pius XII, *Humani Generis* 36. Retrieved from http://www.papalencyclicals.net/Pius12/P12HUMAN. HTM (accessed 10/5/2007).

[4] Guy Consolmagno, *Brother Astronomer.* New York: McGraw-Hill, 2000.

13

New Challenges to Ancient Traditions

Vatican I and the Modern Era

Chapter Overview

In this chapter, we will explore:

▶ The beginnings of the global village in the eighteenth and nineteenth centuries

▶ The American and French revolutions and their effects on the Church

▶ New ideas from the Enlightenment and the Industrial Revolution

▶ Vatican I and the Church's response to the modern world

▶ The Church's teachings on issues of social justice

Sean: Finding Prejudice in the Promised Land

You take a big bite of your sandwich and lean back in the grass. The sun on your face feels wonderful. It was your dad's idea to get the whole family out of town and into the meadow for the day. You don't get many holidays working at the factory, so being away from the machines is a relief. Your mom looks relaxed—a good thing, since with a husband and eight kids, she doesn't usually have time to breathe, much less sit down. Yep, another good idea of Dad's. But his best one of all had been coming to this country.

In the seven years you have been in the United States, you have grown from a 10-year-old boy to a young man. You work for a living alongside your dad in the glass factory and bring home money to your mom every week just like he does. It's hard work, hot and tiring, but you don't mind; you're just glad there's work to be had at all. Back in Ireland, you had seen people starving when their crops failed and they couldn't get work. You thank God every day that your family escaped that. Not that life in America has been easy—the good Lord knows that even with your dad and the four oldest kids working, the family still has barely enough for clothes and food. Like right now, you desperately need new shoes—you could plant a bush in that hole in your right boot—but who has money for things like that? Still, when you compare the little you have here to the nothing back in Ireland, it's easy to see why your dad chose to leave.

Every now and then, he talks about how hard it was to leave behind everyone and everything. He says he knew it would be hard to start over in a new place, and he expected to be given a hard time because he was an immigrant. What he didn't expect was that his faith would cause him problems, too. From the minute your family stepped off the boat, some people looked at you like spies and traitors just for being Catholic. Like that guy Swenson down at the factory, who is always calling you a papist and telling people that you worship the pope and Mary instead of God and Jesus. Sure, you know that Swenson and his friends are just ignorant, but it's hard dealing with the constant name calling and put-downs. Hey, you just want to work hard and make something of your life and hopefully find a way to give your own kids—once you have them—a brighter future. Is that so different from what people like Swenson want?

You don't want to think about the likes of Swenson today, though. In fact, you don't want to think about any problems at all. It's a holiday, and you just want to smell the clean, sweet air and look at the blue sky, so you roll over on the grass, catch your little brother in your arms, and laugh with him as you swing him up toward the sun.

Sean is typical of the Catholic immigrants who came to the United States in the eighteenth and nineteenth centuries. Many arrived with little more than what they were wearing and the hope for a better life. We will talk about how Catholics experienced America in the early history of the country. Struggle was the way of life in the eighteenth and nineteenth centuries, which included such pivotal events as the French Revolution with its devastating effects on the Church. The Church was struggling in other ways, too, as it tried to deal with the new ways of thinking brought on by the Enlightenment and new ways of doing that the Industrial Revolution kicked off. We will see how the Church responded to all this newness, including the convening of the First Vatican Council. Finally, we will look at the vibrant tradition of Church teachings that call Catholics to recognize the struggles of the poor and mistreated and to act for justice in the world. ■

Bringing the World Closer to Home

Today we talk about the world as a global village. We recognize that what happens in a little town in Kansas can affect how people live in Uganda or Peru, mainly through trade and commerce. Let's say you are sitting on a couch; the metal for the frame might come from Ghana, the fabric for the cover from India, the cotton stuffing from Tanzania, with the whole thing assembled in Korea before being sold in the United States—four continents and five countries for just one piece of furniture. The global village was certainly not this advanced in the eighteenth and nineteenth centuries, but we can see its beginnings. Traders were importing and exporting materials, and people in many areas of the world were starting to feel the crunch from competition in far-off lands. A worldwide economy was taking shape, and the competition added new challenges for the working person.

All this contact among peoples had benefits as well. With traders traveling the globe, more and more people were being exposed to the same diseases. That may not sound like a good thing, but in the big picture it is. As people were exposed to the same infections and developed the same antibodies, it became much less common for someone to show up with a new disease that would wipe out entire populations. Famines also became less common and less severe because food could be shipped quickly where it was needed. With information circulating faster than ever, it became easier to know where the needs were. All in all, business around the globe was speeding up, and the world was coming closer together.

Closer together does not necessarily mean happier, however. Consider the countries of Western Europe—they spent most of the eighteenth and nineteenth centuries fighting each other. Now that a number of those countries had empires spread around the globe, they had more to fight about.

France and Britain carried their squabbles around the world, with Britain largely the winner due to several natural advantages: It was separated from the mainland of Europe; small; centralized; and most important, it dominated the high seas. By the eighteenth century, England was planning all its fights and conquests around its sea power. That was bad news for countries like Spain, which had been in a serious slump dating back to Britain's defeat of its Armada in 1588. All the income from its empire kept Spain going for a while, but by the early nineteenth century, colonists throughout Latin America had won independence from both Spain and Portugal. These two countries fade from the world stage after that. Things were also bleak for Germany, which remained a mess of principalities until the second half of the nineteenth century, and Italy was struggling to form itself into some sort of unified country. Things were chaotic in the little part of the globe that controlled so much of the rest of it.

Work and lifestyles were evolving as well. Even with cities and factories becoming important, most people still lived in rural areas and worked on farms, but they did not necessarily do things the way they had always been done. Farmers were beginning to use complex rotation systems for their crops, resulting in bigger harvests. In addition, everyday people were buying more: They took to drinking coffee and tea, which until recently only the rich could afford. They bought soap and began washing more often, lit their houses with candles and lamps, and bought toys for their children and newspapers for themselves. Capitalism was taking root, not only in the ways people worked but also in their attitudes as consumers.

Revolution and Religion

Economics had an impact well beyond the merely personal. Two of the biggest events of the time—the American and French revolutions—had financial underpinnings. In both cases, protests about the way governments were dealing with their finances played a big role in lighting the revolutionary fires.

Setting Up a New Country: The American Revolution

In the dead of night, a group of colonists dressed as Native Americans quietly climb on board a ship. They sneak around and find the ship's cargo—a load of tea—and gleefully toss it into the harbor. This famous incident, the Boston Tea Party, was part of the lead-up to the American Revolution. The tea-tossers were protesting England's taxing of goods coming into America. The colonists were not represented in the English government, so they had no say on their taxes, a situation that made them furious. Most of the colonies were democratic, and everyone—or at least every white male who owned property—had a say in what went on. It stood to reason that eventually they would grow tired of a system controlled by a king across the sea. However, the government back in England wanted to keep control of the colonies, especially because of their profitable business interests. All this made for a situation that went from difficult to dangerous to downright hostile. When this hostility was combined with the "we are all equal" ideas of the Enlightenment, it led to a revolution.

By 1776, the colonists decided they had had enough, and at the Second Continental Congress, they declared their intention to create their own country, one in which individual rights would take center stage. The French, who had been taking a licking from the British all over the globe, were more than happy to help the upstart colonists when they decided to take a military stand against the British.

The American Revolution was not really a big war—General Washington never led more than twenty thousand soldiers into a battle, which was small by military standards—but it was huge in terms of influence. When the colonies won their independence in 1781, they established a representative form of government and created a nation where Church and State were more separate than the Western world had ever seen. The leaders of the French Revolution were inspired by what they saw happening over in America, as were the people who drafted the constitutions of Switzerland, Norway, Belgium, and Canada, among others. Around the globe, people took the ideas of democracy and individual freedom embraced by the American Revolution and made their own countries into places governed of, by, and for the people.

Reinventing an Old Country: The French Revolution

America was not the only place feeling a burst of revolutionary spirit. Over in France, a series of economic and agricultural disasters in the late 1780s led to famine on the one hand and anger against the king's government on the other. Put the two together, and you have a recipe for violence.

Representatives of the common people were called together with clergy members and the nobility to deal with the crisis. When the commoners got tired of dealing with the other two groups, they took their inspiration from the Americans across the Atlantic and declared themselves a National Assembly. The assembly issued the Declaration of the Rights of Man, which stated that all men (and presumably women) have certain rights that cannot be taken away: the right to liberty, property, and security; equality under the law and with regard to opportunity; freedom of association, expression, and the press as well as from oppression or arbitrary arrest; and religious toleration. They declared that only an elected assembly has the right to make new laws, levy taxes, control the armed forces, and supervise the government.

In other words, the National Assembly declared the king null and void.

By 1791, the people of France were hoping the chaos of the revolution would give way to a more stable situation, but instead things just got messier. France declared itself a republic, and the king and queen were executed. This alarmed the monarchs of France's neighbors, and soon the country found itself battling on just about every front and ending up with a civil war to boot. Enter General Napoleon Bonaparte, who decided he would be the one to restore order. Napoleon and two others took command in 1797, but by 1804, the little general had declared himself emperor. Napoleon restored order, repairing roads, constructing new highways, improving communication, stabilizing public finances and the currency, and issuing a new legal code. He also kept up the wars, and by 1807, most of Europe was at his mercy. His good luck came crashing to an end eight years later at Waterloo, and six years after that he died in exile.

The French had to work through more attempts at monarchy after their revolution, but by 1870, the country was a full-fledged democracy. This allowed the French middle class to become a central force in society—a position previously held by the nobility—and helped unify the country. In France, democratic institutions such as elections, representative government, and constitutions were showcased for all of Europe to see, which eventually changed the way European countries looked at government altogether.

Big Problems for the Church

The American Revolution had little impact on the Church; after all, a few colonies in a far-off land breaking away from a Protestant country was not big news to the Catholic Church in Europe. The French Revolution, however, made for hard times for the Church. The revolutionaries tried to get the country out of its financial mess by taking over the Church's property in France, which amounted to about 10 percent of the country's cultivatable land. In the violence and chaos of the revolution, something like thirty thousand clergy members left their posts, and many left the country. Those who stayed were persecuted and sometimes massacred, and many churches and monasteries were destroyed. Before the Revolution, the Church was critically important in French society; by its end, many thought the Church pointless at best and a hallmark of the old oppressive ways at worst. Catholic rulers in other European countries meanwhile decided some of these Church reforms looked good and started putting them in place in their own countries.

Pope Pius VI was horrified by all this but also scared to protest too much for fear of turning countries toward Protestantism as England had done a few centuries before. Then Napoleon invaded Italy. The pope had to agree to a humiliating compromise just so Napoleon would leave Rome alone; in the end, Napoleon sent French troops into the city anyway. They arrested all the cardinals they could get their hands on and carried Pius off as a prisoner; he died in captivity. Once Napoleon's government imploded, the new pope was restored to Rome and was once again recognized as ruler of the Papal States.

All this had a big impact on how future popes thought about their worldly power. Over the course of the next century, the Italians tried to form a unified country, and they needed to include the Papal States in it. After all, the Papal States lay right in the center and included Rome, which had to be the capital of any Italy worth having. However, after the revolution and Napoleon, the popes were convinced they needed the secular power they got from the Papal States just to maintain the freedom of the Church, and this led to many fights close to home.

The fallout for the Church did not stop there. By 1815, there were almost no monks in Western Europe outside of Spain. Some countries had begun allowing civil marriage and divorce; in many areas, the press was free from religious influence; and throughout Europe, people were calling for—and getting—religious toleration. The Church and its ideas were not the center of European society anymore. Pope Pius VII decided the best way to shore up European Catholicism was to restore the Jesuits, which he did in 1814. He also needed the support of European rulers, however, and during the nineteenth century, the Church signed many treaties with European countries as a way of securing the freedom of the Church in those areas.

Thinking about Humanity: The Enlightenment

After years of religious wars tearing up Europe, people were tired of living in deep uncertainty. Once peace was restored, many started thinking about separating the religious questions that had caused such friction from the philosophical and moral issues that affected their daily lives. Reason, people believed, could provide the new grounding they were looking for, and it was a grounding to which everyone—Catholic and Protestant, believer and atheist—had access.

This new thinking filtered into every area of human life: political, social, and economic issues; understandings of history, philosophy, science, and religion. The old view of God as an all-powerful ruler just did not work for Enlightenment people, who were starting to think about the deity as a scientist and architect who had designed the universe to lead humans to happiness. The "God works in mysterious ways" idea seemed outdated, as did the notion that some things are known only because God has revealed them. The Bible is full of miracles and other happenings that do not make sense according to the laws of nature. This had not bothered Christians of the past, but it bothered people now. "God created the laws of nature for a reason; surely he is going to work within them," was the new line of thought. Besides, people were more interested in morality than in faith, so they tended to see the Bible as a book that laid out a moral code and talked about Jesus as a great teacher rather than as a savior.

What does it mean to put reason and morality in the place that faith used to occupy? Among other things, it means that if humans can learn to use reason perfectly, then they themselves can become perfect—no more sense of sin or unworthiness, no more need for a savior to bring about a change that humans are incapable of making on their own. People do not need to be freed from some innate evil; the way to make people better is through education rather than stronger faith, and the purpose of religion is to help people live well here on earth, not to lead them to something greater in some other life.

Granted, the common man and woman continued to hold more traditional beliefs, and much of this "enlightened" debate was taking place mostly among the intellectual elite, but that does not mean these ideas were not powerful. In fact, Western society continues to live in the world that Enlightenment thinkers created. For example, Enlightenment thinkers (let's call them

ETs) wanted reason to be the center of life; we look to science to tell us what is true. ETs wanted the rule of law in politics; this is how all Western democracies are set up. ETs saw industrialization as a good thing; industrialization remains the basis of modern economies.

Some of our deepest struggles have Enlightenment roots, too. We struggle to deal with the truths that lay beyond science, the morality that does not square up with law, and the sense that we must live within nature rather than conquering it. Here in the United States, we are particularly tied to Enlightenment thinking; in fact, it is at the very heart of our Constitution. We find it in the idea that humans can create their own destiny and that a person's abilities and actions rather than his or her birth should determine how he or she lives. It is so much a part of who we are that we often do not realize there was ever any other way of thinking.

What the God of the Enlightenment Looked Like

When Enlightenment thinkers talked about God, they broke from the God images of the early Church or Middle Ages. If God is not a king (why would believers in democracy want a king?) or a savior (what do humans need to be saved from?), then what can be said about the divine? Let's take a look:

God Is the Universe

Seeing God and the universe as the same thing is called pantheism, and it made a lot of sense at a time when people were starting to learn more about the universe. They figured out that it was larger than anyone could ever have imagined, maybe even infinite; that it worked according to specific laws; and that for all its great diversity, everything seemed to work perfectly together. To many people, that sounded like a good definition of divinity.

God Is a Clockmaker

Okay, not really a clockmaker, but that is how people expressed a concept called deism, which is the idea that God created the universe to be self-running. People holding this view believed God got the universe going, set the laws of nature in motion, then stepped back and let everything "tick" without any further interference. This view of God was particularly popular with people who wanted to understand God from the standpoint of science. Quite a few of America's Founding Fathers were deists.

God Is a Big Lie

Atheism, the belief that there is no God, was nothing new in the eighteenth century, but it gained a lot of ground then. Atheists tended to make reason the center of life, and religion the culprit for getting people more interested in the world to come than in making this one a better place. Atheists argued that you do not need to think there is a God to live a moral life.

Of course, none of these conceptions of God fit with Christian belief or Catholic teaching, and Church leaders were alarmed that such ideas were gaining in popularity with the intellectuals. In fact, these ideas reflected a worldview that some Catholics would come to believe needed to be fought with every tool in the Church's arsenal.

Going High-Tech, Nineteenth-Century Style: The Industrial Revolution

While these intellectual debates swirled, closer to the ground people were dealing with another kind of societal change—technological. Technology was developing so rapidly during the late eighteenth and early nineteenth centuries that we talk about this time as the Industrial Revolution. New machines were being created and older ones used on a much wider scale than ever before. The revolution started in England and spread outward from there. England was ripe for such a change because it was creating a lot of wealth, and as people got more money, they started wanting more and finer things. This led business owners to look for better ways to create those things.

The Industrial Revolution changed working life dramatically: More people found themselves working in factories, iron replaced wood in the making of tools, and steam rather than water or human effort was the top energy source. Railroads made it possible to send products over long distances in a short time. Capitalism was taking off and taking over, and many big industrialists were taking advantage of their workforce. The rich got richer by producing and selling more goods while paying starvation wages. Some people began arguing that society had a responsibility to help these workers, and these voices grew stronger as the plight of workers worsened. Still, it took awhile for the idea that workers have rights to make any headway.

The Industrial Revolution literally changed the way nations looked. Instead of vast stretches of countryside dotted with a few cities and towns, cities crept farther into what used to be rural land. Factories and their workers had to become more specialized; instead of making something from start to finish, workers usually participated in only one step of the process. This in turn made all those separate factories and workers interdependent and left the worker more at the mercy of his employer than his farming ancestor had been; after all, a farmer can decide to grow his own crops, but a factory worker cannot build his own factory. For the most part, the relationship between workers and owners worsened, which opened the way for theories like Marxism to call the entire system into question. However, the Industrial Revolution also gave birth to the modern understanding of professions, increased the food supply, sparked a rise in population, and led to the modern capitalist society in the United States.

It is often said that every generation wants to make life better for their children. The Industrial Revolution made that an attainable goal for the first time.

Strengthening the Papacy: Vatican I

Times were troubled, and many Catholics wanted a strong leader to guide them through the chaos; they came to believe that the Church's power and authority needed to be more centralized in the papacy than ever before. What with secular governments trying to get control over the Church in their lands and national churches heading off in all sorts of directions, these Catholics wanted a pope who would rule with a strong hand, someone more like the absolute monarchs of old than the elected presidents of the modern era. These Catholics became known as ultramontanists, literally "beyond the mountain" people, because they believed the highest authority should not come from within their own lands but from "beyond the mountains"—in Rome, where the Pope was. It was this desire for a strengthened papacy that led to the First Vatican Council, which we usually call Vatican I.

The council began in December 1869 under the direction of Pio Nono, with about seven hundred bishops present. No laypeople or representatives from other Christian denominations were invited, although Pio had notified them that he was calling the council together.

Focus On
Stemming the Tide of Change

The Church ran a rugged course in the eighteenth and nineteenth centuries. With new ideas from the Enlightenment and the Industrial Revolution being bandied about, the Church found its teachings, its structure, and even its very reason for being called into question. Some Catholics believed the Church needed to take a stand against these modern challenges, while others believed the only way to survive and be relevant was to allow the new ideas to inform the ancient faith. The Church was in for a rough ride.

From the viewpoint of the laity, the state of Catholicism actually looked good during these centuries. Even though many monasteries had closed, people who wanted the monk's or nun's life had lots of options because new Orders were being created and older ones were actually growing; the biggest growth was in women's Orders and those dedicated to mission work. People searching for a deeper faith experience in the midst of their daily lives were likely to find it in devotion to the Blessed Virgin, which absolutely exploded in the nineteenth century as apparitions of Mary became known around the world. Possibly the most famous appeared in 1858, when the first in a series of eighteen visions of Mary came to a poor French girl at Lourdes, France, which in turn became one of the greatest pilgrimage sites in the modern world. Actually, we can say that Lourdes became a great pilgrimage site *because of* the modern world because the new railways and steamships allowed pilgrims to travel to this and other holy sites.

From the view of the Church's hierarchy, however, the eighteenth and nineteenth centuries looked much more grim. Catholic rulers across Europe were trying to reduce the pope's power and bring the Church in their lands back under their direct control. They wanted to appoint bishops and abbots, dictate what feast days would be observed, control appeals to Rome, and decide which papal statements would be published in their countries. It was like dragging the Church back seven hundred years to the time of the Investiture Controversy, and the popes wanted none of it.

In fact, for the better part of the nineteenth century, the popes were none too happy with most of what was happening in the world. Repeatedly, they condemned what they saw as too much attention to new ways of thinking and too little to the faith of the fathers. For instance, in 1832, Gregory XVI took issue with freedom of conscience, of the press, and of speech. Modern Americans hold these things dear, but Gregory saw them as threats to faith and the authority of the Church. If people have the freedom to decide their religious views for themselves, many will fall into error; if the press and speech are free, lies will be spread. Gregory thought modern people grabbed onto new, liberal ideas without thinking them through. He was willing to fight against this, which meant fighting those Catholics who thought the Church needed to embrace modern thought in order to remain relevant. How, they reasoned, would

continued on page 275

continued from page 274

people take Church teachings seriously if the Church simply rejected modern society outright?

One nineteenth-century pope who took a strong stand against new thinking actually started out embracing modern ideals, but a series of events caused him to change course. Pius IX (1846–1878)—known to the world as Pio Nono—took up the cause of modernization of the Papal States early in his papacy. He brought in rail lines, had gas lighting set up in Rome, convinced farmers to use new methods of agriculture that increased their harvests, put tariffs in place to help trade, and did away with many of the restrictions that had been placed on Jews over the years. He also made serious political reforms in the Papal States, including creating an assembly with lay representatives that was designed to help run the states. However, the revolutions that swept across Europe in 1848 led to a seismic change in Pio Nono's thinking.

Pio Nono took seriously his local role as bishop of Rome, in addition to his universal role as leader of the Church. Rather than staying locked away in the Vatican, he got out among the Romans, visiting schools and hospitals, confirming children, and preaching at small chapels all over the city. He was beloved by everyone— that is, until Italy became embroiled in revolution. When Pio denounced some actions of the Italian revolutionaries, his appeal rating plummeted. The Romans now despised him, calling him a traitor and forcing him to flee from Rome in disguise. He was able to return to the Vatican after two years but only because French troops accompanied him, and the presence of soldiers was a necessity for the remainder of his papacy.

By the time Pio Nono returned to St. Peter's, his thinking about modern ideals had changed dramatically. He no longer believed he was to help bring the Church into the modern world; his role, as he saw it now, was to maintain the ancient faith in dark and troubled times. He was convinced the liberalism he had been so eager to embrace in his younger days merely fueled the fires of revolution and atheism, tearing people away from God and the Church.

And he was ready to fight, which often meant fighting those within the Church itself who believed in the new ideals. In response to Catholics wishing to use modern methods such as archaeology and textual criticism to understand Scripture or Church doctrine, he issued a work commonly known as the *Syllabus of Errors*. In it, Pio railed against secularism, rationalism, socialism, liberal capitalism, freedom of religion, and the idea of progress. If modern society was going to declare war on the Church, then Pio Nono was going to declare war on modern ideas.

The attack did not end there. Less than thirty years later, another pope, Leo XIII, let it be known that the American way of doing things was not going to be acceptable in the Church. To Leo, *American* meant "adapted to the modern world," and not just in the big ideas Pio Nono had condemned. Leo also went after the personal practices he thought were leading people into danger, like seeing the inner workings of the Spirit as more important than the direction provided by the Church or thinking that natural virtues like honesty and loyalty were more important than the supernatural virtues of faith, love, and charity. ■

From the beginning, there was conflict between the ultramontanist bishops wanting a monarch and the liberals who thought the Church should accept and incorporate modern ideas. The battle was a lopsided one because the ultramontanists were in control from the beginning. They showed it by making infallibility—the doctrine that the pope can issue certain kinds of statements that can never be wrong—the central issue to resolve.

Most of the bishops gathered actually supported the idea of infallibility, but not all believed that defining it as doctrine was a good idea. Some thought they needed a way to make sure such statements would be rare, some were not convinced about the theological and historical basis for the concept, some were worried that the bishops' authority was being undercut, and some just thought the timing was bad because it was sure to cause problems in dealing with other Christian denominations. The bishops debated a draft statement for nearly two months, then finally issued a document explaining the pope's infallibility:

> [S]ince in this very age when the salutary effectiveness of the apostolic office is most especially needed, not a few are to be found who disparage its authority, we judge it absolutely necessary to affirm solemnly the prerogative which the only-begotten Son of God was pleased to attach to the supreme pastoral office.
>
> Therefore, faithfully adhering to the tradition received from the beginning of the Christian faith, to the glory of God our saviour, for the exaltation of the Catholic religion and for the salvation of the Christian people, with the approval of the sacred council, we teach and define as a divinely revealed dogma that when the Roman pontiff speaks EX CATHEDRA, that is, when, in the exercise of his office as shepherd and teacher of all Christians, in virtue of his supreme apostolic authority, he defines a doctrine concerning faith or morals to be held by the whole Church, he possesses, by the divine assistance promised him in blessed Peter, that infallibility which the divine Redeemer willed his church to enjoy in defining doctrine concerning faith or morals. Therefore, such definitions of the Roman pontiff are of themselves, and not by the consent of the Church, irreformable.[1]

About sixty bishops who could not in good conscience support the statement left Rome before the final vote; they would not publicly stand against the work of a Church council, but they could not be a part of it, either.

Infallibility is probably the most misunderstood doctrine in the Church. *Infallible* literally means "not able to be wrong," and theologically it means that the pope has a special gift of the Holy Spirit that protects him from error when he is solemnly defining matters of faith and morals. The idea is that at those special moments when he speaks *ex cathedra,* literally "from the chair" of Peter, the pope expresses the mind of the whole Church coming together under the guidance of the Holy Spirit. By definition, an infallible statement is guaranteed to be free from error but is not guaranteed to be the best or fullest expression of the issue. The Catholic belief that the Church is constantly led by the Holy Spirit to deeper understanding of the truths it teaches means that later generations of Catholics may come to see older statements, even infallible ones, as no longer fully expressing those truths.

While the formal definition of infallibility had to wait for Vatican I, the idea that the pope could make infallible statements was first directly expressed in the fourteenth century. You will not find anything specifically about infallibility in the New Testament (NT), but Catholics see the roots of this doctrine in the authority Jesus gave to his apostles, the need to make sure correct doctrine is taught, and the belief that the Holy Spirit guides the Church. Although the infallibility of the pope is a point of contention between Catholics and other Christian groups, most popes never make a statement that comes under the heading of "infallible." This has occurred only twice: in 1854—sixteen years before the doctrine was officially defined—when Pio Nono declared Mary to be the Immaculate Conception; and again in 1950, when Pope Pius XII declared that she was bodily taken up into heaven in the Assumption.

Back at Vatican I, the ultramontanists finished defining the doctrine just in time; one day after the infallibility statement was issued, the Franco-Prussian War broke out and the bishops had to leave Rome. The declaration of infallibility may have been a shining light in the eyes of those Catholics who wanted the popes to be absolute monarchs, but another event of the same war dashed at least some of their hopes: An Italian army captured Rome, and the pope's power as a political ruler came to an end. The Papal States were no more. Almost sixty years later, the pope was once again declared a ruler but this time over a tiny fraction of the area once controlled by the papacy. Vatican City, the world's smallest sovereign state, was created in 1929.

Working for the Workers

Infallibility may have gotten big press in the nineteenth century, but how the Church was coming to understand its role in taking a stand for workers and the poor had a much bigger societal impact. The Industrial Revolution had some great long-term effects, but in the short run, it was a disaster for big chunks of the population, a fact that horrified Karl Marx and led him to imagine a future where workers were in charge. Marx (1818–1883) was a poor German exile living in London when he and his friend Fredrick Engels published the *Communist Manifesto* in 1848. The book did not exactly set the world on fire when it was published, so twenty years later, when Marx wrote *Das Kapital*, a Russian censor found the work so deadly dull and unimportant that he let a translation be published, figuring no one would read it anyway. Not many people did at first, but then Vladimir Lenin—the future father of the Russian Revolution—latched onto Marx's ideas as the solution for Russia's ills, and suddenly the world took notice of Karl Marx.

Marx came to believe that civilization is really the history of class struggle. Economic injustice, he said, is the only cause of human conflict; things like religion or politics are just excuses people use to mask the real issues. The situation Marx saw all around him gave him ample fodder for his ideas: factory owners forcing workers into meaningless jobs that paid starvation wages, child labor a mainstay in factories, runaway capitalism creating more class conflict than any system in history, and the most basic understandings of human worth and dignity ignored as irrelevant throughout the whole structure.

Most people saw these injustices as inevitable—simply the way the world works. Marx, however, believed that if workers banded together and fought for their rights, they could sweep away the old injustices and create a new system in which everyone would be equal. In Marx's communist society, there would be no private property. Religion, which Marx saw as helping the powerful by getting the powerless to focus more on the next world than on this one, would become extinct.

Marx was not the first to imagine humans living together in a class-free society where everyone owns everything in common. In fact, the image calls to mind monasticism and even more looks like the society of the first Christians described in the Acts of the Apostles. However, Marx did not think love of God and neighbor was going to make this sort of sharing possible; it would take all-out war to put the system in place. Marx had no use for the idea of God, or even for human choice, because he thought social conditions rather than our consciences determine who we are and how we live. There was no place for accident, change, or even compassion in Marx's view of history and society.

Marx was not totally wrong in thinking many in the Church were on the side of those wanting to keep things as they were, but some Catholics were coming to realize that things could be—and had to be—different. They recognized that Marx was raising valid questions but worried that his ideas would pull people away from the Church and from Christian understandings about the nature of the human being and the meaning of life. They realized that from the Christian perspective, the Church needed to help protect workers both from greedy industrialists who made their fortunes at the expense of the poor and from Marxists who wanted to better workers' lives at the expense of their souls.

The Church had cared for the poor and discarded since its earliest days, but now it began to realize it needed to do more than try to make their lives better in the current situation—it needed to help change the situation itself. Pope Leo XIII (1878–1903) took a strong stand for workers when he issued the document *Rerum Novarum* in 1891. Leo did not go for the capitalist idea that the market should be the only determining factor in how to deal with workers; this had created too many miseries. Instead, he called for the State to protect workers and declared that workers had the right to organize and to demand higher pay and better working conditions. Eventually this led to the creation of Christian trade unions. However, Leo did not agree with the Marxists either, because he thought that private property was fine and that the family rather than the State was the basic building block of society. Leo also believed changes could be made peacefully. Having criticized both capitalism and socialism, he called on Christians to change themselves and the world around them by getting involved in social justice—a call that has grown clearer and deeper within the Church ever since.

Voices from the Past

Rerum Novarum

▶ Author: Leo XIII

▶ Written: 1891

▶ Audience: Bishops, officially; all people, unofficially

This encyclical is a product of its time, talking about issues in language that can sound traditional and disturbingly paternal to modern ears, but make no mistake—Leo was leaping into the arena of social justice with both feet. In the excerpts below, he lays out what he believes should be the responsibilities of the State, workers and employers:

> Rulers should . . . anxiously safeguard the community and all its members; the community, because the conservation thereof is so emphatically the business of the supreme power, that the safety of the commonwealth is not only the first law, but it is a government's whole reason of existence; and the members, because both philosophy and the Gospel concur in laying down that the object of the government of the State should be, not the advantage of the ruler, but the benefit of those over whom he is placed. As the power to rule comes from God, and is, as it were, a participation in His, the highest of all sovereignties, it should be exercised as the power of God is exercised—with a fatherly solicitude which not only guides the whole, but reaches also individuals.[2]

[T]he following bind the proletarian and the worker: Fully and faithfully to perform the work which has been freely and equitably agreed upon; never to injure the property, nor to outrage the person, of an employer; never to resort to violence in defending their own cause, nor to engage in riot or disorder; and to have nothing to do with men of evil principles, who work upon the people with artful promises of great results, and excite foolish hopes which usually end in useless regrets and grievous loss. The following duties bind the wealthy owner and employer: Not to look upon their work people as their bondsmen, but to respect in every man his dignity as a person ennobled by Christian character. They are reminded that, according to natural reason and Christian philosophy, working for gains is creditable, not shameful, to a man, since it enables him to earn an honorable livelihood; but to misuse men as though they were things in the pursuit of gain, or to value them solely for their physical powers—that is truly shameful and inhuman. Again justice demands, in dealing with the working man, religion and the good of his soul must be kept in mind. Hence, the employer is bound to see that the worker has time for his religious duties; that he be not exposed to corrupting influences and dangerous occasions; and that he be not led away to neglect his home and family, or to squander his earnings. Furthermore, the employer must never tax his work people beyond their strength, or employ them in work unsuited to their sex and age. His great and principal duty is to give everyone what is just . . . Lastly, the rich must religiously refrain from cutting down the workmen's earnings, whether by force, by fraud, or by usurious dealing; and with all the greater reason because the laboring man is, as a rule, weak and unprotected, and because his slender means should in proportion to their scantiness be accounted sacred. Were these precepts carefully obeyed and followed out, would they not be sufficient of themselves to keep under all strife and all its causes?[3] ■

Rerum Novarum was based on a deep belief in human dignity, which is the starting point for all Catholic social teaching. Read it today and it does not sound radical, but it was a huge step for a pope to take. More than that, it laid out a path that Catholic teaching would follow and paved the way for future Church leaders to take up and continue its call.

Carrying the Faith to a New Land

We usually think of early American history as a Protestant time, considering the role the Puritans and others played. That is largely true—even at the time of the revolution, about 85 percent of Americans were Protestant—but Catholics were certainly here and having an impact. Catholic missionaries set up the first stable mission and parish on the continent in St. Augustine, Florida, in 1565—fifty-five years before the Puritans landed at Plymouth Rock. Catholics also could be found in the original thirteen colonies, especially in Maryland and Pennsylvania. In fact, Maryland was founded by an English Catholic, Lord Cecil Baltimore, in 1634. Oddly enough, Lord Baltimore never actually set foot in the colony he founded, or on any American soil for that matter. He stayed in England and sent a group of settlers, mostly Catholic, to the New World. Even there, though, Protestants still outnumbered Catholics by the time of the revolution.

In the beginning, Catholics had an easier time in Maryland than in the other colonies because they were allowed to practice their religion openly and without fear. Maryland passed an Act of Toleration in 1649 that granted religious toleration to all Christian denominations (although it also made denying the divinity of Christ a capital offence). If you wanted to be a citizen in Massachusetts, on the other hand, you had to pledge an oath of allegiance that specifically denounced the pope. Not even Maryland could hang on to religious freedom: the Protestant majority managed to repeal the Act of Toleration within twenty years of the colony's founding. By the turn of the eighteenth century, the only place that Catholics had the same rights as all other citizens was in Rhode Island, which was founded by settlers fleeing the intolerance of the Massachusetts colony.

Once the colonies became a nation, things did not get much better for Catholics. In 1774, the British Parliament gave Catholics full religious rights in Canada. Over the border in the future United States, members of the First

Continental Congress meeting at the same time protested the new law in Canada, saying that giving rights to Catholics was dangerous to the civil rights and liberties of all Americans. Do not think that the revolution brought full freedom to all (white male) Americans; even afterwards, some states would not allow Catholics to participate in the political process.

Big Changes, Big Numbers, and Big Tensions for American Catholics

The Catholic population of the new United States began growing in the last part of the eighteenth century, when the French Revolution and a revolt in what is now Haiti caused boatloads of fleeing Catholics to show up in U.S. cities. The Louisiana Purchase in 1803 also caused a jump in the number of U.S. Catholics, but it was immigrants coming to America in the nineteenth century, especially from Ireland, that really caused the numbers to explode. From 1830 to 1870, the Catholic population grew 1,400 percent, from 318,000 to 4.5 million. Catholics still made up only 13 percent of the population, but they had become the largest single religious denomination in the country—something that still holds true today.

This Catholic influx caused big changes in Catholic life in the United States. Catholic communities had been more or less independent of one another, with only a few bishops to lead them. However, as the number of Catholics grew, so did the Church structure, which became better organized with more bishops to do the work. As immigrants became the biggest part of the American Church, anti-Catholic sentiment grew as well. Many Protestants saw Catholicism as opposed to the very ideals on which their country was founded: democracy, civil liberties, and religious toleration. Catholics had a rough time convincing their skeptical fellow citizens that they really accepted the most basic values of American life.

Often shunned or oppressed by the society around them, American Catholics also had divisions among themselves. The United States was founded on the principle of separating secular government and religious institutions, but this issue divided American Catholics. To some, the benefits of the American way of thinking were clear, but for others and for the Church hierarchy in Rome, this was a terrible idea because it seemed to push religious beliefs away from the heart of social and political life. Things did not get easier once Leo

XIII condemned Americanism. While Leo made it clear that he was going after the spirit of individualism and materialism and not after American political institutions, he did not win Catholics any friends among those in the United States who were already hostile to the Church.

The Church Then and Now

Bringing Justice to Society

The Catholic Church has always taught that faith must be the source of how its members act both in their personal lives and out in the world. Since the time of *Rerum Novarum,* though, the Church has understood this responsibility in a new light: from simply calling on people to act in a loving manner toward one another, to calling on them to be actively involved in the struggle for justice for all with a special preference for the poor and the powerless. Over the course of the twentieth century, many Church leaders and clergy members worked to help people deal with and change the problems affecting their working lives and their societies. Catholic social teaching makes clear that human dignity means that every person has the right to life and the things that sustain and enrich life, like adequate food, housing, health care, education, employment, and choice of faith; it also stresses that every person has the responsibility to work for justice for all.

Let's take a look at some of the main themes in modern Catholic social justice teaching:

A call to participation in the family and the community. The Church sees the family as the center of society, so it teaches that social conditions should support the family in every way. This gives people a firm base for going out in the world to work for the greater good.

Focusing on the poor and vulnerable. The call to give special concern to those most in need runs throughout the Bible, from the prophets of the Old Testament crying out for justice to Jesus encouraging those who have much to share with those who have little. This is the basis for the Church's teaching that personal action is not enough; Catholics must also work in the public sphere for the poor and vulnerable.

Workers' rights. The Church sees work as part of the divine plan, a way for humans to live up to their full potential. This means that workers have the right to fair wages and good working conditions and that they can create unions to help put those rights in place. However, workers also have the responsibility to recognize and respect the rights of owners to their economic initiative and ownership. As a part of these rights and responsibilities, the Church stresses that the work people do and the economies they create must be set up to help people, not simply to make a profit.

Care for God's creation. The Church's very existence is based on the belief that God has placed humans in this world and given them everything they need to live here, but they have the responsibility to use the world's resources wisely in ways that benefit people everywhere and also to respect the intrinsic worth and beauty of all God's creatures.

Put these together, and you get the Church seriously teaching and actively working for a whole range of social issues, both locally and globally: economic justice, health care, education, issues of discrimination, environmental issues, ways to change the societal supports for violence, religious liberty, human rights, issues related to immigrants and refugees, an end to regional conflicts, and many others. Archbishop Oscar Romero, who was martyred for his efforts to help the poor of El Salvador, spoke with the voice of the Church when he proclaimed in a sermon:

> A civilization of love that did not demand justice of people would not be a true civilization . . . It is a caricature of love to try to cover over with alms what is lacking in justice, to patch over with an appearance of benevolence when social justice is missing. True love begins by demanding what is just in the relations of those who love.[4]

Questions and Ideas for Understanding

1. Do you think religion should be separate from questions of morality and philosophy? Why or why not?

2. Enlightenment thinker and American Founding Father Thomas Jefferson created a version of the Jesus story that left out all references to miracles, divinity, or other supernatural elements. The so-called Jefferson Bible looked at Jesus as an ethical and moral thinker, a very different view from that of any of the gospel writers. Is this an

appropriate reinterpretation of Jesus for Jefferson's time or a rejection of Christian truths?

3. Imagine your response to the French Revolution if you were (1) a monk or nun living in France, (2) an overtaxed peasant living in Germany, or (3) a member of the nobility living in Italy. What good might you see in it? What problems?

4. Humanism is sometimes considered a religion in itself, with its own theology and set of beliefs. Research this view of humanism, and write a short essay explaining what religious humanism has in common with traditional Christianity and where it differs.

5. Read what Catholics, Protestants, and others had to say about the declaration of infallibility in the nineteenth century. More than a century after Vatican I, do Catholics and/or Protestants talk about this doctrine any differently than they did at the time it was declared?

Notes

1 *First Dogmatic Constitution on the Church of Christ*, Chap. 4. Retrieved from http://www.catholicbook.com/AgredaCD/Ecumenical_Councils/Vatican1.htm#session4chapter4 (accessed 10/5/07).

2 *Rerum Novarum*, 35. In *Human Dignity and the Common Good*, ed. Richard W. Rousseau. Westport, CT: Greenwood Press, 2002.

3 *Rerum Novarum*, par. 20.

4 Oscar Romero, *The Violence of Love*, trans. James R. Brockman. From a sermon given April 12, 1979. New York: Harper & Row, 1988, p. 157.

14

The Ancient Faith Gets a Modern Makeover

Vatican II

Chapter Overview

In this chapter, we will explore:

▶ The wars plaguing the twentieth century

▶ How the Church dealt with conflict

▶ John XXIII and the calling of Vatican II

▶ What Vatican II means for the Church

▶ How American Catholics moved into the mainstream

▶ How the Church thinks about itself in today's world

Amelia: Face to Face with History

It is October 11, 1962. You wake up excited—and stiff. Finally, the day you have been waiting for: the opening of the Second Vatican Council. For two nights, you and your sleeping bag have been holding your spot in St. Peter's Square, but a little stiffness is a small price to pay to get a space near the basilica so you can see the action. After all, this is why you came all the way from your hometown of Ravenna, right?

You and thirteen others from your university worked odd jobs for more than a year to raise money for this trip. It took a lot of dedication, but every time your parish priest, Padre Giovanni, talked about what this council could mean for the Church and for Catholics everywhere, you got more excited. Besides, you have never traveled this far from home. You can't wait to tell your parents and little sister all about it.

Suddenly, the huge bronze doors of the papal palace swing open, and a long procession of people begins flowing out. You and your sixty thousand neighbors in the square crane your necks to see. It's a good thing Padre Giovanni is here to help explain things. First come the Swiss guards in their wild outfits, then what seem like endless rows of bishops in flowing white robes. They step out into the sunlight, slowly cross the square, and then reverently climb the steps into the basilica itself. They are followed by the people who work in the Vatican, then the beautifully dressed patriarchs of some of the Eastern churches, and behind them the princes of the Church—the cardinals—in their red robes.

Awe—that's the feeling as you sense the spirit of God moving all around you. Finally, you see Pope John XXIII being carried aloft through the square on his papal throne, and your heart overflows. At first he looks uncomfortable, held above the crowd like this, but as you and the thousands around you begin to shout and cheer for the one who has made all this possible, the love and joy in your voices seem to affect the pope, too; tears are rolling down his cheeks as his chair passes by.

You get it; you get his tears. After all, *il Papa* has lived to see his greatest dream fulfilled.

On the opening day of the Council, people like Amelia filled St. Peter's Square. Young, old, pilgrims, scholars, journalists—they came from all over Italy and the world to see history unfolding. It seemed like a moment of hope—something that was sorely needed. Two wars had devastated the world, and the Church had struggled with its own conflicts. The Second Vatican Council would not solve all these problems, but it would turn out to be one of the most transformative events in the history of the Church. We will talk a lot about Pope John and about his council and will wrap up with a look at how the Church understands itself today. ■

Mapping the Twentieth Century

Step into a museum containing all of twentieth-century history, and the most striking exhibit might easily be a collection of world maps. Borders seem to have changed almost daily, with new countries appearing and old ones disappearing. This century witnessed ongoing struggles over control, and many of those struggles involved war.

At the beginning of the century, most parts of the world were still governed by one European nation or another; Britain in particular had an empire that stretched around the world. But then, who needs an empire when a single country can make an empire look small? In 1900, three countries—Russia, the United States, and China—each covered an area larger than the old Roman Empire. Their size alone made them forces to be reckoned with.

When the First World War began in August 1914, a short fight was anticipated. After all, with modern machine guns, submarines, and torpedoes, how could either side last long? However, instead of easy victory there was deadlock—a deadlock that would result in more than 8.5 million soldiers and sailors killed, 20 million more wounded, and 5 million civilians killed. The war started as a European fight, but because European countries had colonies all over the world, the situation was ripe for a regional conflict to become worldwide. Eventually the war ended, with Germany signing an armistice in November 1918, accepting total defeat and humiliating terms of surrender. It was also time for another map. In 1914, Europe consisted of twenty nations; by the time of the armistice, it had thirty-one.

In the decades following the war, the world went from one kind of bad to another. In October 1929 in the United States, the Wall Street stock market crash kicked off the Great Depression. All over the world, the value of money tumbled, international trade went down, and in some industrialized nations, unemployment hit more than 30 percent—a recipe for disaster.

Germans were having a rough time after the First World War. Combine their humiliation at losing with the economic situation of the 1930s, and you have a group of people ready for someone like Adolph Hitler, who would tell them it was once again time to be proud of being German. By 1934, Hitler and his party controlled Germany. Something similar had happened in Italy in the 1920s, with Benito Mussolini seizing control in 1922. In Russia, where people were dealing with the aftermath not only of the war but also of their revolution and conversion to communism in 1917, another ruthless leader was on the rise: Joseph Stalin came to power in 1924 and rapidly began eliminating anyone he thought posed a danger to him—as many as 20 million people during his thirty years in office.

Once Hitler, Mussolini, and Stalin decided the best way to improve their countries was to start attacking others, the rest of the world was in danger. The Second World War started with a German invasion of Poland in 1939, and Russia joined in almost immediately. (The friendship did not last long; Hitler decided in 1941 that he would just take over Russia, too, and his soldiers almost made it to Moscow before they had to turn back.) With Europe in an uproar, Japan decided in December 1941 to begin attacking territories and bases from Burma and Hong Kong in Southeast Asia to Pearl Harbor in Hawaii. Suddenly, war was everywhere, with Germany, Italy, and Japan on one side; the United States, Britain, China, and others on the other; and everybody gearing up for a long and bitter fight.

By the time Germany was defeated in May 1945, the list of casualties was horrific. More than 60 million people, including 38 million civilians, were dead. Six million of these were Jews whom Hitler had methodically rounded up and killed because he considered them subhuman. Millions more bore emotional scars that would never heal.

Yet the defeat of Germany and Italy did not end the war; Japan was still fighting. Ultimately, the United States ended things by dropping an atomic bomb on Hiroshima on August 6, 1945, and another three days later on Nagasaki. Five days following this second atomic bomb, Japan surrendered, and World War II finally ended.

The world following the Second World War was a changed one. In 1940, people had tended to think of science and technology as making the world a better place, but seeing how technology had been used to bring about the Holocaust and create the atomic bomb caused many to question whether "progress" was really such a good thing. Once again, the world map needed to be redrawn. At the start of the war, about one third of the world's population lived in countries that were European colonies, but by the end of the war, most of those colonies had become independent nations, with the last major break for independence coming from India in 1947.

There are many ways to draw a map, however, and following the war, a major division emerged: communism vs. democracy. Russia began gobbling up the countries around it, creating the communist Soviet Union, and then China joined the communist ranks when it went through its own revolution in 1949. The United States headed up the democracies; in fact, Americans were the best and most heartfelt missionaries for democracy that the world had ever known. Many of the conflicts during the latter part of the century, among them the Korean War and the Vietnam War, could be traced directly or indirectly to these conflicting ideologies. By the 1990s, the Soviet Union was breaking up, and once again a new map was needed to figure out what country was where.

Maps were not the only things changing. In that twentieth-century museum, there would be one huge room devoted to discoveries and inventions. The world had never seen such technological growth and geographical exploration as occurred in the twentieth century. Humans traveled to the heights of space and the depths of the ocean, viewing these worlds for the first time. Other technological changes had profound effects on humans as well: the automobile, television, movies, computers, the Internet, space telescopes, medical advances—the list is endless. People could—and would—argue whether science and discovery actually were making things better all the time, but everyone could agree on one thing: they were making things different.

The Church in the Public Eye

In the latter part of the nineteenth century, Church leaders were deeply concerned that Catholics were paying more attention to secular culture than to Christian teaching and thoughts of salvation. When the 1900s rolled around, popes were busy condemning Americanism, calling for Catholics to return to their traditional understandings and forbidding Catholic scholars from applying modern research methods to Scripture and doctrine. When the First World War broke out just fourteen years into the new century, it became clear that the Church of the twentieth century would need to deal with more than internal conflicts.

Even after the horrors of the First World War, nothing could really prepare the popes—or the world—for the onslaught of the Second World War and the chaos of communism. Many twentieth-century popes had a deep-seated and well-founded fear of communism; after all, the Church's first real brush with communism came during the Russian Revolution, when hosts of priests were murdered and the Church in Russian lands was severely persecuted. Moreover, that was just the beginning; wherever communism got a foothold in the Western world, it meant chaos for the Church.

Left-leaning forces in Mexico tried to get rid of Christian influence in general and Catholicism in particular starting in the 1920s. When the Spanish Civil War began in 1936, the murder of more than seven thousand priests and seminarians and the rape of hundreds of nuns by leftist epublicans caused Pope Pius XI to support the opposing forces. This was highly problematic because those "opposing forces" were Fascists loyal to General Franco, who used murder and torture to keep dissenters and ethnic groups in line. Pius and other twentieth-century popes felt like they were between a rock and a hard place—they did not see themselves as supporting the right side in a good cause but rather as opposing those who wanted to destroy the Church. Both Pius XI and his successor, Pius XII, had a real and valid fear that Christianity would be completely eliminated in communist and other left-leaning countries.

The Nazis in Germany were not leftist, but it did not take long for the popes to recognize them as a threat. Pius XI signed a 1933 concordat with Hitler's government protecting the Church's religious freedoms in German lands, but once he saw what the Nazis were really about, Pius wrote a condemnation of the movement as anti-Christian and ordered that it be read from every pulpit in German Catholic Churches in 1937. His successor, Pius XII, had to deal with the full-on war and its consequences. From the time he was elected pope in 1939, Pius tried to prevent the war, but once it broke out, he did his best to promote peace and prevent atrocities without seeming to say that God was on one side or the other of the fight.

Pius XII has taken a lot of heat from those who say he secretly supported the Nazi regime, but this is a simplistic answer to a complex situation. Pius worked directly to help save Jews, obtaining visas for some three thousand people and hiding others in the Vatican and around Rome in monasteries and convents when they were threatened with deportation. He also repeatedly refused to publicly condemn anti-Jewish laws, however, and when he did speak out against atrocities, it was in vague terms.

Pius was trying to act for what he saw as the good of the Church and the good that the Church could do. He seems to have been deeply concerned that if he and other Church leaders publicly condemned the Nazis, the Church in many areas would be persecuted; Catholics would be put at risk and so would the Church's rescue operations for Jews. These were difficult times and difficult decisions, and we can question whether Pius XII made the best decisions possible, but we have every reason to believe he tried to act in as moral and conscientious a manner as he could, working always toward peace.

In the United States, Catholics were gaining ground. The complaint about American Catholics had long been that they were loyal to a "foreign power"— the pope—rather than to their country, but it was hard to doubt the patriotism of Catholics when they lined up to fight for the United States in the Second World War. While most Catholic clergy in America still came from Europe during the 1920s, by the 1940s, it was Americans filling the pulpits as well as the pews—putting another nail in the coffin of the idea that American Catholics were too influenced by foreigners.

In the period during and after the war, American Catholics put their participation in the Church on display in a big way. From 1945 to 1965, the number of men and women entering religious Orders increased 30–50 percent, and the number of U.S. bishops and archbishops rose by 58 percent. One hundred twenty-three Catholic hospitals were opened, along with more than three thousand elementary and high schools and ninety-four colleges. All those new schools helped boost the number of students enrolled in Catholic schools by more than 120 percent, and the GI bill helped push up the number of students in Catholic colleges and universities by more than 300 percent. Catholics were everywhere in American society. One of the biggest leaps forward for American Catholics did not occur within the Church at all: in 1960, the Catholic John Fitzgerald Kennedy was elected president of the United States. With his election, Catholics felt like they had finally been accepted as full members of American society.

A Big, BIG Job

Every other council in history had been called because the Church needed to deal with a particular challenge to its teaching or its unity, but this time the pope was telling everyone that the issue was *aggiornamiento*, which is Italian for "updating." Updating does not mean getting rid of the past but rather taking what has been received and making it relevant to the present. For John and for the council that he called, *aggiornamiento* meant looking at the world at that moment and discerning how the Church should be present in it.

Pope John figured it was the people in the field who knew what was going on and what the council needed to do, so he sent letters to cardinals, bishops,

Living the Call to Action: Dorothy Day

◀ ◀ ◀ ◀ ◀ ▶

The early life of Dorothy Day (1897–1980) may seem an unlikely beginning for a woman the Church may one day declare a saint. She was not raised a Catholic, had numerous love affairs and an abortion, and finally had a child while in a common-law marriage—not the kinds of things Catholics usually associate with heroic virtue. But having the baby affected Dorothy profoundly, and she felt an inner force pushing her to have the child baptized in the Church. It was not long before she converted to Catholicism herself, a move that brought about the end of the marriage and started her on the trek to the social action grounded in Catholic faith that would be her life's work.

All her adult life, Dorothy felt the call to action deep in her bones. While still in college, she came to believe the political and social situation in the United States had gotten completely out of control, leaving workers in desperate straits. She left school to become a journalist and social activist because she wanted to help change things, but she did not find her guiding light until after her conversion to Catholicism. In 1932, she met a remarkable Frenchman named Peter Maurin, a former Christian Brother who had become something of a drifter and workaday philosopher. Through his study of the gospel and Catholic social teachings, Peter had come to believe that every person is of extraordinary value and that living the gospel means putting this knowledge into action. He said individuals should take responsibility for other individuals; in other words, rather than trying to help "the poor" or "the homeless," you should help that particular poor or homeless person right in front of you. Listening to Peter, Dorothy knew she had found her life's work.

Peter and Dorothy started a newspaper, *The Catholic Worker*, in which they described the inequalities of the American capitalist system as well as the profound problems of communism. They wrote about the kind of Christian responsibility that Peter had explained to Dorothy, but they did not stop at writing. While many Christians have read Jesus' words about giving all they have to the poor and turning the other cheek, relatively few have devoted their lives to these teachings, but that is exactly what Peter and Dorothy did. They founded "houses of hospitality" where people who were poor, homeless, mentally ill, alcoholic, or for some other reason at the margins of society were treated as honored guests and given food, clothing, and shelter. One house grew into 2, 2 into 10, and 10 into a network of 185 houses around the world where people continue to live out the vision of Peter and Dorothy.

Dorothy became widely known for her work in support of pacifism, civil rights, and the rights of workers. Age did not slow her down, either: in her 70s, she stood on picket lines and was arrested for her nonviolent activities. Dorothy kept fighting the good fight until her death in 1980.

heads of religious Orders, and Catholic universities and schools around the world asking what issues they thought the Church needed to address. It took three years and eight hundred experts to work through the mountain of replies, but finally an agenda was drawn up, and the opening day of the Second Vatican Council dawned on October 11, 1962.

The beloved pope who had called the council together opened the proceedings with a speech expressing his vision for the work that it would do:

Mother Church rejoices that, by the singular gift of Divine Providence, the longed-for day has finally dawned when . . . the Second Vatican Ecumenical Council is being solemnly opened here beside St. Peter's tomb . . .

Illuminated by the light of this Council, the Church . . . will become greater in spiritual riches . . . [S]he will look to the future without fear. In fact, by bringing herself up to date where required, and by the wise organization of mutual co-operation, the Church will make men, families, and peoples really turn their minds to heavenly things . . .

[Some] say that our era, in comparison with past eras, is getting worse, and they behave as though they had learned nothing from history . . . as though at the time of former Councils everything was a full triumph for the Christian idea and life and for proper religious liberty. We feel we must disagree with those prophets of gloom, who are always forecasting disaster, as though the end of the world were at hand. In the present order of things, Divine Providence is leading us to a new order of human relations which, by men's own efforts and even beyond their very expectations, are directed toward the fulfillment of God's superior and inscrutable designs. And everything, even human differences, leads to the greater good of the Church . . .

The greatest concern of the Ecumenical Council is this: that the sacred deposit of Christian doctrine should be guarded and taught more efficaciously . . . It is necessary first of all that the Church should never depart from the sacred patrimony of truth received from the Fathers. But at the same time she must ever look to the present, to the new conditions and new forms of life introduced into the modern world, which have opened new avenues to the Catholic apostolate . . .

The salient point of this Council is not, therefore, a discussion of one article or another of the fundamental doctrine of the Church . . . For this a Council was not necessary. But . . . the authentic doctrine . . . should be studied and expounded through the methods of research and through the literary forms of modern thought. The substance of

Focus On
Transforming the Church: John XXIII and Vatican II

The world was in a mess: the Cold War, the nuclear threat, the growing gap between rich and poor, the questioning of traditional authority. How could the church respond? According to Pope John XXIII, what the Church needed was a new ecumenical council. He put his plan into practice as Vatican II, causing a major fracas in the Church and thoroughly surprising everyone who had expected this kind and humble man to be nothing more than a chair-filler.

That chair-filler started life as Angelo Roncalli, the fourth of thirteen children in a peasant Italian family. Angelo was not your typical peasant's son; he was always reading, usually best in his class and sometimes getting beaten up for it. His intellectual curiosity served him well later on. After he became a priest, Father Angelo was sent to posts in Bulgaria, Greece, and Turkey, where he experienced firsthand both Eastern Orthodox and Muslim societies. He learned new ways to look at the Bible and theology and was a Vatican observer to the United Nations. All this fostered in him a deep belief that the Church would better live its values and influence world events if it stopped fighting modern ways and paid attention to the world around it.

In 1953, Father Angelo was named patriarch of Venice, a nice retirement position for a 72-year-old. When Pope Pius XII died in 1958, nobody thought Angelo a potential pontiff. When the cardinals could not settle on a candidate, however, they lighted on beloved and uncontroversial Father Angelo.

Three months into his papacy, Angelo, now known as John XXIII, told the world he had been shown in prayer that the Church needed a new ecumenical council to help explain its place in the modern world. This made

waves everywhere. In fact, the man who would follow John as pope, Archbishop Montini of Milan, called up a friend and told him, "This holy old boy doesn't seem to realize what a hornet's nest he's stirring up."[1]

For all his peaceable nature, John did not mind stirring things up. The regal, well-insulated role common to prior popes did not fit John. He would sneak out of the Vatican to visit prisons or hospitals, or maybe to say Mass at a local church. Convention did not bind him.

International affairs were much on John's mind. He wrote about the obligations of rich nations toward poor ones, and as he looked at the struggles in the world—of colonial peoples against their oppressors, of workers for living wages and working conditions, and of women for equality both at home and in the public square—he realized that these needed to affect how the Church lived its mission. Working from the tradition of Catholic social teaching, John explained in the 1963 encyclical *Pacem in Terris* (*Peace on Earth*) that every person has worth and dignity, true peace is only possible when that dignity is recognized, and the purpose of government is to safeguard individual rights.

More than anything, John wanted to find the path to Christian unity. Believing that what divides Christians is not nearly as important as what they hold in common, John met with the heads of other Christian denominations—the first pope to do so. He established the Vatican Secretariat for Christian Unity, devoted to dialogue among Christian groups, and he hoped Christian Unity would be a major focus for the council he called.

John was only pope for five years, but that was all it took for him to become known as "the most beloved pope in history." ∎

the ancient doctrine of the deposit of faith is one thing, and the way in which it is presented is another. And it is the latter that must be taken into great consideration with patience if necessary . . .

The Council now beginning rises in the Church like daybreak . . . We might say that heaven and earth are united in the holding of the Council—the saints of heaven to protect our work, the faithful of the earth continuing in prayer to the Lord, and you, seconding the inspiration of the Holy Spirit in order that the work of all may correspond to the modern expectations and needs of the various peoples of the world. This requires of you serenity of mind, brotherly concord, moderation in proposals, dignity in discussion, and wisdom of deliberation. God grant that your labours and your work, toward which the eyes of all peoples and the hopes of the entire world are turned, may abundantly fulfill the aspirations of all.[2]

Getting to Work

Heaven and earth may have been united, but the bishops themselves were not. Recall the big divide at the First Vatican Council between the conservative ultramontanist bishops who wanted the pope to be a strong monarch and the progressives who wanted the Church to be more in tune with the modern world; the same lines were drawn at Vatican II.

Most of the organizers came from the conservative group. They created ten commissions to work on different issues and suggested sixteen bishops for each one. The body of bishops had to vote the commission members in, but because not many of them knew 160 other bishops, the organizers figured most everybody would go along with their (mainly conservative) suggestions.

They got a shock, however, when the second-oldest cardinal at the council, Cardinal Lienart of Lille, spoke up to say that the bishops really needed to do the choosing for themselves. He suggested they put off voting on the committee members for a few days so that they could get to know one another—and got wild applause from the other bishops for his words. That one suggestion proved to be a turning point: It was the moment it became clear that the bishops themselves—not the organizers, not even the pope calling the council—would run the show.

As it turned out, the final makeup of the commissions did reflect the diversity, both geographical and theological, of the bishops themselves. Those elected were a balanced group of progressives and conservatives, and this was a good thing. The conservative group tended to think the Church needed to face up to the problem of secularization, of people putting less stock in their faith and having less respect for legitimate authority. The progressives, on the other hand, saw the Church as too hierarchical and impersonal, too detached from the modern world to be relevant. Where the conservatives thought it was important to repeat and clarify traditional teaching, the progressives wanted to revisit those teachings to see how and if they met the world's needs. The documents that eventually came out of the council reflect a combination of their views.

The bishops met each fall between 1962 and 1965, leaving time between sessions for the bishops to discuss issues with each other and with people back home and to pray alone and together, and for the committees to revise the proposals. It was a lot of work, and many compromises had to be made, but it is amazing to realize that with 2,500 people voting and some big differences in thinking, most of the documents passed with 99 percent of the vote. The laity did not get a say and women's voices were largely unheard, but this is still an extraordinary example of the Church hierarchy working together.

Pope John XXIII did not get a chance to see all the good that came out of the council. He died on June 3, 1963, just eight months into the first session. Some people who were not too happy with the council hoped it would grind to a halt without John, but the new pope, Paul VI (1963–1978), quickly put an end to that idea, and the council continued as planned.

So while all this was going on in tiny Vatican City, did the rest of the world really pay attention or care? Yes! Council news was plentiful, as more than a thousand journalists from around the world were on hand for the council's first session in 1962—the most publicity any religious event up to that point had ever received. This had the unexpected benefit of giving people a glimpse into the inner workings of the largest Christian organization in the world. The whole process was eye-opening for Catholics as well, and it changed the way they looked at their Church and at themselves. The typical Catholic was used to thinking of the Church Universal as universally in agreement; it was a change to realize that disagreement over theology and morality was a part of life not only between Catholics and other Christian denominations but among Catholics themselves, even Catholics at the highest levels of the Church.

Fitting the Pieces Together: John Courtney Murray

Imagine that you are living in the time before Vatican II and that you have a magical puzzle made out of two pieces. One piece is the First Amendment to the Constitution of the United States of America: "Congress shall make no law respecting an establishment of religion, or prohibiting the free exercise thereof." The other piece is the Church's position at that time that in every country, the government has a duty to protect and promote Catholicism as the official state religion. How do you fit those pieces together?

American Catholics were struggling to make that puzzle work, so a Jesuit priest named John Courtney Murray decided to look at each piece more closely. He thought American courts were misinterpreting the First Amendment. The amendment was not intended to keep religion from influencing society and legislation, he reasoned. After all, believing individuals are part of that society for whom and by whom legislation is made. Instead, Murray argued, the First Amendment was supposed to keep the government from being dominated by any particular set of religious beliefs or from trying to tell people what to believe.

As for the Church's position, Murray understood that the idea of setting up a state religion went against the very foundation on which the United States was created. Murray argued that the Church's position was rooted in its changing human history and was not a necessary component of faith. What the Church was holding as the ideal was really just one way for governments and the Church to interact, not the only or necessarily the best way.

Murray wrote a lot about these understandings during the 1940s, and his ideas caused a ruckus. In 1954, his Jesuit superiors told him he could no longer speak or write publicly on this topic. Nevertheless, his ideas were already out there, and the tide was turning. Attending Vatican II as a theological adviser, Murray helped convince the bishops that they needed to tackle the issue of how the Church and governments interact. It took six full drafts to do it, but finally the bishops produced a *Declaration on Religious Freedom* that says that humans have the right to religious freedom and to seeking the truth in their own way, and that the role of governments is to make sure this freedom is written into law—a far cry from the Church's older position that governments are supposed to promote Catholicism. The bishops took a stand built on the ground that Murray had prepared.

Why the Council Really Is That Important

If you put all the writings from all the councils through the centuries into one big stack, nearly a third of the pile comes from Vatican II. The bishops issued sixteen documents, with the ones called *constitutions* having the highest teaching authority. The documents reflect new ways of thinking applied to ancient beliefs, and they shook many people to the core. To many both outside and inside the Church, it seemed like the council changed everything from the ground up. In some ways it did, but from a theological perspective, the council reaffirmed the fundamental teachings of the faith while updating their presentation and practice. The bishops tried to look beyond the historically conditioned nature of many Church teachings to the basic ideas those teachings were trying to convey, then took those ideas and expressed them in light of modern understandings and ideas. The documents of Vatican II are themselves historically conditioned, and future generations of Catholics will once again need to retrieve the basic ideas presented in them and express them in ways that make sense in their own time. For now, however, these documents give us the best picture possible of who the Church is and how it sees its mission.

The following are the top seven reasons why the council really is that important:

Aggiornamento: Updating the Church

This council was all about renewal, which means restoring something to its original state. This was not an effort to make the Church look as it did in the second century but rather to get back to its roots in figuring out what was most important in its mission. The bishops attempted to show how the traditional teachings were relevant, even vital, to the modern world.

Religious Freedom: Conscience Is Key

Historically, the Church had held the view that every person had a duty to be Catholic and that governments should make Catholicism the official religion; the Church had also taught a legalistic morality that revolved around doing what you were told. The bishops at Vatican II certainly did not tell people to throw Church authority out the window, but they recognized that in the end, people have a duty to develop their own consciences rather than simply follow Church rules. In addition, governments, they said, have a duty to protect the rights of all citizens rather than trying to promote a certain set of religious beliefs. These were huge changes.

Ecumenism and Interreligious Dialogue: Talking to People with Other Beliefs

The Church had been battling other Christian believers and groups for much of its history. Through it all, the Church had seen itself as the sole bearer

Voices from the Past
"A Short Formula of the Christian Faith"

▶ Author: Karl Rahner

▶ Written: 1967

▶ Audience: Educated Catholics

Karl Rahner ranks as one of the greatest Catholic theologians of the twentieth century. Born in Germany and trained as a Jesuit, Rahner had the vocation of a writer: he wrote more than forty volumes on theology and edited many others. However, he did not simply sit at home with pen in hand; both brilliant and busy, Rahner also served as a university professor and, at times, a pastor.

He wrote the "Short Formula" just a few years after Vatican II had transformed the Church. Rahner had been part of that transformation as a theological adviser to the council, and his influence can be found in most of the council documents. In the "Short Formula," we can see a couple of key themes in Rahner's work: that simply in the process of being human, every person experiences the sacred mystery that we call God; and the famous theory of anonymous Christians (which he here calls "advent Christians"), those who do not knowingly accept Christ and the mediation of the Church but whose very search for truth and meaning opens them to receive God's grace.

If the Church wants her mission to be effective in the situation of modern unbelief, she must be able to express the Christian message in such a way that it becomes really intelligible for modern man. This truism, however, demands something very difficult and very often dealt with in an unsatisfactory manner. For the message must be expressed in such a way that the essential stands out clearly from everything secondary and can in fact be "realized." Otherwise a modern "pagan" cannot distinguish this essence of Christianity from the often not very inviting and even repellent outward "image" of the Church ...

In his spiritual existence, man will always fall back on a sacred mystery as the very ground of his being, whether he admits this explicitly or not, whether he lets this truth come through or tries to suppress it. This mystery, which permanently contains and sustains the small circle of our knowing and doing in our daily experience ... lies at the very root of our being ... We call this God ... As the ground of the individual's existence, involved in perception and action, the sacred mystery that we call God is most deeply within us and at the same time so far beyond us that it does not need us. Reverence and worship befit him. Where these are present, where man accepts his existence in full responsibility, where man seeks and expects his ultimate meaning trustingly, there he has already found God by whatever name we may call him, since his ultimate name can forever be spoken only in a love that is speechless before his incomprehensibility ...

This history of man's self-discovery in the ground of his deified being ... reaches its historical climax and final goal which in a hidden way carries this whole historical process, in him whom we simply call the God-Man in this deified humanity. All seek him, not explicitly, yet really, whenever they desire that the ultimate experience of the radical meaning of their being ... and of God's ultimate acceptance become manifest in their history ... To this degree, insofar as we are concerned, every man who is faithful to his conscience is an "advent" Christian.[3] ■

of truth, with other believers misled by their all-too-human pride. At Vatican II, though, the bishops acknowledged that God is not limited to working through the Catholic Church but is found working through other Christian denominations and even in other religions. Vatican II explained that while Catholic teaching gives the fullest human expression of God's truth, God's truth can also be found in these differing beliefs.

The Church's Mission: Living the Good News

The Church has always held that its mission is to share with people the good news of Christ, but too often it has confused the cultural packaging for that good news with the good news itself. Vatican II owned up to this confusion and said that missionaries need to recognize the beauty of the cultures where they are working and express the Christian message in ways that make sense within those cultures. The council also pointed out that there is more to the Church's mission than converting people to Christianity. To live the message it proclaims, the Church must also stand with the poor and the afflicted, educate young people, fight disease and famine, promote better living and working conditions, and work for peace.

Scripture: Read It for Yourself

For centuries, Church leaders did not want the laity to read the Scriptures for themselves because they might misinterpret it and thus threaten their salvation. After all, Protestants split into thousands of denominations based on their differing interpretations. At Vatican II, however, the bishops recognized that Catholics need to ground themselves in the Scriptures. Moreover, while earlier Church leaders had been skeptical of using modern methods of scholarship to study the Bible, at Vatican II the bishops encouraged those methods, as long as the scholars worked within the limits of the Church's teaching authority.

The Faithful: All Working Together to Be Church

Too often people saw the Church as a pyramid, with the pope at the top, the bishops acting as his deputies coming next, and the laity at the bottom simply following orders. The council talked about the different roles within the Church. Bishops, they said, are more than middle managers carrying out the pope's orders; they are teachers and shepherds with a responsibility before

God for their work. The laity are not just worker bees but are absolutely necessary to the Church's work in the world. Lay Catholics need to be active in the lives of their parishes and dioceses and beyond that in society as a whole. Their baptismal faith is a call to action in the world.

On a practical level, the bishops changed the way the Mass was celebrated. People could use their native languages rather than Latin, altars were turned around so that the priest faced the congregation, lay people could be readers and Eucharistic ministers, and the required fast before taking communion changed from midnight on to just one hour. Through these and other changes, the council sought to get lay people more involved in the worship service that was the center of their lives as Catholic Christians.

Diversity: Different Ways of Being the Same Church

For centuries, the Church had thought of unity as meaning that everybody did the same thing everywhere all the time. This usually was translated as everybody doing things the way that European Catholics did them. The bishops at Vatican II saw that true unity could accommodate diversity, not just of culture but also of individual church communities: each is important and brings something to the whole. In other words, the universal Church is really the communion of all the local churches.

Vatican II covered a lot of ground—so much, in fact, that almost half a century later, the Church is still working through what it means. That work has been challenging and not without its critics. While the council created a Church that is more open and participatory, some people feel it weakened what being Catholic really means. They point out that Catholics growing up after Vatican II seem to pay less attention to rituals like novenas or the Stations of the Cross and that some seem to rely so much on their own consciences that they neglect or ignore the Church's teaching that it presents the truest expression of God's will.

Some individuals and groups found the changes so unsettling that they broke away from the Church entirely, claiming it had abandoned being faithfully Catholic in exchange for fitting in with the modern world. Many more Catholics remained in the Church but still felt deeply concerned about the changes. Many other Catholics were so excited that they wanted to imple-

On the Side of the Poor: Liberation Theology

In the Scriptures, God frees his people from slavery; the prophets and Jesus call people of faith to help the poor and needy. Vatican II called on Catholics to live the gospel more deeply, declaring that the Church "joins itself with men of every condition, but especially with the poor and afflicted" and that "Christians ought to interest themselves, and collaborate with others, in the right ordering of social and economic affairs" (*The Decree on the Church's Missionary Activity,* 12).

In Latin America, many bishops and theologians took all this to heart. Believing the Church needed to do more about the terrible poverty and oppression in their societies, they developed a new way of thinking about Christianity known as *liberation theology.*

According to liberation theology, societies sin when they force some to live lives of poverty and oppression so that others can have what they want. Liberation theologians believe it is the prophetic duty of the Church to stand with the poor, to point out the societal sin of oppression and work against it. God wants more than charity from those with plenty, they declare—he wants a more just system where all have enough.

Liberation theologians talk about *orthopraxis,* right action, in addition to *orthodoxy,* right teaching. They talk about *conscientization,* the process by which people and societies learn to look at old problems with new eyes, to link theory and praxis, and to understand their role in the problem and its solution. As the oppressed become conscientized, they learn to reject their status as inevitable and they find their own voice.

At a meeting in Medellin, Colombia, in 1979, the Latin American bishops laid the foundation for this way of thinking about the Christian faith. Since then, liberation theology has taken hold in Africa and Asia and many other places and situations where people are oppressed. It also has influenced feminist theology as a powerful force in Western religious thought.

Liberation theology has its critics. While rooted in Christian faith, it has a strong basis in a Marxist analysis of economic history. Some liberation theologians equate Christianity with socialism or communism—not with particular expressions of these theories as they have been formed into political systems, but with the ideals of the theories themselves. The Church has had good cause to fear communism as a lived experience, and some Church leaders believe that liberation theology is just religious wrapping around a political theory.

Governments and those with wealth and power also have felt threatened by the claim that God stands with the poor and powerless when they work together to create a more just society. In fact, liberation theology has proven so powerful that monks, nuns, priests and others have been martyred for answering the call to work for true justice growing out of their Christian faith.

ment everything as quickly as possible. The late 1960s and early 1970s were rough but exciting times in the Church, and the dust is still a long way from settling. But as Catholics work together to navigate the waters of a more open Church, they are finding that even rough waves carry them to a deeper sense of what it means to be Church.

The Church Then and Now

How the Church Understands Itself Today

The last document produced by the council, the *Pastoral Constitution on the Church in the Modern World,* was also one of the most important. It covers a lot of ground: the dignity of all persons; the role of the individual and society in the common good; the meaning and value of human activity; the Church's role in the modern world; issues relating to marriage and the family; the proper development of culture, economics, and society; the political community; and how to bring about peace and a true community of nations.

In the midst of all this, the document lays out a vision of a Church deeply involved in human history yet also transcending it as a vehicle for God's work in the world. *The Church in the Modern World* is addressed "not only [to] the sons of the Church and all who call upon the name of Christ, but the whole of humanity as well." It is truly the Church's understanding of itself, held up for all the world to see. An excerpt follows:

> Proceeding from the love of the eternal Father, the Church was founded by Christ in time and gathered into one by the Holy Spirit. It has a saving and eschatological purpose which can be fully attained only in the next life. But it is now present here on earth and is composed of men; they, the members of the earthly city, are called to form the family of the children of God even in this present history of mankind and to increase it continually until the Lord comes . . .
>
> In pursuing its own salvific purpose not only does the Church communicate divine life to men but in a certain sense it casts the reflected light of that divine life over all the earth, notably in the way it heals and elevates the dignity of the human person, in the way it consolidates society, and endows the daily activity of men with a deeper sense and meaning. The Church, then, believes it can contribute much to humanizing the family of man and its history through each of its members and its community as a whole.
>
> Furthermore, the Catholic Church gladly values what other Christian Churches and ecclesial communities have contributed and are contributing cooperatively to the realization of this aim. Similarly it is convinced that there is a considerable and varied help that it can

The Vatican II Documents

The Vatican II documents were written in Latin because that is the international language of the Church and later were translated into many languages, including English. Following is a look at each one:

Name	Main Points
Dogmatic Constitution on the Church (Lumen Gentium)	Talks about how the Church sees itself: as the gathering of all those (including non-Catholics) called by God, as an assembly of believers containing both the hierarchy and the laity, and as a fallible human institution continuing the perfect work of Jesus. The Church's role is to create a space for humans to come into relationship with God.
Dogmatic Constitution on Divine Revelation (Dei Verbum)	While God has revealed himself most fully through Christ and his Church, God has also come to humans in many other ways throughout history. Other religions also possess wisdom that God has revealed to them, and Christians need to engage in respectful dialogue with them.
Pastoral Constitution on the Church in the Modern World (Gaudium et Spes)	The Church is a vibrant, living, sacramental sign of Jesus in the midst of history. Progress in society is part of God's design, which includes salvation not only for individuals but also for all of humanity and the entire cosmos. The centerpoint of the Christian life is not heaven but rather working for God through a greater commitment to the world.
Constitution on the Sacred Liturgy (Sacrosanctum Concilium)	The liturgy needs to be updated so that worshippers can truly understand the richness of the Church's traditions and sacraments in language and symbols meaningful for them. The liturgy is a communal event, and the congregation needs to participate in it rather than simply receiving it.
Declaration on Religious Freedom (Dignitatis Humanae)	Each human has the right to religious liberty, a right that governments must safeguard. The main issue in the relationship of the Church and the State is the Church's fundamental right to freedom.
Declaration on the Relation of the Church to Non-Christian Religions (Nostra Aetate)	Believers of all faiths experience similar struggles, and Catholics need to dialogue and collaborate with followers of other religions. Discrimination on the basis of race, color, condition of life, or religion is simply unacceptable.

continued on page 306

continued from page 305

Declaration on Christian Education (Gravissum Educationis)	Everyone has the right to education, and Christians have a duty to educate their children in a Christian manner. Parents, the community, and the Church must work together to provide this education.
Decree on Ecumenism (Unitatis Redintegratio)	Those who follow Christ are not all Catholic Christians. Other Christian communities have also been used by God as a means of salvation. All Christians are called to work for unity among themselves.
Decree on the Catholic Eastern Churches (Orientalium Ecclesiarum)	This document affirms the value of the Eastern churches that are in communion with Rome and gives guidelines for sharing worship with the Eastern Orthodox churches.
Decree on the Church's Missionary Activity (Ad Gentes)	The Church is missionary in its very nature, and Catholics should work closely with other Christians in this most important task. Local churches and bishops have the right and duty to express the Church's message in ways that make sense within their cultural contexts.
Decree on the Pastoral Office of Bishops in the Church (Christus Dominus)	Bishops are the shepherds of their communities, and as part of the hierarchy, they also have a responsibility to the universal Church; gives a general discussion of their roles and duties.
Decree on Ministry and Life of Priests (Presbyterorum Ordinis)	Priests have vital roles to play as helpers of the bishops and in working together with and among the laity; gives a general discussion of their roles and duties.
Decree on the Training of Priests (Optatum Totius)	Seminary training should be restructured to include greater emphasis on the study of Scripture, a deeper understanding of other Christian communities, and more thoughtful use of sociology and psychology.
Decree on the Up-to-Date Renewal of the Religious Life (Perfectae Caritatis)	Religious Orders should be updated to adapt more to the modern world and to the particular cultural contexts in which the brothers and sisters are living. This can include adapting the religious habit to modern conditions.
Decree on the Apostolate of Laypeople (Apostolicam Actuositatem)	The laity have their own Christian vocation. They should participate fully in the life of the Church in roles such as Eucharistic ministers and lectors, and on parish councils, but their apostolate also extends into the sphere of society.
Decree on the Means of Social Communication (Inter Mirifica)	New means of communication have been developed, and the Church must use these to further the work of Christ.

receive from the world in preparing the ground for the Gospel, both from individuals and from society as a whole, by their talents and activity . . .

Whether it aids the world or whether it benefits from it, the Church has but one sole purpose—that the kingdom of God may come and the salvation of the human race may be accomplished. Every benefit the people of God can confer on mankind during its earthly pilgrimage is rooted in the Church's being the universal sacrament of salvation, at once manifesting and actualizing the mystery of God's love for men.[4]

Questions and Ideas for Understanding

1. Leaving aside Vatican II, what do you think would be the most important exhibit for the Church in the twentieth-century museum? Why?

2. Read John XXIII's encyclical *Pacem in Terris,* and evaluate it from the perspective of the early twenty-first century. What does John say that is timeless? What seems conditioned to his time?

3. Research John XXIII's use of the term *aggiornamiento,* and write an essay explaining it as a theological concept.

4. Karl Rahner talked about non-Christians who strive for the truth as anonymous Christians. Write an essay either supporting or refuting the idea that this concept expresses the deepest respect for those of other religions.

Notes

[1] Quoted in Peter Hebblethwaite, *John XXIII: Pope of the Council.* London: Doubleday & Company, 1984, p. 324.

[2] Pope John's opening speech to the c ouncil. Retrieved from http://www.christusrex.org/www1/CDHN/v2.html (accessed 10/05/07).

[3] Karl Rahner, "In Search of a Short Formula of the Christian Faith." In *Readings in the History of Christian Theology,* Vol. 2, ed. William C. Placher. Philadelphia: The Westminster Press, 1988.

[4] *Gaudium et Spes,* 40–42, 45. From *Vatican Council II: The Conciliar and Post-Conciliar Documents,* ed. Austin Flannery. Northport, NY: Costello Publishing Company, 1992. pp. 903-1001.

15

The Road That Lies Ahead
The Church in the Third Millennium

Chapter Overview

In this chapter, we will explore:

- ▶ Pope John Paul II and his impact on the Church

- ▶ The election of Pope Benedict XVI

- ▶ The role of laity and clergy in today's Church

- ▶ Some of the challenges the Church faces in the twenty-first century

- ▶ The Church of yesterday, today, and tomorrow

The Life and Times of . . . You

Here at the beginning I usually write a short story describing a person living through some of the events that will be important in the chapter. Not this time. Now it is your turn, your century, and your story. The events you see in your lifetime, the questions you and others like you want answered, the choices all of you together make—these are the things that will be written down one day as the history of the twenty-first century, and of the twenty-first-century Church. I will begin a discussion of what has happened so far in this century and what issues are likely to affect the Church going forward, but your life is the context for thinking about the Church in today's world.

We will start by looking at John Paul II, the pope who led the Church into its third millennium, and Benedict XVI, the first pope elected in the new century. We will explore the changing roles within the Church for both clergy and laity and for women in particular. Along the way, we will discuss Church authority in relation to university teaching and a massive scandal in the Church in the United States. We will wind up with a quick thought about where the Church's history puts us today. ■

The Pope That Stole the Show: John Paul II

Why begin a chapter on the Church in the new millennium by talking about a pope elected twenty-two years before the century began? Because John Paul II helped create the Church—and the world—we are dealing with in the twenty-first century. He had such a huge impact that the only way to understand where the Church is going is to look at where and how he led it.

A Pope in the Making

Karol Wojtyla, the Polish kid who grew up to be John Paul II, was arguably one of the most well-rounded popes in the history of the Church. Karol was a great student, but he was also an athlete who spent plenty of time playing soccer, swimming, kayaking, hiking, and skiing. The strong muscles he built must have helped when he worked as a physical laborer. Karol was also an actor, singer, poet, and playwright. He co-founded an underground theater troupe that presented Polish works (including some by Karol himself) at a time when that could get you killed during the German occupation of Poland.

Moreover, Karol was deeply religious. He began studying for the priesthood in 1942, with the Second World War in full swing and seminaries forbidden in Nazi-occupied Poland. Karol had to study secretly at night while working at a chemical plant by day. Ordained a priest in 1946, by the time he was 36, Karol had doctorates in theology and philosophy and was teaching as a professor of ethics at a university in Poland.

Karol had serious street smarts, too. Day-to-day life had taught him the horrors of oppression, first under Nazi rule and then under communist rule by the Soviet Union following the war. Jews of his hometown, including personal friends, were killed in the Holocaust, and Karol felt firsthand the persecution of the "Church of silence" behind the Iron Curtain.

In 1958, Father Karol became Bishop Karol of Krakow. When the Second Vatican Council opened four years later, Bishop Karol was able to bring to the table not only a top-notch mind but also a different perspective from most of his counterparts in Western Europe and the United States. Though he was one of the younger bishops at the meeting, Karol was an active participant in all four sessions, and he made particularly important contributions to the discussions of religious freedom and the Church's role in the modern world.

By this time, it was clear that Karol Wojtyla had a bright future in the Church, but few could have known just how bright it would be. One man who did was Padre Pio, the Italian mystic and spiritual healer. When Padre Pio met Karol in 1947, he told the young priest that he would one day wear the papal garments. On October 16, 1978, when he first stepped onto the balcony overlooking St. Peter's Square to greet Catholics as their new pope, the man who would now be known as John Paul II must have held the words of Padre Pio close in his heart.

The Frequent-Flyer Pope

Pope John Paul II was the first non-Italian pope in 455 years, the first Slavic pope ever elected, and the first to have lived all his life up to that point in communist-ruled lands. He brought a new viewpoint to the papacy, as well as a massive intellect; he spoke at least eight languages and could read even more. He used them, too: as pope, he visited every continent except Antarctica, traveling to more than 120 countries. Along the way, he had almost a thousand meetings with prime ministers and heads of state. These were not the main reason for his travels, however. He went to see the faithful, to celebrate Mass with them, and to learn about their lives. Millions turned out to see him, and millions more watched him on television. John Paul II was a globetrotting, media-savvy pope, but it was his personal charisma, profound sincerity, and true interest in those he met that drew people to him.

More than one-sixth of the world's population is Catholic, but John Paul was deeply concerned about the other five-sixths as well. Believing that Christians and Jews needed to find more common ground, he set up diplomatic relations with Israel, traveled to the Holy Land, asked forgiveness for anti-Semitism in the Church's history, and talked with Holocaust survivors. He was the first pope since the time of the apostles to visit a synagogue and the first ever to visit a mosque. He earned the respect of people from many different religious traditions when he prayed with their leaders and honored their sacred writings. While always staying within Catholic doctrine, he stressed that what brings people of faith together is ultimately more important than what drives them apart. Moreover, he publicly repented for those times when Catholics did the driving: the sins committed in the name of the Church against Galileo, the victims of the Inquisition, those massacred during and after the Protestant Reformation, and others. John Paul wanted the light of truth to shine in the Church, and he believed acknowledging the errors of its members would help the Church be more faithful to its mission.

Popes may not have direct political power anymore, but they have enormous influence, and John Paul used his in the service of what he held dear. He asked heads of state to honor human rights in their countries, and he spoke out against the world's powerful, including the United States and its presidents, when they did what he believed to be wrong. He saw Catholic social teaching as a cure for the ills of both capitalism and communism. Where these systems stressed markets and masses, the Church talked about the dignity of human beings and the work they performed. John Paul believed capitalist and communist systems alike created a "culture of death," and he pointed to practices like euthanasia and abortion to prove his point. He called for a new culture of love and reverence for life in all its forms.

John Paul II's impact was felt far and wide but nowhere more than in his homeland of Poland. Having lived so long in the "Church of silence" as it suffered under communism, John Paul came to the papacy determined to stand with those on the side of freedom. He arranged a visit to Poland just a year after being elected; one-third of the country's population turned out to see him. His visit inspired an electrician named Lech Walesa who was trying to create Solidarity, the first independent trade union in a Soviet-controlled country. John Paul saw Solidarity as Catholic social teaching in action and supported it in every way possible. The trade union eventually helped pull down the communist government in Poland, which in turn started the downward spiral of the Soviet Union and the end of communism as a major world power. John Paul II certainly did not do it by himself, but he helped light the fire that eventually destroyed Soviet communism.

A Big Divide

John Paul was much more than a road warrior. If you put all his writings as pope side by side on a shelf, they would take up more than 10 feet. He was a philosopher by training, and it showed in his writings. He held up a consistent ethical and moral viewpoint, one that was not popular with all Catholics. He had a traditional sense of doctrine, especially on social issues. While John Paul was pope, the Western world accepted a freer attitude toward sex, a growing acceptance of homosexual lifestyles, ever-greater reliance on birth control, and an insistence that women be admitted to all levels of leadership within society, but not in the Church under John Paul's leadership. As we will see, he worked to maintain the Church's traditional understandings of sexuality and reproduction, and while expressing his deep belief in the equal worth and dignity of men and women, he made an official pronouncement that women could never become priests.

John Paul took particular issue with the Church in Latin America. At the same time that he was encouraging priests in Poland to stand on the side of workers, he cracked down on clergy members in Latin America who were working for the poor if he thought they strayed too close to Marxism. Some of those embracing liberation theology used a Marxist analysis of social and economic structures as a backdrop for expressing their understanding of the gospel's message of justice and dignity for all. As far as John Paul was concerned, Marxism was just a few inches shy of the communism under which he had suffered and that he believed held nothing but danger and disregard for the Church. He had four Nicaraguan priests suspended from their religious Orders because they had taken high-level positions in a leftist government;

called the entire cohort of Peruvian bishops to the Vatican to defend their support for liberation theology; and pressured many liberation theologians to change their positions and even had some silenced, meaning they were barred from writing or speaking publicly about certain issues.

Many Catholics who were awed and inspired by John Paul's efforts to promote social justice and religious freedom were unhappy with this tendency to shut down opposition voices within the Church. Theologians, priests, religious brothers and sisters, and even bishops felt the heat of John Paul's anger when they publicly expressed views that John Paul believed went against Church teaching. Some of those targeted for their views renounced their vows, feeling they could no longer maintain obedience to John Paul's Church, which they saw as leaving them no room to follow their consciences and the dictates of Scripture; many other clergy and religious, as well as prominent lay Catholics, felt even more bereft of a home in the Church and left it entirely. A divide opened between Catholics who applauded John Paul's efforts to protect the faith and the Church from the errors of modern life and those who believed John Paul was moving the Church away from the reorientation of Vatican II, closing doors the council had specifically tried to open.

John Paul II died in 2005 after a twenty-six-year reign, the third longest in Church history. Increasingly ill with Parkinson's disease in the latter years of his papacy, John Paul still managed to travel, write, and inspire untold numbers. It is estimated that more than 4 million people converged on Rome to pay their last respects to this remarkable man. The pope who followed him, Benedict XVI, took the reins in a Church that had John Paul's fingerprints all over it. John Paul had created a record number of cardinals and bishops; of the 117 cardinals eligible to vote on his successor, John Paul had appointed all but 3. With his enormous body of writings and the people he put in place who shared his vision, John Paul II ensured that his understanding of where the Church was going and what it needed to do would last long into the future. In a nutshell, he set the Church's agenda for the twenty-first century.

The Reformed Reformer: Benedict XVI

When Benedict XVI took over as pope on April 19, 2005, he already knew his way around the Vatican. After all, as Cardinal Joseph Ratzinger he had led the Congregation for the Doctrine of the Faith for the past twenty-four years and was well known in Catholic circles as the Vatican's theological watchdog and enforcer. But this was his role; what about the man who filled the role? On that, most Catholics knew little.

From Germany to Papa Razi

Joseph Ratzinger was born in Germany in 1927. Six years old when the Nazis came to power, he spent his teenage years living through World War II. The Ratzinger family members were not resisters fighting the Nazi brand of German nationalism, but they had no sympathy for the values the party expressed, either. At age 14, Joseph found himself enrolled in the Hitler Youth, a mandatory program for teens in Nazi Germany, but he did not participate. He was headed toward the priesthood, the only profession he seems ever to have considered seriously. Two years later, Joseph the seminary student was drafted along with his entire seminary class into the German army. He worked as part of an anti-aircraft battalion and spent a few months as an American POW before returning to the seminary life for which he was so much better suited.

On June 29, 1951, the Ratzinger household celebrated the priestly ordination of not one but two sons, as both Joseph and his brother Georg were ordained. Father Joseph was headed for an academic career. Becoming a professor in 1958, he taught at a number of German universities and stayed in the academic world for twenty years, publishing an extraordinary number of books and articles along the way. In 1977, he was appointed an archbishop and later that year was made a cardinal. From that point on, he would be a major player not only in the realm of Catholic theology but also in Church politics. Just four years later, he accepted John Paul's call to become the head of the Congregation for the Doctrine of the Faith, a position he maintained until his election as pope twenty-four years later.

A Shift in Focus

If Pope Benedict were a rock star, we would say his big break came at Vatican II, which he attended as a theological adviser to Cardinal Frings of Germany. At the council, Father Ratzinger wrote a speech for the cardinal sharply criticizing the methods used by the Holy Office (formerly known as the Inquisition), declaring them to be a scandal that hurt the faith. The speech was enthusiastically received, and soon after the council, the Holy Office was revamped, its procedures reworked, and its name changed to the Congregation for the Doctrine of the Faith. Joseph Ratzinger, meanwhile, had earned the reputation of reformer.

This is where many observers of Cardinal Ratzinger get a bit lost. Less than two decades following the council, he was named to head the Congregation for the Doctrine of the Faith. Many observers still saw the long shadow of the Holy Office and Inquisition hanging over the congregation, and certainly everyone understood it to be the enforcer of the theological status quo. Cardinal Ratzinger had been a reformer; now he was to take on the role of enforcer. What was up?

According to the cardinal, the answer lay not in a change in his beliefs but in the way reform was being handled. Time and again, Cardinal Ratzinger defended Vatican II, but he believed that much of the theology that grew out of it went in dangerous directions. As he saw it, many radical thinkers had become so engaged with the idea of openness and dialogue that they forgot to be Christian and Catholic. For Cardinal Ratzinger, and for Pope John Paul II, nothing in the Church—including the Second Vatican Council—should be considered an invitation to relativism, meaning that there are no absolute truths. The Church, Popes John Paul and Benedict believe, is founded on truth and must continue to teach truth—and truth is an unchanging absolute. How truth is expressed may change over time, but the core of what is taught does not.

As prefect of the Congregation for the Doctrine of the Faith, Cardinal Ratzinger was the first line of defense against relativism or any perceived theological straying within the Church. The cardinal oversaw crackdowns against dissent called for by John Paul. He silenced more than a hundred dissenters during his time as prefect, including some of his past colleagues in reform. The cardinal was in the forefront of the push to weed out liberation theology and uproot the base communities that had become such an important part of the Catholic landscape in Latin America. In his role as prefect, Cardinal Ratzinger argued that national bishops' conferences lacked teaching authority, expanded the working definition of papal infallibility to include teachings that previously would not have been considered infallible, defined homosexuality as a tendency toward intrinsic evil, and worked tirelessly to maintain the

"Repent and Believe"

"This is the time of fulfillment. The kingdom of God is at hand. Repent, and believe in the gospel" (Mark 1:15). That is how the writer of Mark's gospel sees Jesus' message. Sounds simple, right? However, there is more to repenting than just feeling sorry. The word *repentance* comes from the Latin *penitentia*, which means "an inner transformation." It is this sort of transformation that is at the heart of the Church's modern teaching about the sacrament of reconciliation: a transformation that brings humans into right relationship with God and with each other.

The sacrament of reconciliation, popularly called "confession," is an instance where Catholics confess their sins before a priest, who then makes God's love and forgiveness known to them. For the earliest Christians, this all took place at baptism—if baptism wiped the slate clean, why talk about forgiving sins after that? The answer is that human beings do not always keep the slate clean. Plus, the Church saw sin as driving a wedge between the Christian and his or her community. If a sinner repented and wanted to rejoin the community, Church leaders decided, the penitent ought to stand up in public, confess the sin and why it was wrong, and then go through a public penance—often lasting years—before being received into the community again. God's forgiveness may be immediate, the Church reasoned, but sinners need time to experience the inward transformation of true repentance, and communities need time to mend broken human relationships.

Most early Christians never went through public penance. Over the next few centuries, Christians came to see sin less as a rupture in the covenant between God and humans and more as breaking divine law; since it is much easier to break a specific law than to rupture a whole covenant, now everyone needed reconciliation.

Celtic monks had spread the practice of confessing in private throughout Europe, and by 1215, private confession to a priest was officially recognized as a sacrament.

continued on page 317

traditional Christian understanding of Christ's uniqueness and undercut the theology of religious pluralism that had been gaining ground since Vatican II.

Even more than Pope John Paul, Cardinal Ratzinger became the symbol for the strength of tradition and the demand for uniformity in the Church. Whether that was something to celebrate or grieve depended on a person's theological views.

The Once and Future Benedict

When the white smoke appeared above St. Peter's Square and the news of Cardinal Ratzinger's election was announced, many Vatican watchers imme-

continued from page 316

Originally, penitents could confess to monks or nuns, whose role then was to reassure them of God's love and forgiveness. By the 1200s, however, the Church taught that only an ordained priest could absolve sins in God's name.

Absolution didn't end the process of reconciliation for the penitent, however. Theologians during the Middle Ages saw the priest's absolution as a mark of God's forgiving mercy and saving grace, but God's justice still demanded the penitent do something to put things back in order, that is, penance. Eventually this led to the belief people had to spend time in purgatory to cover all their unrepented sins, which in turn became the justification for indulgences. Luther and other Protestant reformers disagreed strongly with the idea of indulgences, but they did not always agree amongst themselves regarding confession. Was it a sacrament begun by Jesus, or could you just pray and ask forgiveness on your own? Protestants eventually moved toward the latter idea, but in 1551, the Council of Trent reaffirmed the Church's traditional teaching about the priestly role in confessions.

When the sacraments were reworked at Vatican II, Church leaders wanted to get back to the earlier understanding of reconciliation as mending a fractured covenant rather than punishing a broken law. Nowadays the rite is much less about judgment and more about recognizing problematic behavior and the need to change it. Priests offer absolution, but they also offer counseling on how to deal with sin and its consequences, and they give penances as a way of helping people mend their relationships with God, with others, and even with themselves. "Confession" has truly become "reconciliation" again, a way of bringing wholeness to the broken human soul.

diately had visions of the Church Militant on the rise. The watchdog had become master of the house, they thought, and so surely the demand for conformity would grow even stronger. Instead many watchers found themselves somewhat surprised at the even tone and peaceable nature of most of his actions in the first two years of his papacy. When a remark of his regarding the Prophet Mohammed enraged many Muslims, Benedict apologized and met with Muslim leaders to determine how best to convey his respect for Islam and its followers. Under his guidance, the Vatican is attempting to restore diplomatic ties with China, a tricky operation because China maintains a national Catholic Church that is not in communion with Rome.

Casting Light on the Secret Shame

One of the biggest nightmares for the Church in the United States at the end of the twentieth century was the scandal over the sexual abuse of minors by priests. The vast majority of priests would never harm another person this way; less than 1 percent of American priests have been accused in the last ten years—and statistics show that when a child is abused by a church worker, that worker is more likely to be a volunteer than a clergy member, and the church is more likely to be Protestant than Catholic. That said, there is no question that abuse by priests has been a serious problem in the Church and that the Church's image has been severely tarnished in recent years because of it. Furthermore, the cost to the Church is far less important than the damage done to the victims and those who love them.

One survey finds that between 1950 and 2002, more than four thousand priests were accused of abusing more than ten thousand victims. What is more, the Church leadership has been seriously implicated in covering up these crimes. All too often, bishops moved priests who had harmed young people in this way to new parishes, where some continued inflicting this harm on others. There have been legal battles, priests convicted, bishops accused of obstructing justice, and at least a few dioceses declaring bankruptcy after paying damages to victims.

The question that always comes up is how this could happen in a Christian organization, among a group of people dedicated to serving God and helping others. It is a powerful question and one without an easy answer. Some people point to the priests' personal sexual histories, others to the way matters of sexuality are handled during preparation for the priesthood, and still others to issues of power. At the heart of all of these are psychological questions that we just cannot answer here.

However, we can look at why these instances of abuse turned into a crisis for the Church in America. Bishops did not just blithely turn a blind eye to the abuse; very often, they sent priests into treatment and made settlements with the families of those abused. What they did not do was turn the matters over to the criminal justice system. Wanting to protect the Church,

continued on page 319

This does not mean Benedict had moved away from his theological foundations. In fact, the battle against what Benedict had called the "dictatorship of relativism" may end up being the hallmark of his papacy. Also, while he seeks to revive waning Christian faith in what was traditionally the Church's heartland, Europe, Benedict has often made the statement that the Church may need to be smaller to remain faithful to the gospel. He has no interest in reaching out to those drifting away from the Church by making the demands of faith any easier. It is not likely that there will be any major changes in policy or direction under his leadership, but history will have to give the final word on what effect Benedict's papacy has on the worldwide Church.

continued from page 318

they covered up what needed to be out in the open, and in the end, that secrecy caused even more harm. When everything started coming to light in the late 1990s, the public had the sense that the Church had dodged the laws of the land, trying to administer its own justice—or ignore the need for it—rather than allowing the judicial system to do its work. Lay Catholics felt betrayed by priests acting inappropriately and bishops making decisions without taking the people's wishes and needs into account. Angry and sad, quite a few lost confidence in the Church's leadership.

In 2002, the U.S. Catholic bishops adopted the Charter for the Protection of Children and Young People, a blueprint for how to deal with allegations of abuse and how to prevent it from happening in the first place. Bishops now have help from review boards set up to advise them on these issues, they report all instances of abuse of minors to the proper authorities, and they remove priests accused of abuse from ministry even before any allegations are proven or admitted. However, it goes beyond this: The charter also calls for proper screening of candidates for the priesthood and background checks for all Church employees dealing with young people. In addition, outreach to victims has to be central in the Church's response to these problems. This can include working with victims and their families, holding healing Masses for them, and letting victims have a say in how future cases are handled. The Church also has a responsibility to care for the abusing priests. While they must stand accountable for their actions, Catholic teaching explains that they also deserve Christian love and forgiveness and that the Church has a responsibility to give them the help they need.

The fact that children have been abused is shameful and horrific, but the fact that these things are now coming to light is good. Catholics understand that these sins must be acknowledged so that the covenant of the Church's leadership with its people can be renewed. The Church all too often turned to secrecy in trying to deal with an issue that could harm its image; now it must use honesty in showing its deep contrition and greater commitment to living out the gospel.

Who Does What: The Changing Roles of Bishops, Priests, and Laity

The Church is a hierarchy in a world that increasingly values democracy and individual decision making, and that does not always make for an easy fit. Even within the Church there is more than a little conflict over exactly who gets to do what. Traditionally, this conflict has been between those higher and lower within the Church's hierarchy, but nowadays the conflict is often between the hierarchy and the laity. The number of lay Catholics taking on roles in the day-to-day running of parishes and dioceses that used to be reserved for those in religious life has increased dramatically, and that kind of shift in practical power is always going to be accompanied by some difficulties. Still, there is a growing recognition and acceptance among both clergy and laity that the only way the Church is going to live out its mission in the twenty-first century is if everyone works together.

Fewer and Farther Between: Bishops and Priests

We saw that the Second Vatican Council expressed a broad-reaching concept of the rights and duties of bishops, but in the Church under Pope John Paul II, power and decision making were very much centralized within the Vatican. So what should be valued most: the fact that bishops are called to be teachers and shepherds in their own right, or the need for unity of understanding and action among those who lead the Church? It is a hard balance to find and one that Catholics will continue to work through in this century.

Bishops are not the only ones trying to figure out the boundaries of their responsibilities. Go back to a typical parish in 1960, and you would find the priest as the undisputed ruler over everyone and everything that went on. Vatican II changed all that, and now priests participate in their parishes rather than ruling them, working with rather than just for the laity. There is a strongly pragmatic aspect to this new arrangement as well, as a drastic priest shortage means more work to do than priests available to do it.

The need for priestly celibacy is a hotly debated topic. Especially in the Western world, a growing majority of lay Catholics are comfortable with the idea of allowing priests to marry. Married priests were the norm in the earliest centuries of the Church, and in some parts of Latin America and Africa, it is commonplace for priests to have longstanding sexual relationships that are roughly equivalent to marriage, even though these are not accepted by the Church. Many people have long thought that allowing priests to marry would be the best way to ease the priest shortage. However, popular thinking and Church teaching are worlds apart on this issue; the Vatican is vehemently opposed to ending mandatory celibacy, and it does not look likely to budge on this issue anytime soon.

From Pew to Pulpit: Lay Catholics in Parish Life

The rise of the laity to new levels of participation and responsibility in parish life is a direct result of Vatican II. The bishops at the council wrote that the liturgy is the work of all the faithful, clergy and laity, and they said that lay Catholics must be active in the mission of the Church, not just recipients of the ministry of the clergy. Lay Catholics the world over took these ideas and ran with them, seeing in them the theological foundations for their desire to participate more fully in the Church they loved.

Not only have the laity taken on roles previously reserved for priests or religious, but they also have created new ministries. For instance, the base communities so popular in Latin America are small groups of Catholics who come together once or twice a week to sing, pray, and study the gospel. This is a ministry of the laity to the laity, and it can be a powerful force, influencing how participants understand and implement Catholic doctrine in their lives. Other grassroots organizations are more directly vocal about their desire for greater participation in the way the Church is run. In the United States, a group called Voices of the Faithful, for instance, grew out of anger and frustration with the Church's leadership over its handling of the recent sex-abuse scandal; while it accepts the authority of the Church's hierarchy, this group advocates greater lay participation in the governance of the Church at all levels. This and similar calls for greater participation are not always welcomed by the clergy, however; some priests and bishops are deeply concerned about these movements because they do not fall directly under the guidance of the hierarchy.

Over the last forty years, the response of the Church's leaders to the roles the laity have taken on has been a mixed bag of optimism and concern. In 1975, Pope Paul VI issued *On Evangelization in the Modern World (Evangelii Nuntiandi),* in which he talks about the laity consecrating their time to Church service, which implies that the work of lay ministers is not simply helpful but also holy. More recently, though, Pope John Paul issued his *Exhortation on the Vocation and Mission of the Lay Faithful in the Church and in the World (Christifideles Laici).* In this 1988 encyclical, John Paul is much more cautious in tone than Paul was; he wants to make it clear that ordained ministers are in charge and that lay members are under the guidance and supervision of the ordained when they take on ministerial roles. Lay ministers serve the Church, yes, but they are not in a parallel position to the clergy; theirs is definitely a subordinate status. Some people see John Paul's writing as restating the true and traditional Catholic understanding of ministry, while others believe this is one more area in which he pulled the Church back from the openness of Vatican II.

What is becoming clear, though, is that lay ministers see their work as more than just a job. Surveys of lay ministers in U.S. Catholic churches find that they usually feel a sense of being called to their role and of receiving a charism, or special grace, for their work. That does not always mesh with how members of the clergy or other lay members of the parish see them, though. Many people in the pews view lay ministers as simply stand-ins for overworked priests rather than as people who are called to their work.

The Distaff Church: Women's Roles

While the Church's hierarchy remains entirely male, a strong majority of Catholics participating in lay ministry are women. In fact, about 85 percent of all Church roles that do not require ordination are held by women. There are many reasons why women have taken on so many responsibilities within the Church: a shift in cultural attitudes has led to people being more accepting of women in leadership roles; more parishes have created outreach ministries to groups with whom women have traditionally worked, such as children and the elderly; and women are often more willing to accept parish salaries, which are typically lower than those for similar work in the secular world. Since women cannot be ordained as priests or deacons, they cannot take on the clerical roles that are open to men; if they feel called to work in the Church, they must do so either as nuns or in lay ministry.

Women's ordination is a big issue in the twenty-first-century Church, despite the fact that John Paul II declared the subject to be off limits. After resisting the inclusion of women in anything resembling a leadership role for centuries, the Church developing out of Vatican II began allowing women to take on liturgical roles such as readers and Eucharistic ministers, let girls become altar servers, and started admitting women to degree programs in theology and related areas at Catholic universities. Suddenly, women were theologians and parish administrators, professors teaching Catholic history and doctrine, experts in canon law and liturgy; they could now be found filling many roles that would have shocked a Catholic from two or three decades prior. All this created forward momentum for the idea of even more roles opening up for women within the Church, and many saw ordination as deacons and priests as the ultimate and reasonable goal.

In 1975, the Canon Law Society of America declared that there was no theological reason why women could not be ordained, and the next year the Pontifical Biblical Commission decided that nothing in the New Testament made it clear that women could not be priests. On the popular front, the calls for women's ordination were growing, supported by the arguments that it was unjust to deny women a role open to men simply based on biology and that opening ordination to women could resolve the priest shortage in no time at all. To some Catholics, both laity and clergy, women priests seemed like an idea whose time had come; to others, all this talk was solid proof that the Church had strayed too far from its roots.

John Paul II made no bones about where he stood on the issue. In 1985, he issued *Mulieris Dignitatem (On the Dignity and Vocation of Women),* in which he emphasized the deep importance and worth of women but also stressed that the biological differences between men and women are the foundation of spiritual differences as well. He allowed the reestablishment of the diaconate program for lay men but excluded women. Some theologians surmise that he did not want to give the impression that women could eventually move toward ordination. In 1994, John Paul laid all his cards on the table with the encyclical *Ordinatio Sacerdotalis (On Reserving Priestly Ordination to Men Alone);* he declared both that the Church had no authority to confer ordination on women and that this teaching must be definitively held by all Catholics.

Still, this did not end the debate. In response to the uproar the encyclical produced, the Congregation for the Doctrine of the Faith, under the direction of Cardinal Ratzinger, claimed that the teaching in *Ordinatio Sacerdotalis* was infallible even though it had not been declared *ex cathedra*. At this point, the heated uproar became an inferno, with even theologians not in favor of women's ordination provoked to action by the claim of infallibility. Still, while the debate may rage in certain theological circles and while polls may show that most U.S. Catholics, among others, would accept women priests, according to the hierarchy this issue is no longer an issue at all.

Asking for Approval

"As a professor of a Catholic theological discipline . . . I am committed to teach authentic Catholic doctrine and to refrain from putting forth as Catholic teaching anything contrary to the Church's magisterium." This text is part of an official approval known as a *mandatum* that Catholic professors of religion must get from their local bishops in order to teach at American Catholic colleges and universities. The U.S. bishops started requiring the *mandatum* in 2000 in response to the call of John Paul II in his 1990 papal bull *Ex Corde Ecclesiae* for Catholic theologians to be faithful to the Church's hierarchy and teachings.

The Church has a duty to make sure that people teaching Catholic doctrine in Catholic universities are doing so properly, but what if the theologian and the local bishop disagree? Maybe the theologian believes the Church's respect for a person's conscience is more important than its teaching about artificial contraception, and the bishop believes just the opposite. The bishop might refuse to grant that theologian a *mandatum*. The *mandatum*, then, raises questions about academic freedom and what it means to faithfully follow the Church's teachings. The whole issue has caused a stir, with some professors accepting the need for a *mandatum*, others refusing to ask for it on principle, and still others thinking that the whole thing is getting blown out of proportion. Whether you are for it or against it, though, the *mandatum* is part of the reality of American Catholic life in the twenty-first century.

Looking Inward, Looking Outward: The Church at Home and Abroad

As the Church enters its third millennium, it faces a new challenge: less interest in the areas where it has traditionally been strong and unprecedented growth in places that used to be thought far-flung and exotic. In response, the Church must figure out how to repackage its ancient message for the eyes of the modern Western world, open its understanding to new ways of being Catholic and being Church, and seriously dialogue with those of other religions who are now the friends and neighbors of a growing number of the world's Catholics.

Outward Bound: The Church's Growth in Africa and Asia

At the turn of the twentieth century, Earth was home to about 1.5 billion people; by 2001, that number was about 6 billion. As a species, we have been growing exponentially, and the Catholic population is growing faster than most; the population of the globe rose by 117 percent in the last half of the twentieth century, but the number of Catholics shot up by 139 percent. In fact, there are more than a billion Catholics now—about 18 percent of the global population.

Asia and Africa saw the biggest population explosions, and the number of Catholics in those areas has been growing rapidly. Asia has 861 percent more Catholics now than at the beginning of the twentieth century, and the Catholic population in Africa grew by a whopping 6708 percent. Not that you are likely to see a Catholic church on every street corner in Calcutta or Dar es Salaam—Catholics still make up a small percentage of the inhabitants of both continents, but that percentage is growing.

For a long time, Catholics in Africa and Asia had little voice in the Church, but this too is changing. African and Asian Catholics face different challenges than do Western Catholics, and over the course of the twenty-first century we are likely to see the Church taking notice. Africa is afflicted with the highest HIV rate in the world, as well as by terrible poverty and appalling wars. The Church knows that witnessing to the gospel in Africa means helping people live lives of dignity in the midst of tragedies, as well as helping find ways to end those tragedies. As for Asia, Catholics there find themselves in the midst of a continent that contains the countries with the largest Islamic, Hindu, and Buddhist populations in the world and many other thriving religious traditions as well. Asian Catholics have to work out how to live in harmony with those around them who have dramatically different ideas and beliefs.

Looking at Africa and Asia shows us a lot about the future of the Church. From being a big deal in a few areas of the world, it is fast becoming one part of the religious landscape in much of the world. The Church must adapt to living and working with people of many other beliefs and to the different understandings that Catholics in non-Western areas bring to their faith. Many practices that Western Catholics take for granted are really just how the West goes about being Church. This can cause a problem when Catholics all over the globe are forced to do things the same way.

Today the Church is talking about "inculturation"—taking universal ideas and beliefs and allowing people to develop rituals, practices, and symbols meaningful for their particular cultures. It can be a sticky process; sometimes it is hard to know the line between simply expressing the same belief but in a different way and expressing an entirely different belief. Moreover, what looks like inculturation in Africa or Asia can seem far-fetched to those far away in Rome, meaning there have been more than a few heated battles between the Vatican hierarchy and the locals in those two continents. One of the main challenges the Church is going to face in the twenty-first century is how to maintain the integrity of its unity while recognizing the reality of its diversity. It may not be an easy road, but it is one that will lead the Catholic Church to become truly catholic—that is, universal.

Less of a Good Thing—Shrinking Interest in the Catholic Heartland

About 40 percent of Europe is Catholic, along with about 63 percent of the total population of North and South America, but these numbers are changing. Latin America has been overwhelmingly Catholic for half a millennium, but now evangelical forms of Christianity are making big inroads. The number of Catholics is on the rise in the United States (partly due to the increase in immigration from Latin America), but so is the number of people who do not think religion is important at all—a trend called secularization. Jump over to Europe—the historic heart of Catholic Christianity—and you will find practically an epidemic of people turning away from Christianity.

What is behind this? Did Westerners just suddenly wake up one morning and decide that religion was unimportant? The answer is "kind of yes." Westerners have turned more and more to the belief that science can explain the world and that religion is no longer necessary. Even many people who express a religious preference have an essentially secular point of view, thinking of religion as a "Sunday thing" that does not affect how they see the rest of their lives or the world. More than a few people see religion of any kind, and Christianity in particular, as being too big a part of our world's violence. Then there is sex: some scholars would say that more people in the Western world have been turned off by the Church's views of sexuality than by any other issue. From these viewpoints, it is just a short hop to believing that religion has no value at all.

As more people in non-Western areas are turning to Catholic Christianity, more people in traditionally Christian areas are turning away from it. This is a big problem for the Church and one it is having a hard time changing. How can the Church show secular Westerners that it is still needed in society? How can it convince people thinking about leaving the Church that it gives them something they cannot find anywhere else? It does not seem likely that the Church is going to be able to answer these questions any time soon.

Talking It Over: Dialogue with Other Religions

Since Vatican II, the Church has put much effort into talking with members of other religions, not to convert them but to encourage mutual understanding. By doing this, the Church shows its belief that everyone brings something to the table and that no one side has the lock on truth. Some Catholics have a hard time with this; after all, hasn't the Church spent centuries telling everyone that it is the only path to God? Others agree that God's work in the world goes beyond the Church but worry that Church beliefs may get watered down or neglected in dialogue. In the end, the Church sees dialogue with other religions as not only valuable but also inevitable. Western Catholics are much more likely to encounter people of other religions than they were a hundred years ago, and dealing with people of differing beliefs is part of daily life for Catholics in other areas. In the twenty-first century, the need for understanding and harmony between Catholic Christians and those of other faiths will only continue to grow.

When Islamic radicals crashed airliners into American targets on September 11, 2001, it drove home for Americans how much people are willing to live, die, and even kill for their beliefs. It is a lesson that people in the Middle East, Ireland, Serbia, and many other areas had already learned. Part of the Church's need for dialogue is to find ways for people of different traditions to live together in peace.

One of the biggest reasons for religious dialogue is that more and more Western Christians find themselves drawn to other religions, especially the religions of Asia. Hindu understandings of reincarnation and the sacredness of all life and Buddhist messages of compassion and right action have found their way into the consciousness of the Western world, and their influence is growing among Christians. So while the Church is working for true understanding and harmony with people of other beliefs, it also wants to understand what draws Christians to these beliefs and how it may best help Catholics hold strong to their faith.

The Church Then and Now

The Church of Yesterday, Today, and Tomorrow

So there you have it—the whole of Catholic history, or at least the highlights. I stated at the beginning of this book that Catholics see the Church as the continuation of the community that grew around Jesus during his life and stayed strong in its faith after his resurrection. I hope you now understand what that community is all about, how the Church strives to carry on the ministry of Jesus, where it succeeds in its mission, and where it falls short. If you are Catholic yourself, maybe you have a deeper sense of why Catholics look at their history—the good, the bad, and the ugly—and see the Holy Spirit moving throughout all of it and continually calling the Church toward a deeper commitment to the gospel.

As we settle into the new millennium, Catholics are still going to struggle as they try to be part of their world, with its constant change and moving definitions of morality, while remaining faithful Christians who hold fast to the ancient faith. The Church will continue to work at finding the balance between recognizing its own authority and not stepping on God's, being part of history yet not being swayed by changing fashions, and standing up for truth clearly and honestly without becoming rigid or demanding that all follow its path. We have seen times when the Church simply repeated its teachings and demanded allegiance, refusing to deal with the world around it. That may have made things seem easier but not better. The Church of the twenty-first century cannot return to such a time and would not want to if it could. It has a harder job now: not to be aloof from the world but to be down on the front lines, calling people to the gospel and showing them how to live it. The road that lies ahead may be harder to navigate, but if it carries the Church to greater compassion and a fuller expression of God's will, then it is the only path worth following.

Questions and Ideas for Understanding

1. Pope John Paul II traveled the globe and talked to people of many different faiths and ideologies. In doing so, he became one of the most recognizable faces on the planet. Is this sort of visibility helpful to the

Church, or does it put the Church's leader too much on the level with any other celebrity?

2. The Polish Solidarity movement and Latin American liberation theology both aimed to help those who are poor and oppressed, and grew out of deeply rooted Catholic thinking, but they were received very differently in the Church led by John Paul II. Research these two movements, and write an essay comparing them with Catholic social teaching.

3. For John Paul and for Benedict, relativism, the idea that there is no absolute truth, is one of the most damaging of modern ideas, destroying belief and leaving people with no firm grounding on which to base their lives. Do you think Vatican II opened the Church to relativism? If so, do you agree with John Paul and Benedict, or do you think differently? Why?

4. Do you think the deeper involvement of lay Catholics in running parishes and dioceses will lead to a more democratic Church, or does the structure of bishops, cardinals, and pope ensure that this will not happen? Should it happen?

5. According to Church teaching, the fact that women are not allowed to be priests is a by-product of the differing and complementary roles of men and women, not an issue of power and subordination. Write an essay exploring the Church's position and either supporting or refuting it.

6. The Church was a vocal and important participant in the 1994 population conference in Cairo and helped set the direction for the United Nations Population Fund. Whether or not you agree with the Church's position, do you think it is a good idea for a religious body to have a major voice in this sort of global public policy debate? Why or why not?

Major Events in Church History

ca. 5 CE	Jesus is born
ca. 30	Jesus is crucified
ca. 33	Pentecost
ca. 50	The Council at Jerusalem
ca. 50–180	The New Testament is written
ca. 64	Saint Peter and Saint Paul are martyred
ca. 70	The destruction of the Temple at Jerusalem
ca. 107	Saint Ignatius of Antioch dies
ca. 155	Justin Martyr writes his apology
203	Perpetua is martyred
270	Saint Antony of Egypt goes into the desert and begins the tradition of Catholic monasticism
313	Constantine issues the Edict of Milan, ending the Roman persecution of Catholics
325	The Council of Nicaea
330	Saint Peter's Basilica is constructed
341–420	Life of Saint Jerome, early biblical scholar
354–430	Life of Saint Augustine of Hippo, influential theologian of the early Church
381	The Nicene Creed is affirmed by the Council of Constantinople
431	The Council of Ephesus declares that Mary is the mother of God
432	Saint Patrick becomes bishop and does missionary work in Ireland
451	Council of Chalcedon affirms apostolic doctrine of two natures in Christ
480–543	Life of Saint Benedict of Nursia, founder of the Benedictine Order
540–604	Pope Gregory the Great brings unity and order to the Church
589	The filioque is added to the Nicene Creed
700	Boniface does missionary work in Germany
800	Charlemagne is crowned Emperor of the Romans
993	Ulrich, bishop of Augsburg, is named a saint in the first formal canonization
1054	The Orthodox Church separates from the Catholic Church; the Great Schism occurs
1096–1254	The Crusades take place
1182–1226	Life of Saint Francis of Assisi, founder of the Franciscan Order
1225–1274	Life of Saint Thomas Aquinas, master philosopher and theologian of the Church
1294	John of Monte Corvino arrives in China
1347–1380	Life of Catherine of Siena, doctor of the Church and mystical writer
1431	Joan of Arc is burned at the stake
1492	Columbus claims the New World for God and Spain
1517	Martin Luther posts his 95 theses
1545–1563	The Council of Trent
1549	Francis Xavier arrives in Japan
1564–1642	Life of Galileo Galilei
1605	Robert de Nobili arrives in India
1618–1648	The Thirty Years' War
1626	Saint Peter's Basilica is consecrated in Rome
1634	The Catholic colony of Maryland is established
1774	British Parliament gives Catholics full religious rights in Canada
1790	John Carroll becomes the first bishop consecrated in the United States
1854	The dogma of the Immaculate Conception is declared by Pope Pius IX
1870	Vatican Council I declares papal infallibility
1891	*Rerum Novarum* is released
1929	Creation of Vatican City, the world's smallest sovereign state
1936	Pontifical Academy of Science is founded
1950	The dogma of the Assumption is declared by Pope Pius XII
1962–1965	Vatican Council II
1970	Saint Teresa of Ávila and Catherine of Siena are named the first women doctors of the Church
1978	Pope John Paul II, the first non-Italian pope since 1523, is elected
1986	First World Youth Day
1992	The current edition of the *Catechism of the Catholic Church* is released
2002	The Peace Pledge is signed by spiritual leaders from around the world
2005	Benedict XVI is elected

Index